W9-BCJ-237

D. Stewis

International Resource Management:
the role of science and politics

THE FRIDTJOF NANSEN INSTITUTE

International Resource Management: the role of science and politics

Edited by
Steinar Andresen and Willy Østreng

Belhaven Press
(A division of Pinter Publishers)
London and New York

© Fridtjof Nansen Institute 1989

First published in Great Britain in 1989 by
Belhaven Press (a division of Pinter Publishers),
25 Floral Street, London WC2 9DS

All rights reserved. No part of this publication
may be reproduced, stored in a retrieval system,
or transmitted by any other means without the prior
permission of the copyright holder. Please direct all
enquiries to the publishers.

British Library Cataloguing in Publication Data
A CIP catalogue record for this book is available from
the British Library

ISBN 1-85293-097-7

Library of Congress Cataloging in Publication Data
CIP applied for

Typset by The Castlefield Press, Wellingborough, Northants
Printed and bound in Great Britain by Biddles Ltd.

Contents

List of figures and tables

List of contributors

Steinar Andresen is Programme director at the Fridtjof Nansen Institute, and is a political scientist from the University of Oslo.(1979) He has worked on various aspects of ocean management, issues concerning the law of the sea, and international resource management. Among his publications is *Power and Law of the Oceans*, Norwegian University Press, Oslo, 1987 (in Norwegian). He has been affiliated with the Fridjof Nansen Institute since 1979, since 1987 as senior research fellow. In 1987-1988 he was visiting research scholar at the Institute for Marine Studies, University of Washington.

Halldór Asgrímsson is Minister of Fisheries and Justice in Iceland. He graduated from the Cooperative's Commercial College, Iceland (1965), and studied at Commercial Colleges in Bergen and Copenhagen (1971-73), he was a lecturer at the University of Iceland (1973-75). He was a member of Parliament from 1974-78 and from 1979, becoming Deputy Leader of the Progressive Party in 1980. He has been a member of the Board of Directors at the Central Bank of Iceland and also of the Nordic Council. He has been Minister of Fisheries since 1983 and Minister of Justice and Ecclesiastical Affairs since September 1988.

Per Bakken is a Senior Executive Officer in the Norwegian Ministry of the Environment, and has a Master of Science from the University of Oslo. He has been associated with the Norwegian State Pollution Control Authority (1978-84), and is presently with the Ministry of the Environment where he works on various issues of international cooperation on air pollution. He was head of the Norwegian delegation in the negotiations leading up to the Vienna Convention and the Montreal protocol.

Helge Ole Bergesen is a Senior research fellow and a political scientist from the University of Oslo (1977). He was Assistant Professor (1978-79) at the University of Odense, Denmark, and since 1980 has been at the Fridtjof Nansen Institute where he established and directed its research programme on international energy policy. He has worked in various fields covering human rights issues, North-South relations and international energy issues. Among his publications is *Natural Gas in Europe: Markets, Organization and Politics,* (with Javier, Estrada; Arild, Moe; and Anne Kristin, Sydnes; Pinters Publishers, 1988).

Sonja Boehmer–Christiansen is research fellow at the University of Sussex, Great Britain, with an MA and D. Phil. from the same University. She has been a lecturer and teacher of geography in Australia from 1962-69, and has been associated with the Open University in Great Britain from 1970-74 and the Institut füt Volkrecht (at the Institute for International Law) at the Maximilian University in Munich, West Germany (1981-84). She has published extensively on various issues of pollution control.

Leif E. Christoffersen is Division chief in the World Bank. Completing his undergraduate studies at Edinburgh University, Scotland in 1961, he pursued his graduate studies in international economics at the Fletcher School, Tufts University, USA. He joined the World Bank in 1964 and has served that organization in various managerial capacities, mostly related to agriculture, rural development and natural resources management. He is currently leading the environmental division, Africa region.

Brit Fløistad is research fellow at the Fridtjof Nansen Institute, and a political scientist, at the University of Oslo. She has been associated with the Fridtjof Nansen Institute since 1982 and she has mostly worked with international cooperation in managing marine living resources after the establishment of exclusive economic zones. Among her publications is *Fish and Foreign Policy; Norway's Fisheries Relations with Other States in the Barents Sea, the Norwegian Sea and the North Sea;* the Fridtjof Nansen Institute, 1987.

Edward Miles is Director at the Institute for Marine Studies, University of Washington, and took his Ph.D. in international relations at the University of Denver 1965, where he was became Assistant and Associate Professor 1966-74. Since 1974 he has been Professor of Marine Studies and Public Affairs at the University of Washington. His fields of specialization are international law and organization; science, technology and international relations; marine policy; and ocean management. He has published extensively in these fields and one of his publications is *The Management of Marine Regions: The North Pacific,* 1982.

Dietrich Sahrhage is Doctor and Professor in Fisheries Biology. He was a fisheries biologist at Federal Fisheries Research Center in Hamburg 1953-65, and was associated with the Food and Agriculture Organization (FAO) of the UN, 1965-74. Since 1974 he has been Director of the Institut für Seefischerei in Hamburg, retiring in November 1988. His main research contribution has dealt with fisheries biology mainly in the North Atlantic and Antarctic waters. He was editor of the book *Antarctic Ocean and Resource Variability,* 1988.

Thorvald Stoltenberg is Minister of Foreign Affairs in Norway. He studied international law and international relations in Austria, Switzerland, USA and Finland from 1952-54, becoming a lawyer in 1957. He joined the Ministry of Foreign Affairs in 1958 holding various positions throughout the 1960s. He has been state secretary in several ministries and was Minister of Defence (1979-81). He is a member of the Labour Party and has held a number of positions in different organizations both nationally and internationally. In 1978-79 he was chairman of the North-South Committee in the UN. In 1987 he was appointed Minister of Foreign Affairs.

Lloyd Timberlake is Director of External Affairs at the International Institute for Environment and Development (IIED). His previous positions include writer/ senior editor, at IIED, Editorial Director, with Earthscan, science editor, then Chief Nordic Correspondent, Reuters News Agency. Among his chief publications is *Only One Earth*, 1987.

Arild Underdal is Professor of Political Science at the University of Oslo, and holds a D. Phil. from the University of Oslo, where he was Assistant Professor 1974-76, research fellow at the Norwegian Council for Science and the Humanities 1977-78, Associate Professor at the University of Oslo from 1979-85 and Professor at the Norwegian School of Management 1986-87. Among his major publications is *The Politics of International Fisheries Management*, Norwegian University Press, 1980

Jørgen Wettestad is research fellow at the Fridtjof Nansen Institute, and is a political scientist from the University of Oslo (1984). He has been associated with the Fridtjof Nansen Institute since he graduated, and has worked in various aspects of environmental politics both at the national and the international level, with special emphasis on organizational aspects. Among his publications is *Multilateral Aid Agencies and the Environment: Principles, Implementation and Possible Nordic Policy Options*, the Fridtjof Nansen Institute, (in Norwegian), 1987.

Oran Young obtained his Ph.D. from Yale in 1965. He was Assistant Professor and Professor of Politics at the University of Princeton 1966-72, Professor of Government, University of Texas at Austin 1972-76 and Professor of Government and Politics, University of Maryland 1976-82. He was Director at the Center for Northern Studies from 1983-86, and he is now a Senior fellow at Dartmouth College and the Center for Northern Studies. He has worked in various aspects of international resource regimes and his numerous publications include *Resource Regimes: Natural Resources and Social Institutions,* 1982.

Willy Østreng is Director of the Fridtjof Nansen Institute, and a political scientist from the University of Oslo (1971). He was research fellow at the Fridtjof Nansen Institute from 1971-78 and has been Director since. He was research fellow at Harvard University, in 1974, and at the University of California, Berkeley in 1987. His main research interests are polar politics, ocean law and politics, international resource management and international security. He has published extensively in all these fields and his publications include *Soviet Oil and Security Interests in the Barents Sea* (with Helge Ole Bergesen, and Arild Moe,) Pinter Publishers, 1987.

Preface

To mark the occasion of the thirtieth anniversary of the Fridtjof Nansen Institute in Norway, an international symposium was arranged for 10-11 October 1988 at the Norwegian Academy of Sciences and Letters. The title of the symposium was 'The Management of International Resources: Scientific Input and the Role of Scientific Cooperation'. The symposium gathered some 100 participants from seven countries.

There are several reasons why this topic was chosen. Fridtjof Nansen himself was a prominent natural scientist. At the turn of the century, he was one of the founding fathers of the International Council for the Exploration of the Sea (ICES). Today, the study of international resource regimes is the major focus of research activities at the Fridtjof Nansen Institute. An important aspect of the Institute's philosophy is to improve communication and understanding between researchers and groups interested in applying the scientific findings. Consequently it is seen as important to bring together people with different backgrounds to discuss these problems. Among the participants at this symposium were natural and political scientists, representatives of research councils, civil servants, members of government and representatives of international organizations.

Although the symposium forms the point of departure for this book, this is not a volume of conference proceedings. The speakers at the symposium have all· submitted separate papers to this volume; the editors have attempted, through the organization of the book, through comments to the papers and through extensive use of cross-references, to link the different articles together so as to create an entity.

All the contributors to the book have responded promptly to our comments and, despite other pressing commitments, have managed to stick to their deadlines — for which the editors are very grateful. However, without the help of a number of key persons, we would not have been able to produce this book according to plan.

Anne-Christine Thestrup has done the typing and editing very efficiently while Dag Harald Claes and Grete Haram has provided equally efficient assistance in the computer work. We also wish to express our gratitude to Øystein Thommesen, who has been responsible for making the appendixes and to Per Oue Eikeland for efficient work with the index; to Susan HØivik, who has provided language assistance, to Marit Bockelie, who made a beautiful drawing of the institute for the symposium programme; to Arild Moe for his help in the initial phases of this book; and to Brit Fløistad and Jørgen Wettestad for commenting on some of the papers.

This book could not have become reality without the teamwork of all the staff at the Fridjof Nansen Institute during the symposium and the active support of the Board of the Institute, not least from its chairman, Alf Sanengen. Hard work and support are important, but material contributions cannot be overlooked either. We were fortunate enough to receive financial support for the symposium from the following sources: Bærum Municipality, the Norwegian Academy of Sciences and Letters, the Norwegian Marshall Fund, the Norwegian Research Council for Fisheries, the Norwegian Research Council for Science and the Humanities, the Royal Ministry of the Environment, the Royal Ministry of Foreign Affairs and the Scandinavian Airlines System.

Finally, let us add that none of those mentioned are responsible for any shortcomings of this book. Although the authors are responsible for their individual contributions, the editors alone bear the responsibility for the book as such.

Willy Østreng
Steinar Andresen
Lysaker, February 1989

Foreword: Foreign policy and science*

Thorvald Stoltenberg

When the Fridtjof Nansen Institute was established thirty years ago, there was a cold war in Europe and between East and West. Already in 1958, however, there was an obvious need for increased contacts between East and West to reduce tensions and to discuss common problems. The question as to how we could promote a better climate for cooperation on common problems was an important concern among the group of people who took the initiative in establishing an institute in the name of Fridtjof Nansen. The same motive was behind the attempts to break the impasse in East/West contacts initiated in the same period by the Norwegian Foreign Minister, Halvard Lange, and his Polish colleague, Adam Rapacki.

For one who took part in both these events during the late 1950s, the shift in the East/West climate during the last few years has been dramatic. The superpower dialogue between Washington and Moscow has led to a number of important East/West agreements. The agreement between the European Communities and COMECON is potentially very important for trade and economic relations in Europe, and the CSCE process offers hope for much more open human contacts across the old East/West divide. On arms control and disarmament, there is a new momentum towards agreements on reductions aiming at creating a more stable balance of power with lower levels of armament than before.

In looking back on the events of the last few years, it may be argued that it all started in 1984. For me and others who grew up with George Orwell's famous book *1984* as an ominous warning of a sinister future for mankind, this is a special paradox. The year 1984 for us stood as a codeword for all the negative trends in modern society, as a symbol of humanity's inexorable move towards an inhuman world.

Instead of fulfilling George Orwell's nightmarish vision, the year 1984 may become a symbol of a positive landmark in European history. Since 1984, we have seen important shifts and changes in many key areas of international politics. We do not know today the end result of these changes. Indeed, we will almost certainly experience backlashes and new problems in one field or another. What is important is that there is now a new mood of optimism and hope in international relations. There is again a sense that international problems can be tackled through talks, negotiations and peaceful settlements. The foundation has been laid for a period of constructive international cooperation on the many common challenges facing international society today.

Let me make a brief run though of the list of important events during the last few years.

In 1984, a new dynamism in the process of Western European integration was created by the EC/EFTA declaration on a 'European Economic Space' (EES), which was followed by the European Single Act of the twelve members of the European Community in 1985. This act also set up the target of creating a European internal market by the end of 1992.

In 1985, General Secretary Gorbachev came to power in the Soviet Union. Faced with the results of a long period of economic and political stagnation, he has initiated a process of reform encompasing almost every field of Soviet policy. 'Glasnost' and 'perestroika' have become familiar concepts even outside Russia. The human rights situation is significantly improved, and the general openess in discussing both internal and external policy is dramatically changed.

The year 1986 saw the start of an active dialogue between the United States and the Soviet Union, a process which brought four summit meetings between President Reagan and General Secretary Gorbachev in less than three years. The INF Agreement became the most visible and concrete result of these contacts, but the superpower dialogue has also been instrumental in promoting specifically the Soviet withdrawal from Afghanistan and in general a broader understanding to encourage peaceful settlement on other regional conflicts, such as the Iran/Iraq war, the Angolan/Namibian conflict and others. One important beneficiary of these developments has been the United Nations. Only three years ago the world organization was in the middle of the worst crisis of its existence. Its political prestige had never been lower, at least not in many Western countries, and financially the organization was on the verge of bankruptcy.

Today, even this has changed. The superpower dialogue has reached even the UN, and the Security Council has once again become a key arena for discussion of issues of international peace and security. New peacekeeping operations and observer missions have been established in Afghanistan, on the Iran/Iraq border, and are being prepared for Namibia and Western Sahara. The UN services for mediation and negotiations are being requested in several other difficult international conflicts.

Why have all these changes occurred in a span of only four to five years? There are several interrelated factors involved. In this article, there is space and time only to mention a couple of the most significant ones.

The most important factor behind the basic change of attitude towards international cooperation is probably the fact that the world in the 1980s has become truly global. In some sectors, such as the nuclear field, we have already known for many years that we are all in the same boat. But the 1980s have seen a convergence of many other trends which all point in the same direction. Together they have created a new global awareness, a perception in almost all countries that nations, peoples and individuals of the earth are becoming truly interdependent. Most of all, these trends indicate that foreign policy today is becoming less a question of relations between states and more a matter of how nations should cope with common problems.

The need for effective international cooperation is nothing new to Norwegians, who make up only 0.1 per cent of the world population. We have long been dependent on international cooperation for our security, for giving us free access to economic markets for our goods and services, etc. Other small middle-power or like-minded nations have long ago joined forces in a plea for a more organized world society, with a stronger United Nations, more multilateral cooperation, and a world society ruled by law and a common code of behaviour.

What is new is that the perception of global interdependence is now growing even among the great powers. The necessary reforms of the Soviet economy can no longer be achieved by turning inwards. If the Soviet economic system is to take advantage of the vitality, technological innovation and growth potential of the emerging global economy, it must become part of this economy. And if the United States is to close the enormous budget deficits which have accumulated during the 1980s and which have turned the United States from a creditor to a major debtor nation, it can only do so by a closer coordination of economic policies with that of other industrialized nations.

An important factor in explaining this new global awareness lies, however, in the problems of the environment. In Scandinavia, the fall-out from the Chernobyl accident and last summer's algae invasion from the North Sea were powerful reminders of a new kind of threat to our security. In the rest of Europe forests are dying and pollution of air and waterways has accumulated to a point which nature can no longer absorb. In other regions the rain forests are being cut down at an alarming rate, and population growth, desertification, soil erosion and water degradation are becoming keywords in a growing list of threats to our global environment. To round it off, we have only in the last year or so become really aware of a dangerous depletion of the ozone layer in the stratosphere and of the possibilities of global climatic change.

Science and technology are key factors in this development. The subject of the International Symposium of the Fridtjof Nansen Institute is therefore particularly relevant. Science and technology are powerful forces for change in the international system. Technology has made the world smaller and more integrated at the same time as it has given us more powerful tools for research and further advances of human knowledge than ever before. The network of cooperation and exchange of information between scientists in all countries has been a driving force behind the process of internationalization.

If we are to have any hope of tackling the many important problems facing us, scientific cooperation will be an important prerequisite. To mention one example, research into the enormously complicated issue of global climatic change will require a huge cooperative effort, with coordination from international organizations and with participation from scientists all over the world.

Science is also a necessary instrument in the conduct of foreign policy. Scientific research gives us a base for policies and decisions regarding the exploitation of natural resources such as oil, fish, whales, etc. In the polar regions, which in the spirit of Fridtjof Nansen have always been close to the heart of research activities of the Nansen Institute, research programmes and scientific cooperation have provided essential input for necessary policy decisions.

I have come to appreciate the ability of the Fridtjof Nansen Institute to combine independent and excellent research with its role of providing practical ideas on how Norway and other nations should act in the management of international resources.

It gives me great satisfaction to announce my support for the proposed research project on energy strategies in the Third World to be conducted by the Fridtjof Nansen Institute and ECON-Center for Economic Analyses. The aim of this project is threefold: first to analyse developing countries' planning in the energy sector, secondly to connect this to the recommendations of the World Commission on Environment and Development and thirdly to evaluate the functioning of the UN system within this issue area. In our view this is an excellent way to combine interesting political and foreign policy issues with interdisciplinary research cooperation. I wish the Nansen Institute and ECON success with the project.

*Opening address, Fridtjof Nansen Institute Symposium on the Management of International Resources, Scientific Input and the Role of Scientific Cooperation, Oslo, 10–11 October 1988

Introduction

Steinar Andresen and Willy Østreng

The main purpose of this book is to analyse the role of science in political processes of international resource management. Two key problems will be addressed:

- the role of science in initiating political processes and international cooperation, and
- the role of science in political decision-making.

The common denominator of these two problems concerns the ability of scientists and scientific knowledge to play a part in shaping and influencing political decisions on resource management. To initiate policy and integrate scientific knowledge into the decision-making processes is highly dependent upon the organization of the relationship between science and politics. In most international resource regimes, decisions are supposed to be based on scientific advice and scientific bodies are set up as integral parts of the decision-making systems. Thus, existing arrangements usually provide the necessary *legal* means for science to influence the political processes of international resource management.

However, not all knowledge acquired by scientific methods commands sufficient consensus among the parties to serve as a guide to their joint public *policy*. In certain issue areas it is more or less up to the parties to 'pick and choose' whatever they like from the scientific debate to support their own national positions. Science is being politicized and used for partisan rather than universal interests. This poses the need to define the purpose of science.

Dr. Fridtjof Nansen, who was himself a politician, diplomat and scientist, pinpointed this issue in a metaphorical way by stating:

If I should ask you to tell me what is the purpose of clothing, I hope most of you would reply: its purpose is to protect the body. But I am afraid that many would say that its main purpose is to beautify the body. Similarly, if we were to ask what is the purpose of jewellery, some would say ornamentation and beautification, while others would say demonstration of wealth. We all agree that there is an answer to that type of question, though we may not agree on what it ought to be.

In line with this reasoning, what we are focusing on here is whether the purpose of science is to protect the body of politics from the intrusion of harmful influences on the common good of the international community, or to beautify the body of politics by bestowing legitimacy on decisions alien to the preservation of the common good. There is of course a third option: science might be used both for the protection and beautification of the body of politics. And to complicate matters even further it has also been maintained that the purpose of politics, under certain conditions, is to protect and beautify the body of science.

From these points of departure, our aim here is to provide some insight into questions of this kind: To what extent do we have at our disposal adequate, unitary, legitimate and (politically) usable scientific knowledge to enable regime parties to make complex decisions on resource politics? What is the importance of scientific consensus and legitimacy of scientific bodies as regards the decision-makers? Under what circumstances do scientific recommendations shape the content of resource management decisions? How do scientific bodies relate to political decision-makers? How strongly do characteristics of international organizations affect the relationship between science and politics? To what extent have scientific knowledge and initiatives contributed to political processes? To what extent has scientific cooperation across boundaries contributed to cooperation among politicians? What factors — if any — appear important in producing such spill-over effects?

These issues will be discussed within the framework of one section dealing with international regimes in general, and three sections comprising three empirical areas: environmental protection (Sections 2 and 3), the management of the living resources of the ocean (Section 4) and the polar regions (final part of Section 1).

The Foreign Minister of Norway, Thorvald Stoltenberg, describes in his article how international politics are gradually changing to become the relationship of states to mutual problems, rather than to each other. Transboundary pollution, the depletion of the ozone layer and global climate change are among the new international agenda-setting issues facing the governments of the world.

In Section 1 Oran Young addresses the complex relationship between science and social institutions, aiming to derive some lessons of practical value to policy-makers. Young's article is followed by that of Steinar Andresen who asks whether increased public attention towards international resource regimes is likely to hamper or promote the inclusion of scientific premises in decision-making processes. In the next article Edward Miles deepens the nexus between scientific/ technical knowledge and politics, whilst Willy Østreng discusses the relationship of research to national interests and the ability of science to influence and initiate political processes in the polar regions.

In Section 2 Lloyd Timberlake assesses why science and scientists assumed the role of referees rather than that of initiators in drawing up the Report from the UN World Commission on the Environment and

Development. Helge Ole Bergesen discusses measures to prevent science from becoming a tool in the hands of political actors, whilst Leif E. Christoffersen elaborates the problems of how to put to good use the technological tools of computers and satellite-based remote sensing in enhancing the global environment.

Section 3 is opened by Sonia Boehmer-Christiansen, who discusses why pollution control involves a complex process of public policy-making influenced by a broad range of factors. Jørgen Wettestad concentrates on the North Sea environmental cooperation and develops an analytical framework for studying the relationship between science and political decision-making in more general terms. Per M. Bakken addresses the interaction between scientists and governments in recent endeavours to protect the ozone layer.

Section 4 is devoted to living resources. Dietrich Sahrhage focuses on the complex interaction of science and politics in the international management of fish resources, while the Icelandic Minister of Fisheries, Halldor Asgrimsson, analyses the background to the 1982 decision of the International Whaling Commission for a zero catch quota. In comparing the characteristics of the International Whaling Commission and the International Council for the Exploration of the Seas, Brit Fløistad highlights differences in how scientific advice is provided and mediated in the management of whale and fish stocks.

The concluding article, by Arild Underdal, unites theoretical and empirical aspects of the previous sections, combining them into an overall, generalized perspective on international resource management.

SECTION 1:
Science and International Regimes

SECTION
Search information and routines

1

Science and social institutions: lessons for international resource regimes

Oran R. Young

The purpose of this article is to discuss the relationship between science and social institutions, with particular reference to international resource regimes. This is obviously a tall order, and I can do no more than scratch the surface of this always intriguing and sometimes puzzling subject. None the less, I shall press on in the hopes of posing some provocative questions and stimulating others to think hard about the relationship between science and social institutions in order to challenge my tentative conclusions. In the process, I will endeavour not only to deepen our understanding of this important relationship but also to derive some lessons for policy-makers who must wrestle daily with concrete issues relating to the human use of natural resources and environmental services at the international level.

To avoid unnecessary misunderstandings, let me start by defining several key terms. *Science*, broadly construed, encompasses both a collection of knowledge claims that are widely accepted as scientific by virtue of the fact that they conform to certain procedural canons (for example, falsifiability, reproducibility) and a set of human beings engaged in the production and refinement of such knowledge claims who, taken together, may be thought of as the scientific community. Defined in this way, science includes the social and behavioural sciences as well as the life sciences and the physical sciences.

Regimes are social institutions, which is to say that they are networks of rights and rules that serve to structure interactions among the occupants of more or less well defined roles in and between human societies. Resource regimes are institutional arrangements governing the human use of natural resources and environmental services; international resource regimes are those resource regimes that deal with natural resource and environmental issues cutting across the jurisdictional boundaries of the members of international society or involving the global commons.[1] Such regimes may be geographically specific (as in the case of the Antarctic Treaty System[2] functionally circumscribed (as in the case of the emerging regime for the protection of the stratospheric ozone layer[3] or limited in terms of membership (as in the case of the international whaling regime).[4] But international resource regimes may also be cast in broader terms as exemplified by the complex of arrangements for the oceans and marine areas[5] formalized in the 1982 Convention on the Law of the Sea or as envisioned in recent proposals for an international regime for the atmosphere which would encompass ozone depletion, global warming, acid precipitation, transboundary radioactive fall-out, and so forth.[6]

Science takes on significance for international resource regimes in at least four distinct contexts: (1) agenda setting, (2) regime formation, (3) social choice and (4) compliance. I shall have something to say about the role of science in each of these contexts in the substantive sections of this essay.

Agenda-setting

It has become commonplace to observe that scientific knowledge tends to become a public (or collective) good in the sense that it is difficult to exclude others from reaping the benefits of such knowledge once it becomes available to anyone in a community.[7] Somewhat less well known, however, is the fact that science produces a steady stream of externalities or, in other words, unintended side effects whose costs and benefits are not considered seriously in initial decisions regarding the investment of human as well as financial resources in the production of scientific knowledge. Those who think about such matters at all are apt to take it as an article of faith that the balance of these externalities will prove positive rather than negative. As it turns out, however, this is not always the case, especially when it comes to those side effects of science affecting institutional arrangements.

Science, especially as applied in the form of technology, can and often does expand human capabilities in ways that erode existing institutional arrangements and give rise to compelling pressures to restructure international resource regimes. The extraordinary advances of the post-war period in technologies usable to exploit marine resources, for instance, simply swamped the traditional institutional arrangements governing maritime activities (codified in large part, as recently as 1958 in the Geneva Conventions on the Law of the Sea) and led directly to the efforts to restructure these arrangements that engendered the third United Nations Conference on the Law of the Sea (UNCLOS III) which, in turn, eventuated in the negotiation of the 1982 Convention on the Law of the Sea.[8]

Let me be more specific about the role of science and technology in undermining the traditional order of the oceans. The advent of high endurance stern trawlers combined with increasingly sophisticated techniques for navigating these vessels (for example, satellite navigation) and locating fish (for example, aerial reconnaissance) quickly overwhelmed the prevailing arrangements for the marine fisheries based on open-to-entry common property and featuring the allocation of harvestable fish on a first-come, first-served basis.[9] The ensuing pressure to establish fishery conservation zones within which coastal states exercise exclusive management authority soon proved irresistible.[10] Similar comments are in order regarding offshore oil and gas development. Advances in science and technology producing the capability to exploit hydrocarbons efficiently in offshore areas immediately triggered pressures to replace the traditional high seas arrangements in sizeable areas extending beyond the (then) three-mile limit.[11] Taken together, these science-based advances in technologies applicable to fishing and outer continental shelf development surely played a determinative role in the remarkably rapid transition from the traditional arrangements reflected in the 1958 conventions to the promulgation of exclusive economic zones (EEZs) as codified in the 1982 Convention.[12]

In expanding human capabilities, moreover, science and the technological advances to which it gives rise regularly engender compelling pressures to create new resource regimes at the inter-national level where none previously existed.[13] Prior to the invention of the radio and the consequent development of commercial broadcasting, for example, there was no need to think about arrangements governing the allocation and use of frequencies in the electromagnetic spectrum. Before the introduction of communications satellites, no one felt a need to come up with a regime to govern the use of the geosynchronous orbit for international telecommunications.[14] Likewise, the contemporary concern about the development of a regime to deal with transboundary radioactive fall-out is a product of the harnessing of nuclear energy to produce electricity and the concomitant danger of nuclear accidents. For its part, the problem of protecting the stratospheric ozone layer simply did not exist until science and technology made it possible to produce chlorofluorocarbons (CFCs) and other gases capable of destroying ozone molecules in the stratosphere. Yet today each of these concerns, along with a number of other similar problems, occupies a prominent place on the agenda of issues requiring the development of new international resource regimes.

To return for a moment to the concept of externalities, it is worth pondering the fact that, for the most part, the institutional impacts of science and technology to which I referred in the preceding paragraphs were unintended and, more often than not, unforeseen by those responsible for producing the relevant knowledge. We can infer from this that the social costs associated with the production of scientific knowledge are seldom reflected in the decisions of science policy-makers. With all due respect to the benefits of science, moreover, these costs are far from trivial. It takes little insight to realize that efforts to restructure existing international regimes or to create new institutional arrangements at the international level are costly in terms of time and energy under the best of circumstances and that these efforts can easily lead to protracted and expensive stalemates.[15] What is more, since science and technology typically progress more rapidly than regime (re)formation, it is pertinent to ask in specific cases whether the relevant players can devise institutional arrangements quickly enough to prevent serious damage to natural resources and the environment resulting from the unrestricted use of new capabilities.[16]

On a more positive note, science regularly plays an important role in agenda setting by identifying and highlighting previously unknown and often cumulative problems arising from the human use of natural resources and environmental services whose solution requires the creation of suitable institutional arrangements. In this connection, it is interesting to note that the scientific community is far more effective with respect to some international resource and environmental issues than others. It appears, for instance, that scientists have contributed greatly to the impetus behind efforts to negotiate the 1985 Convention on the protection of the ozone layer, to add the 1987 Protocol to this convention, and to reopen the protocol to introduce even more stringent restrictions on the production and consumption of chlorofluoro-carbons.[17] Conversely, it is hard to escape the conclusion that the scientific community has played a more ambiguous and less effective role with regard to the problem of acid precipitation, presenting the relevant scientific evidence in ways that both sides in the debate over acid precipitation have been able to exploit for partisan purposes.

In my judgement, the keys to the effectiveness of the scientific community in this context lie less in the state of scientific knowledge about specific issues than in the ability of those scientists working on a given issue to reach consensus among themselves and to overcome the natural tendency of members of the scientific community to exhibit extreme caution in the interests of avoiding any appearance of overstating the inferences to be drawn from the available evidence.[18] It is not clear, for example, that the current state of scientific knowledge regarding ozone depletion is markedly superior to the state of knowledge regarding acid precipitation. But scientists working on the issue of ozone depletion have achieved remarkable success in influencing the course of the public debate on this issue not only by vigorously exploiting dramatic events relating to ozone depletion (for example, the seasonal 'ozone hole' over Antarctica) but also by presenting a united front to the world at large concerning the causes and effects of ozone depletion.[19] There is some evidence that scientists working on the global warming trend are taking note of this success and beginning to map out steps to heighten their influence over the public debate about global climate change in an effective manner.[20] The success or failure of this effort may well have dramatic consequences for the prospects of devising institutional arrangements at the international level to cope with climate change in a timely manner.[21]

Undoubtedly, the idea of seeking consciously to reach consensus is foreign to scientists socialized to value the thrust and parry of competition among conflicting ideas as a method of advancing knowledge. So too is the notion that the scientific community should seek to participate in a sophisticated manner in policy arenas rather than simply publish scientific results to be used by policy-makers as they see fit. None the less, it is increasingly clear that the behaviour of the scientific community itself is an important determinant of the role of science in the process of creating international resource regimes.

Before moving on, let me pause briefly to note a new development that may affect the role of the scientific community in setting agendas relating to international resource regimes. The fact that human activities, in the aggregate, have become a major source of change in large ecosystems or in the biosphere as a whole (in such forms as stock depletions, habitat destruction and global warming) means that there will be growing opportunities for social scientists to join natural scientists in identifying needs and opportunities for the development of international resource regimes. Whereas natural scientists can sound the alarm with regard to the effects of acid precipitation, ozone depletion, or global warming, social scientists can point to individual incentives and institutional pressures that, in combination with advances in science and technology, are likely to necessitate a restructuring of existing resource regimes or the creation of new regimes where none now exist.[22]

The implications of this development are surely worth exploring in some depth. While the knowledge claims of social scientists are typically more tenuous than those of natural scientists, it is also true that social scientists often possess a more sophisticated grasp of policy-making processes and the determinants of collective action in human societies. Perhaps for these reasons, natural scientists are apt to draw a sharper distinction between analysis and praxis than social scientists. Whatever its other consequences, this means that there may well be scope for the development of a constructive partnership between natural scientists and social scientists not only in the search for knowledge regarding international resource and environmental issues but also in the effort to bring this knowledge to bear on public decision-making in an effective manner.[23]

Regime formation

Raising an issue to a position of prominence on the international agenda is a necessary condition for regime formation in international society, but is not sufficient. As in other social settings, collective action problems abound at the international level, and there is no basis for assuming that the members of international society will enjoy a particularly high success rate in solving these problems.[24] It will come as no surprise, then, that the success of some efforts to form international regimes[25] (for example, the arrangements for Antarctica or the protection of the stratospheric ozone layer) is matched by the failure of efforts to establish similar arrangements in other areas (for example, in the Arctic, acid precipitation in North America or biological diversity). What factors determine whether such efforts result in success or failure? More specifically, what is the role of science in this connection?

The formation of some international resource regimes is essentially science driven. That is, the process of regime formation is carried by the scientific community, operating in scientific forums and employing scientific procedures widely accepted across national and cultural boundaries. In the case of Antarctica, for example, the Comité Spécial de l'Année Géophysique Internationale, operating under the auspices of the International Council of Scientific Unions, played a key role in planning and coordinating the International Geophysical Year (1957-58) which, in turn, became an important way station on the road to the creation of the Scientific Committee on Antarctic Research (SCAR) in 1958 and the formation in 1959 of the Antarctic Treaty System itself.[26] Similar comments are in order regarding the origins of the international regime for the protection of polar bears. A particularly interesting feature of this case is the role played by the International Union for the Conservation of Nature and Natural Resources (IUCN) in providing a scientific forum, in the form of a Polar Bear Specialist Group, within which scientists from the five relevant countries were able to reach consensus on the substantive terms of an international polar bear regime.[27] Much the same is true of the creation of the regime governing trade in endangered species set forth in the 1973 Convention on International Trade in Endangered Species of Wild Fauna and Flora (CITES). In this instance, the IUCN was able to provide critical backing through the listing of endangered species in its authoritative *Red Book* as well as through the provision of an impartial arena within which key scientists could hammer out the terms of an agreement unhindered by the biases of various interest groups.[28]

The key question in cases of this sort involves the ability of scientists to influence the response of the relevant governments to the institutional arrangements proposed by the scientific community. When the proposed arrangements do not impinge on the concerns of powerful interest groups, this may not be a major problem. Perhaps we can account for the relative success of the international regime for the protection of polar bears in this way. Frequently, however, groups possessing considerable political influence drag their feet or openly oppose the recommendations of the scientific community, with the result that policy-makers are unwilling, or even unable, to follow through on the recommendations of the scientific community. It is easy to see such forces at work in the frequent battles concerning regional fisheries arrangements calling for the application of scientific management criteria like maximum sustainable yield or optimum sustainable yield or optimum sustainable population.[29] And there are good reasons to doubt whether some of the members of CITES would be able to suppress the illegal trade in endangered species even if they were to make a concerned effort to do so.

A much more complex situation arises, by contrast, when science becomes involved in efforts to form international regimes covering human activities that are highly politicized from the outset. These are cases, like arrangements relating to fur seals, acid precipitation or global warming, in which powerful interest groups oppose each other with regard to the provisions of proposed regimes as well as numerous other issues.[30] When these conditions prevail, it is not possible for members of the scientific community to devise the terms of appropriate regimes in more or less apolitical settings and then to present the finished products to governments for their approval. Rather, scientists must choose between remaining aloof from the process of regime formation on the premis that science and politics do not mix, or entering the political process directly in the hope that scientific findings can have at least some beneficial impact on the outcome.

Scientists who do become involved in the political process in such cases typically encounter several problems. While it is comforting to think of scientists as disinterested suppliers of objective knowledge claims, it is virtually impossible for the scientific community to avoid becoming — and being perceived by others as becoming — another interest group in the politics of international regime formation. The fact is that the scientific community, like other interest groups, is made up of human beings who have distinct values and policy preferences. As a result, this community regularly engages in efforts to promote institutional arrangements, which its members prefer for normative reasons on the grounds that they are necessitated by scientific considerations alone. Consider, in this connection, the role of scientists in general and of SCAR in particular in the campaign to set aside Antarctica as a continent for science, thereby prohibiting or sharply restricting the activities of others in the Antarctic region.[31] There is nothing inherently wrong with the scientific community operating as an interest group in the political process. None the less, it is hard to play such a role and to retain credibility as a source of objective or disinterested analysis at the same time.

Even more disturbing is the exploitation of science and scientists by interest groups seeking to direct processes of regime formation to their own advantage. The problem here arises from fundamental differences in modes of operation between the political process and scientific procedures. Politics is an adversary process in which various players or interest groups use information selectively (or even manipulatively) in order to influence others or to assemble winning coalitions. For their part, scientists are generally cautious about the inferences to be drawn from their work and chary about asserting direct cause and effect relationships as opposed to probalistic connections. The result, more often than not, is a situation in which scientists are deployed in such a way as to promote the interests of key players in the political process and in which scientific knowledge claims are used selectively or out of context to strengthen the case of various interest groups. Exploitation of this sort is not confined to the political right or to the political left. Conservatives in the United States and elsewhere, for instance, routinely exploit the cautious attitude of scientists regarding cause and effect relationships in their opposition to the establishment of effective international regimes to control the long-range transport of air pollutants. For their part, those desiring to ban the consumptive use of wild animals regularly use scientific findings selectively to make the case that such activities threaten the viability of species.[32]

All this presents members of the scientific community with a difficult choice. If they remain aloof from the political process, they must accept the risk that their findings will be used in a seriously distorted manner by those desiring to promote partisan causes. If they seek to minimize this danger by becoming involved directly in the political process, on the other hand, they may well be exploited by players whose grasp of this process far exceeds their own. Under the circumstances, it is easy enough to understand why many scientists today seek to acquire a sophisticated grasp of the political process, even while maintaining their primary commitment to the advancement of scientific knowledge. Even so, this hardly constitutes a simple solution to the dilemma, since the time and energy required to achieve sophistication regarding the political process ordinarily involves significant opportunity costs measured in terms of distractions from the pursuit of science as such.

Before proceeding to the next set of relationships between science and social institutions, let me pause again to note that the process of regime formation itself is a suitable subject for analysis on the part of social scientists.[33] Even a cursory examination of the record is sufficient to demonstrate that efforts to create international resource regimes succeed under some conditions (for example Antarctica, ozone depletion) but fail under other conditions (for example, acid precipitation in North America, biological diversity). The result is exactly the sort of puzzle that scientists find intriguing as a point of departure in their quest for enhanced understanding of the world. What is more, it is easy to see how advances in our understanding of the determinants of success and failure in regime formation would be distinctly helpful to policy-makers endeavouring to cope with issues relating to natural resources and environmental services at the international level.

Research in the social sciences regarding this topic is still in its infancy. Thus, it is relatively easy to point to shortcomings in existing accounts of regime formation at the international level.[34] The accounts of those who focus on the behaviour of rational utility maximizers, for example, commonly fail to come to grips with collective action problems that can and often do lead actors who behave in an individually rational fashion to arrive at collective choices that are suboptimal (sometimes drastically suboptimal) for all concerned. Similarly, propositions advanced by political realists to the effect that the presence of a hegemon (that is, a single preponderant actor) is necessary to the achievement of success in regime formation at the international level are relatively easy to falsify in the realm of natural resource and environmental issues. But this does nothing to alter the potential of social science in improving our understanding of processes of regime formation at the international level. Rather, it suggests that we should be devoting more resources to research on this subject in the interests of filling major gaps in our current understanding of dynamics of regime formation.

Social choice

International resource regimes generally encompass procedures for making social (or collective) choices regarding the human use of natural resources or environmental services.[35] Some of these choices involve the allocation of scarce resources or, in the vocabulary of economics, factors of production among alternative users. In many fisheries, for instance, it is necessary not only to determine total allowable catches (TACs) on a yearly basis but also to apportion allowable catches among commercial, subsistence and recreational users.

A second range of social choices relating to the human use of natural resources and environmental services involve the distribution of economic benefits or the incidence of costs among the members of international society.[36] Should the International Seabed Authority, for instance, endeavour to collect economic returns on deep sea-bed minerals and, if so, what sort of mechanism (bonus bids, royalties, corporate taxes) should it employ to achieve this goal?[37] Who should pay for programmes designed to repair the damages caused by transboundary radioactive fall-out or to compensate innocent victims of such fall-out for the damages they sustain? Should some international agency play a role in this area through the establishment of a clean-up fund or the imposition of regulations on polluters or pollution charges?

Undoubtedly, there is a large and significant role for science in establishing a sound basis on which to confront these social choices. The calculation of maximum sustainable yields from fish populations and optimum sustainable populations for marine mammals is essentially a matter for scientific analysis.[38] So also is the assessment of the number of communication satellites that can occupy the geosynchronous orbit simultaneously without interfering with each other. And similar comments are in order regarding efforts to calculate the effects of the long-range transport of air pollutants on various ecosystems. In all these cases, it would hardly make sense to proceed directly to allocative or distributive choices without first factoring in the contributions of the scientific community.

Having said this, however, it is important to emphasize that international society cannot simply turn over decisions about the human use of natural resources and environmental services to the scientific community without further ado. In fact, social choices in this realm invariably turn on normative or value preferences. Science may be able to tell us how many fish to harvest if we wish to achieve maximum sustainable yield or maximum economic yield, for example, but it cannot say which of these harvest levels we should strive for when the two criteria yield different results. If we assume a given social rate of discount, science may well be able to map out an optimal use rate for non-renewable resources like offshore oil or manganese nodules, but it cannot specify what the social rate of discount should be.[39] Similarly, science can tell us something about the number of extra skin cancers likely to result from increases in ultraviolet radiation associated with the depletion of stratospheric ozone, but it cannot determine how much ozone depletion is socially acceptable.

The problem in this context is to arrive at and maintain a clear sense of what scientific analysis can and cannot do for us in making allocative and distributive choices about natural resources or environmental services. We should seek to benefit from scientific analysis as much as possible in determining total allowable catches in the marine fisheries, but we should not expect science to tell us how to allocate the resultant TACs among commercial, subsistence and recreational users. We should apply scientific analysis rigorously in our efforts to determine the cumulative impacts of acid precipitation on complex ecosystems, but we should not expect science to tell us what sort of liability rules to establish in order to avoid or control such impacts.[40]

Yet, maintaining this distinction is not easy. Partly, this is due to the fact that we commonly pose policy issues in such a way as to subsume scientific and non-scientific questions at the same time. In part, however, the problem arises because groups whose interests are at stake in a given issue area exhibit a natural tendency to disguise their value preferences in the form of arguments stressing scientific findings in order to give their views an air of objectivity. Surely, this problem should not lead us to dismiss the valuable contributions of science in dealing with natural resource and environmental issues. But it obliges us to be alert at all times to the distinction between what science can and cannot do in this realm.

While the preceding observations focus on the role of the natural sciences, it would be inappropriate to leave this topic without noting that there is a large and rapidly growing body of literature in the social sciences seeking to assess the allocative and distributive consequences of institutional arrangements in general and social choice mechanisms more specifically.[41] The result is what might be termed a comparative statics of resource regimes, including those operative at the international level.[42]

This work, too, walks a fine line between scientific analysis and arguments intended to justify value preferences.[43] Those trained in economics, for example, tend to focus (sometimes exclusively) on questions of allocative efficiency in evaluating the relative merits of alternative social choice mechanisms.[44] Not surprisingly, they are attracted by the virtues of transferable and marketable permits for allocating TACs in the marine fisheries and by the advantages of pollution charges (or even marketable pollution rights) over regulatory approaches in efforts to combat air and water pollution.[45] To be more specific, those who think first of allocative efficiency find it hard to justify reserving choice tracts on the deep sea-bed for the Enterprise, setting aside orbital slots for possible future use by developing countries, or imposing across-the-board cuts in the production of chlorofluorocarbons. Yet efficiency is hardly the only criterion that we may wish to employ in evaluating the relative merits of social choice mechanisms. Equity and ecological balance, for example, are surely relevant in this context, and there may well be other criteria of equal merit in normative terms. To some analysts, for instance, a major virtue of pollution charges lies in the fact that public agencies can make use of them to generate sizeable revenue flows which they can subsequently employ to compensate innocent victims of pollution or to conduct research on the development of cleaner technologies. Similarly, many commentators object to the traditional first-come, first-served approach to allocating TACs in the marine fisheries not only because it fails to produce any economic returns to designated agencies treated as owners/managers of the resource, but also because it generates incentives to engage in high technology pulse fishing of a sort that is destructive to marine ecosystems. To the extent that we endeavour to apply several of these criteria of evaluation simultaneously, moreover, we must come to terms with the fact that social choice mechanisms that seem preferable in terms of one criterion will often look much less attractive in terms of other criteria. At this juncture, scientific analysis cannot help much in coming to terms with the resultant trade-offs.[46]

The intermingling of science and politics is particularly pervasive in the area of social choice. There is, in fact, a double danger in this realm. As I have already suggested, interest groups regularly endeavour to mask their preferences as scientifically proven propositions. There is no cause for surprise, therefore, when inshore fishers blame poor harvests on alleged depradations of high seas fishers or when those whose actions have contributed to desertification attribute the problem to global climate change. At the same time, it is not uncommon for scientists themselves to become confused about what science can and cannot contribute to the making of social choices. It is easy for scientists who know a lot about the dynamics of animal populations, for instance, to make pronouncements about socially appropriate harvest levels or for scientists who have studied the role of ultraviolet radiation as a cause of skin cancer to become advocates of sharp reductions in the production and consumption of chlorofluorocarbons. Certainly, this does not mean that we should dismiss or even discount the contributions of scientific analysis to making collective choices in an informed manner. But it does suggest that the balance between science and politics in arriving at social choices concerning the human use of natural resources and environmental services is destined to be a delicate one.

Compliance

It is common knowledge that institutional arrangements which prove unable to elicit high levels of compliance on the part of those subject to their constituent rights and rules quickly become dead letters. Such a fate has befallen many efforts to build regimes at the international level, as well as in other social settings. Consider, for example, the arrangements pertaining to peacekeeping set forth in Chapter 7 of the United Nations Charter or the more specific provisions relating to international trade in commodities incorporated in the commodity regimes for sugar, coffee, tin and so forth.[47]

None the less, misconceptions about compliance in international society abound. Those who style themselves realists frequently seize on specific acts of non-compliance and infer from them that international regimes do not ultimately matter because powerful members of international society will simply ignore the dictates of such arrangements whenever it is inconvenient for them to comply with the terms of specific regimes. But no one would apply such a standard of perfection in evaluating compliance in domestic society, drawing sweeping conclusions from the occurrence of specific acts of non-compliance rather than focusing on the fact that most members of society comply with the dictates of a wide range of institutional arrangements as a matter of course. And there is considerable evidence to suggest that the members of international society, like their domestic counterparts, exhibit high levels of compliance with the provisions of many international resource regimes on a regular basis.[48]

Those who are sceptical about the significance of institutional arrangements in international society are also prone to exaggerating the role of enforcement or the deployment of sanctions on the part of central authorities in eliciting compliance from the individual members of society. No social system that relies predominately on enforcement to elicit compliance with rights and rules can long survive. Nor is the role of sanctions in connection with compliance confined to the actions of central authorities. Thus, students of society have long been aware of the behavioural significance of socialization and social pressure. While studies of these phenomena have typically focused on domestic society, there is much evidence to suggest that such phenomena are important in international society as well.

The scientific community can and, in my judgement, should participate actively in the pursuit of compliance with the rights and rules incorporated in international resource regimes. Partly, this is a matter of the role of science in developing and deploying verification procedures or monitoring systems. Studies of compliance regularly suggest that increases in the probability of non-compliant behaviour being detected depress rates of violation, independently of the probability that more tangible sanctions or penalties will follow detection. In other words, actors are more likely to violate prescriptions, including those characteristic of international resource regimes, if they believe they can do so without detection and adverse publicity. It follows that any improvements in detection mechanisms or monitoring systems should result in a lowering of rates of violation.

As it happens, science and technology have much to offer in this realm, especially in the development of monitoring systems capable of verifying compliance or detecting violations in a non-intrusive manner.[49] Thus, the use of tamper-proof transponders to verify that fishing vessels are operating within permissible areas; the deployment of advanced seismographic techniques to distinguish between earthquakes and underground nuclear tests; the deployment of landsat images with sufficiently high resolution to support detailed inferences about activities occurring on the ground; and the emergence of advanced forms of chemical analysis capable of identifying the origins of non-point source pollutants can all contribute to enhancing our ability to verify compliance or detect violations at the international level. What is more, the application of such procedures need not involve intrusive practices of the sort that would provoke strong reactions from the guardians of state sovereignty, much less the establishment of some central authority that opponents could denounce as an incipient world government.

Additionally, the scientific community can play a significant role in the pursuit of compliance at the international level by operating as an organized interest group.[50] This community is unusually, perhaps uniquely, transnational in character. It is, as well, remarkably well organized (through organizations like the International Council of Scientific Unions) and highly skilled in the art of communicating across national boundaries. The scientific community is therefore capable not only of transcending the parochial concerns of individual states, but also of bringing pressures to bear on national governments that exceed the pressures more localized groups can muster. The role of this community in ensuring high levels of compliance with the provisions of the Antarctic Treaty System is comparatively well known. But there are clear indications that the community of scientists has been active and quite effective in promoting compliance with the provisions of numerous other arrangements, like the nuclear safeguards system operated by the International Atomic Energy Agency, the pollution control procedures set forth in the Mediterranean Action Plan and the arrangements for the protection of endangered species under the provisions of the Convention on the International Trade in Endangered Species of Wild Fauna and Flora.[51]

Perhaps this is also an auspicious point at which to re-emphasize the importance of forging an effective partnership between the natural sciences and the social sciences in connection with the operation of international resource regimes. Whether we think about it in conjunction with international arrangements or in connection with institutions in any other social setting, compliance is a suitable topic for study on the part of social scientists.[52] Certainly, many aspects of this topic are not well understood at present. But it is easy enough to see how advances in our understanding of compliance could facilitate efforts to implement the provisions of international resource regimes and, at the same time, enlarge the role of natural scientists in this domain. If it turns out, as I have suggested, that enforcement becomes an important determinant of compliant behaviour only at the margin, for instance, we will know that it is necessary to devote more attention to the study of other bases of compliance. Similarly, if investigations in this field continue to point to the probability of detection as a key determinant of compliant behaviour, we should redouble our efforts to make use of scientific knowledge in developing non-intrusive verification procedures and monitoring systems. No doubt, we will often be confronted with the need to make public decisions about such matters in the face of considerable scientific uncertainty. Even so, the benefits flowing from an effective partnership between the natural sciences and the social sciences in this realm will surely outstrip any costs associated with this course of action.

Conclusion

My central theme is that the relationship between science and social institutions, including international resource regimes, is a complex one. Science is hardly an unmixed blessing in this realm. Scientific advances and the technologies to which they give rise can undermine existing resource regimes and create a need for the establishment of institutional arrangements where none previously existed. Given the difficulties involved in regime (re)formation, the resultant costs to society are far from trivial. What is more, interested parties or interest groups sometimes manipulate scientific findings, not to mention scientists themselves, in their efforts to promote their preferences in connection with the operation of existing resource regimes and with the design of new arrangements. Given the subtleties of the political process, scientists will often find themselves facing a difficult choice between acquiring a mastery of this process at some considerable cost in terms of pursuing their scientific research, or eschewing the political process and accepting the risk that their findings will be used by others in a distorted fashion.

None the less, science and scientists (including social scientists) have much to offer to those concerned with the formation and operation of international resource regimes. Among other things, they can provide early warning of the need for new institutional arrangements, mobilize informed opinion behind efforts to hammer out the terms of appropriate regimes, identify the determinants of success in processes of regime (re)formation, backstop the operation of social choice mechanisms incorporated in specific resource regimes, and contribute to the development of verification procedures or monitoring systems designed to improve compliance with the provisions of specific regimes. Beyond this, the forging of an effective alliance between natural scientists and social scientists would enhance the role of the scientific community in the development and operation of international resource regimes. It would also yield a legacy of great value in our efforts to solve complex problems in other realms.

Notes

1. Young, Oran R., 1988, *International Cooperation: Building Regimes for Natural Resources and the Environment,* Cornell University Press, Ithaca.

2. Østreng, Willy, 1989, 'Polar Science and Politics: Close Twins or Opposite Poles in International Cooperation', in this volume.

3. Miles, Edward, 1989, 'Scientific and Technological Knowledge and International Cooperation in Resource Management', in this volume.

4. Asgrimsson, Halldor, 1989, 'Developments Leading to the 1982 Decision of the International Whaling Commission for a Zero Catch Quota, 1986-90', and Fløistad, Brit, 1989, 'Scientific Knowledge in the Management of Fish and Whale: Global or Regional Organizations, Single and Multi-species Approach', both in this volume.

5. Wettestad, Jørgen, 1989, 'Uncertain Science and Matching Policies: Science, Politics and the Organization of North Sea Environmental Cooperation', in this volume.

6. Soroos, Marvin S., 1988, 'The Atmosphere as an International Common Property Resource', paper prepared for the 1988 Annual Meeting of the American Political Science Association, and Bankes, N.D., 1988, 'The Ozone Convention and Protocol: Further Steps Towards an International Law of the Atmosphere', Resources, **22** (Spring), pp. 1–30.

7. In fact, this was not always the case. Until well into the nineteenth century, monarchs and other patrons of science, operating under the influence of a mercantilist view of the world, often endeavored to sequester scientific knowledge as proprietary information.

8. Hollick, Ann L., 1981, U.S. *Foreign Policy and the Law of the Sea,* Princeton University Press, Princeton.

9. Warner, William W., 1983, *Distant Water: The Fate of the North Atlantic Fisherman,* Little, Brown, Boston.

10. Young, Oran R., 1982, *Resource Regimes: Natural Resources and Social Institutions,* University of California Press, Berkeley.

11. MacLeish, William H., 1985, *Oil and Water: The Struggle for Georges Bank,* Atlantic Monthly Press, Boston.

12. Pontecorvo, Giulio (ed.), 1986, *The New Order of the Oceans: The Advent of*

a *Managed Environment*, Columbia University Press, New York.

13. Brown, Seyom, Cornell, Nina W., Fabian, Larry L., and Brown Weiss, Edith, 1977, *Regimes for the Ocean, Outer Space and Weather*, Brookings Institution, Washington DC.

14. Demac, Donna A. (ed.), 1986, *Tracing New Orbits: Cooperation and Competition in Global Satellite Development*, Columbia University Press, New York.

15. Sandler, Todd and Cauley, Jon, 1977, 'The Design of Supranational Structures: An Economic Perspective', *International Studies Quarterly*, **21**, pp. 251-76.

16. The interlocking problems that have led some observers to advocate a new international order for the atmosphere illustrate this concern.

17. Gleick, James, 1988, 'Treaty Powerless to Stem a Growing Loss of Ozone', *New York Times*, 20 March, 1.30.

18. Henrickson, Alan K., 1986, 'The Global Foundations for a Diplomacy of Consensus' in Alan K. Henrickson (ed.), *World Order: The Artisanship and Architecture of Global Diplomacy*, Scholarly Resources, Wilmington, pp. 217-44.

19. Titus, James G. (ed.), 1986, *Effects of Changes in Stratospheric Ozone and Global Climate*, vol. 1, United States Environmental Protection Agency and United Nations Environment Programme, Washington DC.

20. Jager, Jill, 1988, 'Anticipating Climatic Change: Priorities for Action,' *Environment*, September 1988, pp. 12-15 and 30-3.

21. For a striking account of the quest for international cooperation in public health during the nineteenth century, which makes a similar point, see Cooper, Richard N., 1988, 'International Economic Cooperation: Is It Desirable? Is It Likely?', unpublished paper.

22. For an early and clear account of the need for partnership between the natural sciences and the social sciences in this realm, see Caldwell, Lynton K., 1972, *Defense of Earth: International Protection of the Biosphere*, Indiana University Press, Bloomington.

23. Jacobson, Harold K. and Shanks, Cheryl, 1987, *Report of the Ann Arbor Workshop on an International Social Science Research Program on Global Change*, Institute for Social Research, University of Michigan.

24. For a general account of collective action problems see Hardin, Russell, 1982, *Collective Action*, Johns Hopkins University Press, Baltimore.

25. Andresen, Steinar, 1989, 'Increased Public Attention: Communication and Polarization', in this volume.

26. Polar Research Board, 1986, *Antarctic Treaty System: An Assessment*,

National Academy Press, Washington DC. See also Østreng, Willy, 1989 in this volume.

27. Larsen, Thor, 1978, *The World of the Polar Bear,* Hamlyn, London.

28. Kosloff, Laura H. and Trexler, Mark C., 1987, 'The Convention on International Trade in Endangered Species: No Carrot, But Where's the Stick?', *Environmental Law Reporter,* 1710222-10236.

29. Gulland, J.H., 1974, *The Management of Marine Fisheries,* University of Washington Press, Seattle.

30. For relevant background on all these issues, consult Caldwell, Lynton Keith, 1984, *International Environmental Policy: Emergence and Dimensions,* Duke University Press, Durham.

31. Polar Research Board, 1986. For a different viewpoint see Østreng, Willy, 1989, in this volume.

32. Herscovici, Alan, 1985, *Second Nature: The Animal-Rights Controversy,* CBC Enterprises, Montreal.

33. Krasner, Stephen D. (ed.), 1983, *International Regimes,* Cornell University Press, Ithaca.

34. Young, Oran R, forthcoming, 'The Politics of International Regime Formation: Governing the Global Commons', *International Organization.*

35. For a survey on the broader literature on social or collective choice see Mueller, Dennis C., 1979, *'Public Choice,* Cambridge University Press, Cambridge.

36. As economists have often noted, markets yield distributive outcomes as a by-product of the performance of their primary role in allocating scarce resources among alternative uses. Haveman, Robert H., and Knopf, Kenyon, A. 1978, *The Market System,* 3rd edn., Wiley, Santa Barbara.

37. Devanney, J.W., 1975, *The OCS Petroleum Pie,* MIT Sea Grant Report no. MITSG 75-10, Cambridge.

38. For an account that emphasizes the complications that arise in efforts to calculate maximum sustainable yields under real-world conditions see Larkin (1977).

39. Scott, Anthony, 1973, *Natural Resources: The Economics of Conservation.* McClelland and Stewart, Toronto, Chapter 8.

40. For a more general analysis of liability rules see Calabresi, Guido and Melamed, A. Douglas 1972, 'Property Rules, Liability Rules and Inalienability: One View of the Cathedral'. *Harvard Law Review,* **85**, 1089-1128.

41. Russell, Clifford S. (ed.), *Collective Decision Making: Applications from Public Choice Theory,* Johns Hopkins University Press, Baltimore.

42, Young, Oran R., 1988.

43. Asgrimsson, Halldor, 1989, in this volume.

44. Eckert, Ross D., 1979, *The Enclosure of Ocean Resources: Economics and the Law of the Sea*, Hoover Institution Press, Stanford.

45. Kneese, Allen V., and Shultze, Charles L., 1975, *Pollution, Prices and Public Policy*, Brookings Institution, Washington DC.

46. Young, Oran R., 1982, Chapter 5.

47. Zacher, Mark W., 1987, 'Trade Gaps, Analytic Gaps: Regime Analysis and International Commodity Trade Regulation,' *International Organization*, **41**, 173-202.

48. Young, Oran R., 1979, *Compliance and Public Authority: A Theory with International Applications*, Johns Hopkins University Press, Baltimore.

49. A particularly striking recent example is the Nuclear Test Ban Verification Demonstration Agreement negotiated by the Natural Resources Defense Council (NRDC) in the United States and the Institute of Physics of the Earth of the Academy of Sciences in the Soviet Union.

50. For a case in point see Haas, Peter M., 1987, 'Do Regimes Matter? A Study of Evolving Pollution Control Policies for the Mediterranean Sea', paper prepared for the 1987 Annual Meeting of the International Studies Association. The concept of epistemic communities that Haas and his colleagues are currently developing is also relevant to this discussion.

51. Scheinman, Lawrence, 1987, *The International Atomic Energy Agency and World Nuclear Order*, Resources for the Future, Washington DC.

52. Young, Oran R., 1979, and Fisher, Roger, 1981, *Improving Compliance with International Law*, University Press of Virginia, Charlottesville.

2

Increased public attention: communication and polarization

Steinar Andresen

Purpose and scope

As a general rule, the need for scientific advice is recognized within the various international resource regimes which have been set up. Different types of expert or scientific bodies usually form an integral part of the decision-making systems, and decisions are to be based on scientific advice.[1] Thus, as a point of departure, scientific premises are considered legitimate and constitute one set of criteria when decisions are taken in international resource regimes. However, research has shown — not least as highlighted in several contributions to this book — that scientific input often has little or no impact upon the regulations finally adopted.[2]

The type and strength of the *interests* at stake may be the single most important variable to focus on in discussing the impact of scientific advice. This is clearly demonstrated by Willy Østreng in his article on the polar regions: when economic and political interests are strong, policy variables tend to dominate and there is often little room for (independent) scientific input.[3] The *organization* of the scientific input may also affect the weight attributed to scientific advice.[4]

More recently a new dimension has surfaced that may affect the relation between science and politics in international resource regimes: the increased *public attention* paid to many issue-areas dealt with by these regimes. By public attention, I mean attention from such actors as the public at large, the mass media and international organizations. Although perhaps ambivalent and difficult to measure, this is likely to influence the relation between science and politics in international resource regimes.

Is such increased public attention likely to hamper or promote the inclusion of scientific premises in the decision-making process? What is the response of scientists to this development? What options do they have at their disposal? In order to grasp the total implications of the participation of the new actors, I will not confine this article to the formal decison-making fora only. The more general relationship between these actors and the scientific community will also be taken up. My empirical references deal mostly with the management of the the marine environment and living resources.

The premise of this article is not that 'the more science the better politics'. Scientists have their often (very) limited field of expertise, whereas aggregation and evaluation of different policy alternatives is the responsibility of the decision-makers, who have to take account of several considerations other than scientific ones. The decision-makers may also choose to disregard scientific recommendations. However, both the decison-makers and the concerned public should get the opportunity to consider scientific advice in complex issue-areas.

As attention is growing, it seems natural that the pressure and demands upon the scientists for more information will increase correspondingly. This represents an important challenge to the scientific community, who may now get a much larger audience than they have been used to. To adopt the phrase used by Oran Young, it may increase the scientists' role as *agenda-setters* in the international society. This is, however, one side of the coin only. Important characteristics of the scientific community, such as *uncertainty, disagreement, caution* and *difficulty of simple communication,* may make it difficult to respond to such a development. The demand for simple and certain answers that often follows increased public attention cannot always be met by the scientific community.

Thus, some scientists may prefer to withdraw to their ivory towers instead of participating in the debate. However, if they choose to do so, this may exclude the scientific premises from the public debate. On the other hand, if they choose to participate actively, their scientific integrity may be endangered. Before looking into this dilemma, let us examine to what extent there has been increased public attention towards international resource regimes.

Increased public attention?

Although I have no figures to substantiate this assumption, I am quite certain that counting the number of times major international newspapers referred to issue-areas dealt with in this book would yield figures considerably higher in the last few years than some years ago. The combination of accidents, scientific discoveries and strong international environmental groups has brought about a new environmental awakening among the public. As a part of this development has been an expansion of what is considered 'environmental', it includes most of the empirical topics covered in this book — with certain variations between the issue-areas as to how much attention they get.[5]

As such, public attention towards environmental matters is not of new date. Up until quite recently however, attention has been rather sporadic and cyclical.[6] When major environmental disasters are perceived to have happened — like large blow-outs on the continental shelf, major oil-tanker accidents or radioactive fall-out — the outcry from the media and the public has been significant. However, attention has usually soon faded away. The political answer to such attention has frequently been a new convention, an international conference or a sharpening of existing rules. Whether these have served their intentions, we often do not know.[7]

Over the past few years, however, a more fundamental change appears to have been brought about; environmental issues have been figuring increasingly on national and international agendas, with a more permanent position. Although the time lapsed is too short to know whether this will be a lasting phenomenon, the combined effect of a number of incidents/discoveries indicates that attention will not fade away soon. The Chernobyl accident, the discovery of the hole in the ozone layer above the Antarctic, the greenhouse effect, the algae blooming and the death of the seals in the North Sea all have contributed to the environmental awakening among the public, scientifically justified or not. This may be especially pronounced in the industrialized world; but the considerable attention given to the UN-based Brundtland Commission on Development and Environment may signify a greater emphasis on environmental matters in the Third World as well, although this raises difficult distributional questions.

If this proves to be a lasting trend, one consequence seems obvious: the politicians of many nations will pay more attention to various issue-areas with environmental implications; the heart of the matter may well be votes at the next election. In other words, a more direct and stronger link can be expected between the concerned public and the policies being adopted by international resource regimes. As pointed out by Jørgen Wettestad, the apparent success of the Second North Sea Conference as regards a more strict environmental regime can be viewed in such a perspective.[8] Lloyd Timberlake in his article also points out the influence of the public in the making of the Brundtland Report.[9]

For those concerned with the health of the environment or protection of resources, such a development will generally be applauded. But where does it leave the scientists? As a point of departure it may increase their role as agenda-setters in the international society.

Agenda-setting: closing the gap?

As pointed out by Oran Young, 'science plays an important role in agenda setting by identifying and highlighting previously unknown . . . problems'.[10] This is undoubtedly true, but why traditionally has there been a considerable time-lag between the discovery of these problems by the scientists and the time they reach the international political agenda? Many of the problems we are wrestling with today in the international society were discovered by scientists long ago. A few examples serve to illustrate this point: the link between the sooty skies over industrial Manchester and acidity found in precipitation was discovered by a British chemist in 1852; twenty years later he first used the term 'acid rain'. Yet it took approximately one hundred years before this question reached the international political agenda.[11]

As regards living resources and the marine environment, international marine scientific cooperation — through the International Council for the Exploration of the Sea (ICES) — was established just after the turn of the century, more than 60 years before issues of pollution of the marine environment, over-exploitation of fish and rational management of the oceans and its resources reached national and international agendas. Similarly, the whaling issue has been a hot international political issue for almost two decades now. However, concern over the effect of whaling on stocks does not originate in the 1970s and 1980s. As early as 1910, it was brought up at an International Zoological Congress.[12]

The most obvious reason for this time-lag is that potential or actual problems threatening the environment or some class of resource identified by scientists need not be perceived as *political* or *economic* problems. If the relevant and dominant actors are not negatively affected, they will see no reason to take action. The management of whales as well as fish resources may serve as an illustration: although scientists had warned that many Antarctic whale species were seriously depleted, no concrete action was taken by the whaling nations until they found themselves unable to fulfil their quotas.[13] Similarly, as pointed out by Dietrich Sahrhage in his article later in this book, 'It was less on the strength of the arguments presented by the scientists but rather by the obvious collapse of fisheries that actions for the protection of the resources were finally taken.'[14] Thus, national interests may be an active barrier towards science as agenda-setter.

In fact, listening to scientists may be considered harmful for perceived short-term economic and national interests. As pointed out by one analyst, 'To demand of a politician that he accord large weight to the welfare of later generations . . . is rather like asking him to commit suicide.[15] Irrespective of how accurate scientists are in their descriptions and predictions, decision-makers may choose to disregard their advice.

Increased public interest in international resource management makes it more difficult for decision-makers to overlook scientific warnings, however. Generally the time-lag between the scientific community and other arenas appears to be narrowing. Although problems like the greenhouse effect and the hole in the ozone layer have been discussed in scientific circles much longer than they have been the concern of the public and the politicians, the gap is closing. Major new research results on such issues are bound to be met with considerable public interest — but how will this affect the role of science and the scientist?

The premiss horizon

In general, the increased public attention has brought about more openness regarding the work and functioning of international resource regimes. On the one hand, this means that new actors and new concerns are included in the scope of premisses when decisions are taken. As a point of departure, the premiss horizon is widened.[16] Also, according to values highly prized in the Western industrialized world, openness and increased participation implies more democracy, which as such is considered good. Actors who may be affected by decisions are seen as having a right to influence the premisses for decisions.

On the other hand, strong public attention may contribute to distort and simplify complex-issue areas and make them into simple battles over beliefs and ideology. Increased public involvement often implies increased *polarization*; according to Edward Miles, the impact is negative on 'the rational searching for management in the context of political confrontation'.[17] He maintains that conflicts are likely to be strengthened with active involvement from public and pressure groups as compared to when the conflict is limited to nation states.[18] Thus, the rational and complex science component may be the one to suffer in such a context. If this is correct, the premiss horizon may not necessarily be widened as a result of increased public attention: some premisses will be added but others may disappear. In fact, the premiss horizon may be *narrowed* if the conflict boils down to a simple 'yes' or 'no' to a certain activity.

The tendency towards increased attention and public involvement promotes important values, but it also poses a challenge for the scientific community. What experience do they have in responding to this development; what has been the traditional role of science in the international community?

More demand, closer scrutiny

'In theory, good science is conducted in a completely objective fashion, unimpaired by all manner of human biases.'[19] For a long time, this was the general perception of scientists. According to one analyst, 'Up until approximately 1965, the benefits to and obligations of both scientists (as producers of knowledge) and society were clear and perceived as legitimate by both groups.'[20] To the extent that the relation between scientists and society was considered at all, great faith was expressed in the ability of science — often through the production of high technology — to solve important problems facing society. The strong support of science following World War II in Western industrialized societies also reflected the scientific and technological achievements which had helped the Allies to win the war.[21]

Gradually a more critical and analytical view of the role of science in society developed. However, warnings of the potentially destructive and harmful aspects of science had also been expressed much earlier. According to Jonathan Swift in *Gulliver's Travels* (1726): ' . . . Since science sees itself as as a . . . superior form of knowledge, it may succeed in undercutting common sense.'[22] More recently, former US President Eisenhower in his famous 'Farewell Address' in 1960 expressed the apprehension that 'public policy could itself become the captive of a scientific-technological elite.'[23]

Over the past two decades, increasing concern over the undesirable impact of science and technology has dampened the celebration of scientific progress. Many powerful interest groups have taken the position that scientists hold values different from the public at large with respect to what is right and what is in public interest. This negative reaction towards science as such can probably be understood in light of the previous uncritical praise; the classical pendulum reaction. A more balanced and analytical view is presented in most social science studies of the role of science, as represented by Oran Young; in international resource regimes science exists both for good and for bad.[24] The important point is that science does not exist in a vacuum. Scientists may have their preferences and their research is destined to be applied. Thus, value free and neutral scientific advice is more a conceptual ideal than a practical reality. According to one student of international regimes, 'One should be very cautious in assuming that knowledge is synonymous with the discoveries of natural scientists . . . superior to politics or a substance that makes experts wise and politicians clowns.'[25]

Although a more critical view on the role of science in international resource regimes (as well as elsewhere) has developed, the increasing complexity and interlinkages in international society have increased the demand for various types of technical advice, not least when it comes to the environment and natural resources. Thus, on the one hand scientists are exposed to more critical scrutiny; on the other hand, the demand for scientific expertise is growing.

The scientific community may find it difficult to respond to this development. The increased attention gives the scientists an opportunity to become agenda-setters in an unprecedented way, but are they willing and/or able to adopt this role? They are not used to being in such a position, and the demand for quick, certain and simple answers may be difficult to accommodate with the time needed for systematic scientific work and the scientific tradition of caution and uncertainty.

Scientific uncertainty

First, we need to clarify what kinds of scientists are operating in international resource regimes. Traditionally science has been regarded as synonymous with natural science. The purest natural sciences are the basic experimental sciences like physics and chemistry where one depends upon controllable variables. Most ocean sciences like oceanography, meteorology and fisheries biology are not such basic sciences since the variables cannot be controlled; meteorologists cannot change the winds in order to control their experiments. Although few would deny that the ocean sciences are 'real' sciences, [26] uncertainty is inherent in their very nature due to the fact that they are not exact sciences. Even if there is an increasing understanding of the interlinkages in marine ecosystems — and between the marine sciences — there is still a long way to go before precise cause-effect relationships can be predicted.

Fishery science is old compared to the environmental sciences, and Jørgen Wettestad is probably correct in assuming that it is more developed.[27] Still, as the following quotations from the recently published book on *Fishery Science and Management: Objectives and Limitations* show, the sources from which erroneous observations and predictions can be derived are many:

Estimating the state of a stock usually must contend with poor data from a poorly sampled population . . . A significant portion of the stock may be illegally or accidentally caught as by catch or not reported . . . Predicting response of the stock to different levels or patterns of exploitation faces other problems. Poor data must be fed into oversimplified models whose assumptions in some cases are unrealistic; . . . the stock is not at equilibrium with fishery, it is not oblivious to the presence and abundance of predators and prey and its rate of growth and recruitment are affected by environmental conditions in ways that are not now predictable.[28]

Thus, fishery scientists may seem quite instrumental and 'useable' in that they give quantitative advice, often perceived as criterion for what is 'science'; but the assumptions on which they base their advice are often less than certain. Nor is their advice always correct.

Similarly, the following quotation concerning the management of whales demonstrates the need for science as well as its limitations:

Without accurate, sophisticated and relatively detailed information concerning these biological subjects, management goals can be achieved only by coincidence . . . (However) . . . it is exceptionally difficult to obtain even the most basic biological information . . . because these species are totally aquatic . . . Consequently it is very difficult to determine either the number of whales or changes in stock size.[29]

Turning to the marine environment, where systematic research has been undertaken for less than two decades, uncertainty is even more pronounced, as extensively documented by Jørgen Wettestad in his article on the North Sea.[30] Uncertainty is not restricted to the possible harmful effects of pollution; according to the last Quality Status Report for the North Sea, 'it should be noted that all figures for input, with the possible exception of dumping, are subject to considerable uncertainty, the extent to which is variable and difficult to quantify.'[31] As the North Sea is one of the most studied ocean areas in the world, it is reasonable to assume that uncertainty concerning the input and effects of pollutants is even greater in other ocean areas.

As a point of departure, it seems reasonable to expect that scientific uncertainty on international resource management would decrease over the years, as science progressed and more knowledge was acquired. However, there is not necessarily a positive correlation between *increased understanding* and *reduced uncertainty* as to scientific advice. In fact, it may be the other way around: as new links are discovered, complexity and uncertainty may become more evident. For example, it used to be believed that the intensity of fishing was the major explanation for the variability in stock abundance. Now, 'It has become accepted that fishing is not the only, and perhaps not even the most important, influence on stock abundance.'[32] Environmental variability plays an important role. Thus, more knowledge has been gained as to what affects the size of the fish stocks, but as yet this has not necessarily reduced uncertainty concerning scientific advice. This insight was brought about by new groups of scientists entering fisheries sciences. While marine biologists used to dominate, oceanographers and other natural scientists have received increased importance. Such a development towards increased interdisciplinary research is welcomed and supported by most funders of research. It is expected to increase insight and discover new linkages, which it often does; but at least in the short run, the advice given is not necessarily more precise.

New and more professions may also create problems of *coordination* and *communication*. Such problems have been pointed out between fishery biologists, oceanographers and meteorologists resulting from cultural and educational differences.[33] Similar problems have been observed as regards communication between mathematical model-creators and more practically inclined marine biologists in the International Whaling Commission (IWC).[34]

Moreover, the scene is no longer completely dominated by natural scientists. Over the past few decades, the social scientists have also become preoccupied with international resource management. This may be most pronounced in the management of fish resources, where especially economists, but also lawyers, anthropologists and political scientists play a part. Oran Young in his article in this book points out various ways in which their contribution can be a valuable addition to the ones presented by the natural scientists,[35] and at least few social scientists would disagree with him. Although many natural scientists probably welcome cooperation from social scientists, this is not necessarily so for everybody. In connection with a research project on the effectiveness of measures to protect the environment, it was noted that some of the social scientists met cultural resistance in their effort to study the role of scientific elites; in some cases 'there was strong resistance towards this "non-science" concern'.[36]

Although this expansion of the research family dealing with

international resource regimes as such is both useful and positive, it may pose certain problems. One concerns the values conveyed by the different professions. 'Each profession involved . . . is predisposed to accept certain basic values, and these values represent unwritten objectives that have a profound influence on the menu of options and evaluations presented to decison makers'.[37] For example, economic efficiency is a key standard in economics, while maintaining a healthy fish population may be an ethical commitment in fisheries biology. Both types of expert advice are needed, but greater demands are put on coordination and cooperation among scientists. Also, if different advice is provided, the tendency for recipients to pick and choose may increase. In other words, more expert advice where new concerns are considered need not necessarily mean that the influence of the scientific premises is increasing.

As such, the tendency towards an increased *multidisciplinary* approach within the ocean sciences represents a step towards a more *holistic* scientific framework. And, indeed, from the concepts that have been elaborated, it seems that management goals are now far more 'scientific' and often more comprehensive than some decades ago.

One example is the maximum sustainable yield (msy) adopted in the management of both fish resources and whales. On this basis (seemingly) precise quantifications and recommendations have been made. However, as has also been clearly demonstrated, the msy concept is no magic word that will reduce uncertainty and solve management problems. It is very difficult to operationalize; it ignores the complex social costs and benefits of harvesting; and the data fed into the models are often inferior. More recently, the optimum yield (oy) concept has been elaborated, which is broader than msy and includes aspects other than the biological ones.[38] As such it reflects *inter alia* that new groups of scientists have given input to fisheries management. However, according to one analyst, 'optimum yield means different things to different people at different times . . . '[39] The same scholar expresses concern about the progress made in fishery sciences as to the elaboration of new concepts: 'We are beginning to sound like the scholars in the humanities, of whom it is said that they only move the bones around in the graveyard.'[40]

If conceptual and scientific shortcomings are obvious in fisheries sciences, this is even more so as regards the marine environment. Concepts like 'ecological needs' and 'marine ecosystems' are increasingly used by politicians and environmentalists alike; but how these concepts can be used for management purposes is not equally clear.[41]

Thus, although progress has been made, within the foreseeable future uncertainty is bound to be a reality within the ocean sciences: they are not exact sciences. The scientists realize these uncertainties. Increased multidisciplinarity increases understanding but does not necessarily result in more precise advice, and there is still a long way to go before concepts are elaborated that may serve as reasonably precise guidelines for management. These features provide parts of the explanation why scientific premisses are not always easily integrated in international resource regimes — even if the decision-makers were inclined to do so. Also, these characteristics may make it difficult for the scientific community to influence the public debate over these issues. However, the various groups of scientists have more insight in these matters than does the average politician or environmentalist. In a period of increased attention and interest, how do they go about communicating their knowledge?

Communication and attitudes

Considering the existence of scientific uncertainty and the many qualifications which have to be made, one cannot expect scientists and their results to be easily accessible for the layman. This situation is often worsened by the fact that scientists tend to use a jargon comprehensible only to a few, most notably their own colleagues with the same professional background. As previously noted, even the differing professions working within the ocean sciences may have serious problems of communication. If this can be the case, one can hardly expect politicians, civil servants and the public at large to be able to comprehend all the nuances in the information they provide.[42]

Also, consensus among scientists — which usually faciliates the integration of scientific premisses — is the exception rather than the rule. Even if we disregard incidents where scientists in an international setting reach differing conclusions as a result of close government ties, the very idea of consensus is contrary to the nature of science. As pointed out by Oran Young, 'the idea of seeking consciously to reach consensus is foreign to scientists socialized to value . . . competition among conflicting ideas as a method of advancing knowledge.'[43] Although this is legitimate indeed, it may not be very instrumental when it comes to practical advice. An illustration was offered by Norwegian scientists after the Chernobyl accident. While some scientists stated they had kept their children indoors out of the (potentially dangerous ?) rainfall, others announced they would gladly eat meat from reindeer and sheep which the authorities had decided to destroy because it might be dangerous.

Another problem to those interested in using the findings of scientists is their cautiousness in drawing firm conclusions. This reticence is as a result of the nature of their job and training, and the inherent uncertainty in the ocean sciences previously described. Scientists will be cautious in employing 'facts' to reach an incontravertible conclusion . . . after all at $p=0,05$, one in 20 "facts" is incorrect.'[44] Thus it is often not easy to find the bottom line for the concerned public — if there is one.

The communication process relates partly to the ability of scientists to convey their message in an understandable manner. However, it also relates to the *attitudes* held by scientists. Traditionally, scientists have not sought the limelight; they have not been used to public scrutiny, and some of them have tended to be rather elitist and arrogant towards the knowledge of the public, the media and international organizations.

For those who think that this is exclusively a trend of the past, a few recent quotations from the journal *Marine Pollution Bulletin* may serve to illustrate this point. 'Whilst interplay between the scientists and the decision makers already contain elements of difficulty, the addition of the public, conservation groups and the media to the scenario provides ample opportunity for farce, tragedy or disaster . . . ' The public, for its part, generally remains blissfully ignorant of environmental issues until they are covered in detail by the media; ' . . . media plays an important and increasing role in educating the public, unfortunately, however, the education process is often lost in efforts to produce more 'punchy' news,' ' . . . amateur groups cannot significantly contribute to decisions on important issues, serving only to "muddy the waters" by their use of unscientific generalizations and insufficiently supported assumptions'.[45] Nor are responsible politicians given much credit by some of the scientists; according to one, 'Regulations are drafted by lawyers and negotiated and put into effect by politicians, neither group being well suited by background and training to evaluate technical issues.'[46]

Certainly these attitudes are not representative of the whole scientific community; but at least they illustrate one extreme of a continuum of attitudes on part of scientists, the 'exclusive, ivory tower ideal'. New actors who have entered the scene are seen as having such qualities that communication is considered 'dangerous'. Scientific methods and traditions are not considered compatible with the simplicity and the demands for quick and simple solutions advocated by these new-comers. In the next paragraph we shall see that other scientists have chosen the opposite strategy, active participation in the public debate.

Participation and politicization

The self-imposed distance to the dirty game of politics is now increasingly difficult to maintain. Although there might be some truth in the foregoing quotes, such attitudes are hardly conducive to a fruitful dialogue between interested parties. And indeed, many scientists have also chosen a more active strategy; they have mobilized fellow scientists, they have participated in the political process or have turned directly to the public.

A Swedish soil scientist in the late 1960s started to campaign to inform the international scientific community about acid rain. 'His campaign, pursued with missionary zeal, kindled an interest in acid rain among reputable scientists.'[47] Today we can confidently state that he was highly successful on that account.

In international cooperation concerning Antarctica, as pointed out by Willy Østreng, scientists have played a prominent role; these 'science politicians' ' . . . also took part in the political process'.[48] As long as the

Antarctic issue was of relatively low salience on national agendas, these roles could be juggled reasonably well. However, as the Antarctic moved more into the centre of national and international interests this became increasingly difficult.

Some scientists have also appealed to the public and to international organizations, thereby entering a political minefield which might be difficult both to comprehend and to control. However, this strategy has been chosen by some scientists in connection with the international management of whales. Since this issue-area may be the prime example of strong public and media attention, I will dwell somewhat on the effect this seems to have created for the relation between science and politics in international resource management, although the issue is also dealt with by others in this book.[49]

In the IWC in the mid-1960s some scientists — as well as representatives of non-whaling nations — appealed to the public and environmental organizations to mobilize against the depletion of the large whales in Antarctic waters. 'The Committee members, as scientists, believe that there is no justification for increasing the serious risk of extinction of the main stock of the largest living animal . . . In this they are in company with other scientists and organizations, several of which have strongly expressed this view publicly and in letters to the Commission.'[50]

Seen in the light of the history of depletion of whales in the Antarctic, this *moral* argument — on the part of some scientists — is easily understood. However, the massive public movement which grew up and rallied against the killing of whales was probably much stronger than many of those making this appeal had expected. One of those who had appealed to the public in the mid-1960s, the (former) US Commissioner to the IWC, a few years later seemed concerned about the direction and strength of the movement which had been unleashed: 'There is a danger that overzealous and uninformed people will continue to promote the notion that whaling continues unchecked and that a total moratorium is the answer.'[51] He mentioned that recent publicity 'has verged on the irresponsible' and that most people think 'that whales are an endangered species' even though 'of the approximately 100 different kinds of Cetaeca, less than 20 are being taken commercially, and less than 10 of these . . . can be considered endangered.'[52]

The strong public concern and emotions over the whaling issue, however, continued to grow and were soon to reach the international political agenda. During the UN Conference on the Human Environment in Stockholm in 1972, a 10-year moratorium on commercial whaling was called for. The whale was about to become the symbol for the environmental movement: 'saving the whale is for millions of people a crucial test of their political ability to halt environmental destruction.'[53]

The phrase 'millions of people' may sound somewhat exaggerated, but it was — and is — not. When the Soviet Union and Japan in the mid-1970s formally objected to some regulations adopted by the IWC, international protests were strong and US conservation groups organized boycotts of imports from the two countries. '21 American conservation . . . and environmental groups, with more than 5 million members, had pledged to support the boycott.'[54] The increase in the number of observing international organizations to the IWC meetings illustrates this growing public attention. Five organizations sent observers to the IWC meeting in 1965; by 1978 the figure had risen to 24, and in the 1980s some 50 non-governmental organizations have usually been present.

The whale was chosen as a symbol by the environmental movement for a number of reasons, one of them being the fact that 'whales . . . make excellent fund raisers . . . '[55] As to the effect of this development on the role of science, it appears that the strong polarization brought about by the increased attention have *reduced* its significance as decision premiss. While the influence of scientists appeared to be increasing throughout most of the 1970s, illustrated through the adoption of the New Management Procedure in 1974,[56] the strong public attention seems to have muddied the waters between science and politics.

As pointed out by Halldor Asgrimsson and by Brit Fløistad, science played no major part when the moratorium on commercial whaling was adopted in 1982. The Scientific Committee of the IWC made no recommendation for a general moratorium prior to its adoption in 1982. The UN Food and Agricultural Organization (FAO) was outright against a moratorium. At the IWC Special Meeting in March 1982, the FAO stated that 'There seems to be no scientific justification for a global moratorium . . . A justification . . . can be put forward on aesthetic or moral grounds, but these seem outside the term of reference of the Commission.'[57] It has also been argued that 'This (moratorium) has never had much scientific backing because, even more than old measures like the Blue Whale Unit, it makes no distinction between stocks'.[58]   Others, scientists and decision-makers alike, would strongly disagree with such a statement, and it is not correct that the moratorium — or the opposition towards catch for scientific purposes — has *no* scientific backing. Many — some highly reputable — scientists in the Scientific Committee strongly supported the moratorium. Also, the majority of scientists in the Scientific Committee have been against catches for scientific purposes after the moratorium. Thus although the moratorium was basically a *political* decision brought about by the joint forces of the environmental movement and the non-whaling nations, these could also claim scientific backing.

Although much more time was spent on scientific work and special sessions were frequently held, by the end of 1970s it had become increasingly difficult for the Scientific Committee to agree on recommendations; 'it was unable to agree if the effect of a moratorium would increase or decrease the flow of information, whether whale biology would be hastened or retarded.'[59]

It appears that scientific discussions in the Scientific Committee on politically sensitive issues are often characterized by *mutual distrust, tactics* and *communication difficulties.*'[60] The scientists are no longer scientists only: they become participants in the political game whether they like it or not. According to a report from four independent scientists (from institutions previously not involved in IWC work), it was very difficult for the Scientific Committee to supply independent scientific advice as it was 'unduly exposed to the repercussions of political disputes.'[61]Another illustration of the blurring of lines between science and politics is the fact that scientists from North America and Europe with strong anti-whaling views have represented small island states from the Caribbean and the Indian Ocean.[62]

Some scientists may enjoy being in the line of fire as active participants in debates over the management of whales; others experience this only as a strain and would prefer to leave this field altogether.[63] When pressures reach those levels, there is little room for independent and open-minded scientific discussions. In the highly polarized atmosphere where the line often does not go between scientists and decision-makers but between an alliance of scientists and diplomats from whaling and non-whaling nations respectively, science loses much of its credibility. This has nothing to do with the ability or skill of the scientists involved, as there are excellent scientists on both sides.[64]

One key element which has made this polarization possible is the scientific uncertainty as to the size of the different whale stocks. Although there is general agreement among scientists that uncertainty exists — as always as regards the ocean sciences — the interpretation and weight attributed to this uncertainty varies considerably. *Conservation-scientists* maintain that, in view of the lack of precise knowledge, no harvesting should be allowed. *Whaling scientists* on their side maintain that enough knowledge exists to permit harvesting of certain species, if 'normal' criteria for the harvesting of living resources are applied.[65] However, their intense controversy would not have received much attention (perhaps it would not even existed?) if it had not been for the high polarization of the issue.

Concluding remarks: lessons to be learned

The intense attention and mobilization in connection with the whaling issue seem to have narrowed the premiss horizon largely at the cost of scientific input. A scientifically very complex issue has been made into a simple one: 'yes' or 'no' to commercial whaling. This would lend support to the assumption that the impact is negative on 'the rational searching for management in the context of political confrontation.'[66] (This must not be mixed up with an evaluation of whether this is good or bad from an outcome perspective, however.)

Edward Miles and Sonia Boehmer-Christiansen draw similar conclusions as regards the dumping of low-grade radioactive waste.[67] In discussing the political objections to sea-dumping, Miles claims 'All of these positions are impervious to scientific and technical evidence but they can all be powerful political symbols which can be used to mobilize large segments of the population.'[68] Again, increased attention seems to imply a narrowing of the premiss horizon (a yes or no to dumping) at the expense of scientific premisses.

When science runs contrary to common belief and attitudes and when scientists are strongly divided in issue-areas with great attention, science seems to play a minor part in international resource regimes. If scientists present evidence more in line with popular belief or strong pressure groups, the chances seem higher that they will be listened to. A case in point is the environmental North Sea regime. Up until quite recently, public attention towards the North Sea was moderate. Scientists generally believed the health of the North Sea to be good and decision-makers responded correspondingly.[69] Lately, as public interest has increased, it appears that the North Sea states are ready to reduce their input of North Sea contaminants considerably. As pointed out by Wettestad, the scientists have similarly increased the threat perception somewhat of the North Sea environment, although not in a manner that justifies the change in public and political perceptions.[70] Scientific advice has been considered, but has probably not been the decisive factor here.

The effect of increased public attention on scientific premisses depends partly upon the ability of the scientific community to tackle this new situation. As demonstrated, there is no easy response to this challenge. Active participation, as in the whaling issue, may reduce scientific credibility. This seems to be the case when polarization is high. According to Østreng, the 'science politicians' within the Antarctic cooperative framework appeared to be able to handle dual roles as long as national interests remained moderate. On the other hand, a traditional elitist attitude may omit scientific premisses altogether from the public debates.

Is there then some intermediate strategy whereby scientists can give useable advice without compromising their scientific ethics in a setting of strong public attention and demand for more information? Some pertinent ideas have been suggested by a Canadian marine biologist, H.A. Larkin.[71] One important aspect concerns scientists dealing with *uncertainty*. Larkin stresses the distinction between 'best' scientific advice available versus complete information. As the latter can never be attained, he claims that the plea for unsufficient data is a 'cop-out', or a sign of insecurity on part of the scientist. Scientists must use the data to the best of their ability; if not, others often less knowledgeable will step in their place. Scientists cannot always be correct, but they should be credible.

As to the aspect of *communicating* scientific recommendations, Larkin makes a distinction between research biologist and management biologist. 'The research biologist should be involved in advancing theory while advice on specific application should come from the management biologist.'[72] It is important to note that the management biologist must be as conversant with theory as the research biologist. In addition, he/she must have a thorough understanding of bureaucratic realities, be willing to work under pressure and have the ability to translate into lay-talk. To those who might object to such 'unprincipled scientific behaviour', Larkin claims that this is exactly the opposite. The management biologist is 'highly principled, but equally pragmatic because he is dealing with the human element of fish management every bit as much as he deals with the fish stock themselves.'[73]

It might be objected that scientists with such qualities are not easy to find. Although probably true, this does not necessarily reduce the value of the idea. Such scientists seem close to what Lloyd Timberlake calls policy researchers; and according to his experience those were the only scientists with any impact on the Brundtland Report. It is also interesting to note that the need for strong integration between qualified administrators and scientists has been underlined in the setting up of the Task Force for the North Sea.[74]

Another objection may be that such an approach may be feasible in some areas, but it will not be easily transferred to more polarized issue-areas. The management of fish resources is not among the issue-areas where public attention is very strong. This is certainly a valid objection, but it is probably even more important to attempt this approach in such a setting, if scientific premises are to be considered at all. The 'intermediate' strategy does not, however, solve the problems of coordination and communication between the different scientific professions. This is an organizational challenge as well as a challenge for the scientific community as such.

Notes

1. This is reflected in the treaties upon which the international regimes are based, for example the International Convention for the Regulation of Whaling (ICRW). Amendments to the Schedule 'shall be based on scientific findings' (Article V, ICRW).

2. See for example, Østreng, Willy, 1989, 'Polar Science and Politics: Close Twins or Opposite Poles in International Cooperation?', and Miles, Edward, 1989, 'Scientific and Technological Knowledge and International Cooperation in Resource Management', both in this volume.

3. Østreng, Willy, 1989, in this volume.

4. This is most clearly demonstrated by Wettestad, Jørgen, 1989, 'Uncertain Science and Matching Policies: Science, Politics and the Organization of the North Sea Environmental Cooperation', in this volume.

5. Generally, the management of living resources has not received as much attention as 'traditional' environmental issue-areas. However, as pointed out later in this article, a major reason for the strong public attention

towards the management of marine mammals is the fact that these have been included in the environmental sphere. The same has not — to the same degree — happened with fish resources.

6. Hamilton, E.I., 'Science - A Time for Change?', *Marine Pollution Bulletin,* vol. 17, no 7, July 1986, pp. 295-8.

7. For a general discussion of success and failure of international negotiations, see Underdal, Arild, 1984, 'Causes of Negotiation Failure', *Internasjonal Politikk,* Oslo, Temahefte I, pp. 81-97. For a discussion of problems of methods and measurements as regards the evaluation of outcomes of international regimes, see Young, Oran, 1982, *Resource Regimes: Natural Resources and Social Institutions,* University of California Press, Berkeley.

8. Wettestad, Jørgen, 1989, in this volume.

9. Timberlake, Lloyd, 1989, 'The Role of Scientific Knowledge in Drawing up the Brundtland Report', in this volume.

10. Young, Oran, 1989, 'Science and Social Institutions: Lessons for International Resource Regimes', in this volume.

11. Park, Chris C., 1987, *Acid Rain Rhetoric and Reality,* Methuen, London and New York, p. 6.

12. McHugh, J.L., 1974, 'The Role and History of the Whaling Commission' in W.E. Schevill, (ed.), *The Whale Problem: A Status Report,* Harvard University Press, Harvard, p. 322.

13. Andresen, Steinar, 'Science and Politics in the International Management of Whales', *Marine Policy,* no 2, 1989, pp. 99-117.

14. Sahrhage, Dietrich, 1989, 'The Role of Science in International Management of Fish Resources', in this volume.

15. Elster, Jon, 1983, *Explaining Technical Change. Studies in Rationality and Social Change,* Cambridge University Press, p.207.

16. For an elaboration of this concept, see Underdal, Arild, in 'Integrated Marine Policy; What, Why and How?', *Marine Policy,* no. 3, July 1980, pp. 159-69.

17. Miles, Edward, 1987, 'Science, Politics and International Ocean Management', *International Affairs,* University of California, Berkeley, p. 70. The statement is based on — and supportive of — findings of Wildawsky, A. and Tenenbaum, E., 1981, *The Politics of Mistrust: Estimating American Oil and Gas Resources,* Sage Publications, Beverly Hills and London.

18. Miles, Edward, 1989, in this volume.

19. Marascco, Richard J. and Miller, Marc L., 1988, 'The Role of Objectives in Fisheries Management', in Warren, Wooster (ed.), *Fishery Science and Management: Objectives and Limitations,* Springer-Verlag, New York, p.179.

20. Rich, Robert F., 1981, 'Knowledge in Society' in Robert F. Rich, *The Knowledge Cycle,* Sage Publications, Beverly Hills and London, p. 24.

21. Ibid., pp. 11-12.

22. Ibid., p. 22.

23. Ibid., p. 26.

24. Young, Oran, 1989, in this volume.

25. Haas, Ernst, 1980, 'Why Collaborate? Issue-Linkage and International Regimes', *World Politics,* vol. 32, no. 3, p. 367.

26. Some, however, may have doubts about this. In an interview at Berkeley on 2 December 1987, Professor Wayne Getz — with extensive and highly acknowledged studies in resource management — stated that the ocean sciences could hardly be labelled 'real' sciences due to the inherent uncertainty. He also claimed that this could result in recruitment problems, with the 'best' scientists going to the 'real' sciences.

27. Wettestad, Jørgen, 1989, in this volume.

28. This collection of quotations is from Wooster Warren (ed.), 1988, pp. 1-2.

29. Scarff, J.E., 1977 'The International Management of Whales, Dolphins and Porpoises: An Interdisciplinary Assessment', *Ecology Law Quarterly,* vol. 6, p. 333. For a more recent account of research on whales, see Gulland, J., 'The End of Whaling?', *New Scientist,* 29 October 1988, pp. 42-7.

30. Wettestad, Jørgen, 1989, in this volume.

31. From the Summary of the Quality Status Report made in connection with the second North Sea Conference, p. 7.

32. Wooster, Warren and Miller, Marc, 1988, 'On Fishery Science and Management', in Warren Wooster (ed.), p. 290.

33. Wooster, Warren, 1986, 'Immiscible Investigators: Oceanographers, Meteorologists, and Fishery Scientists' in Edward Miles, Robert Pealy, and Robert Stokes, (eds.), *Natural Resource Economics and Policy Applications,* University of Washington Press, Seattle and London, pp. 374-87.

34. This has been pointed out by a Norwegian representative to the Scientific Committee in the IWC in an interview, November 1988.

35. Young, Oran, 1989, in this volume.

36. Jacobsen, Harold and Kay, David A., (eds.), 1983, *Environmental Protection: The International Dimension,* American Society of International Law, New Jersey, p. 322.

37. Huppert, Daniel D., 1988, 'Comments on the Role of Objectives in Fisheries Management', in Warren Wooster, (ed.), 1988, p.184.

38. The 'optimal yield' criterion has for example been adopted in US fisheries legislation.

39. Larkin, Peter A., 1988, 'Comments on the Workshop Presentations', in Warren Wooster, (ed.), 1988, p. 288.

40. Ibid., p. 287.

41. For somewhat differing views on how the concept of marine ecosystems can be used for management purposes, see Belsky, Marin H., 1988, 'Marine Ecosystem Model: The Law of the Sea's Mandate for Comprehensive Management', and Morgan, Joseph, 1988, 'Large Marine Ecosystems: A Response'. Both papers presented at the 22nd Annual Law of the Sea Institute Conference, Rhode Island, USA, 13-16 June 1988. Forthcoming in proceedings from the conference.

42. It should be noted, however, that civil servants working with these matters are often very well informed and also may have scientific training.

43. Young, Oran, 1989, in this volume.

44. Phillip, David J. H, 1986, 'Are Environmental Conservation Organizations Necessary?', *Marine Pollution Bulletin,* vol. 17, no. 9, pp. 387-8.

45. Phillip, David J.H., 1986. It should be noted that this author elsewhere in the text presents a more nuanced picture of these actors.

46. Clark, R.B., 1984 'North Sea Review', *Marine Pollution Bulletin,* vol. 15, no. 7, pp. 237-8.

47. Park, Chris C., 1987, pp. 6-7.

48. Østreng, Willy, 1989, in this volume.

49. Primarily in the article by Asgrimsson, 1989, which is exclusively devoted to analysis of the IWC, but also in the article by Fløistad, 1989, both in this volume.

50. IWC/16/3 1964 Report of the Scientific Committee, p. 9, pt. 14.

51. McHugh, J.L., 1974, p. 335.

52. Ibid., p. 335.

53. Holt, Sidney, 'Whale Mining, Whale Saving', *Marine Policy,* vol. 9, July 1985, no 3, p.12.

54. Scharff, J.E., 1977, p.369.

55. Gulland, John, 1988, p.45.

56. For an account of the New Management Procedure, see Asgrimsson, Halldor, 1989, in this volume.

57. Birnie, Patricia, 'Countdown to Zero', *Marine Policy,* vol. 7, no. 1, January 1983, p. 64.

58. Gulland, John, 1988, p. 45.

59. Birnie, Patricia, 'IWC — Survival and Growth', *Marine Policy,* vol. 4, no. 1, January 1980, p. 75 (reference to ECO, vol. 14, no. 3, July 1979, p. 1).

60. Conclusion drawn by author on the basis of interviews with Norwegian representatives in the Scientific Committee, November 1988.

61. *The State of the Northeast Atlantic Minke Whale Stock,* p. 67.

62. Small island states which have been represented by such scientists include Antigua and Barbuda, St. Vincent and the Grenadines and Seychelles. Information obtained from the IWC secretariat, November 1988.

63. Statement by a Norwegian representative to the Scientific Committee in an interview, November 1988.

64. According to Norwegian scientists in the Scientific Committee, some of the best scientists are undoubtedly on the 'conservation' side. Stated in interviews, November 1988.

65. Based upon viewpoints presented by Norwegian scientists in interviews. It has also been stated that if rules applied in the IWC (prior to the moratorium) had been applied in the North-East Atlantic, many stocks would not have been allowed to harvest. Rørvik, J.C., 1982, 'Hvalfangstkommisjonen, hvalfangst og hvalforskning', *Fiskets Gang,* no. 23, p.735.

66. Miles, Edward, 1987, p.70.

67. Miles, Edward, 1989, and Boehmer-Christiansen, Sonja, 1989, both in this volume.

68. Miles, Edward, 1989, in this volume.

69. Wettestad, Jørgen, 1989, in this volume. See also Andresen, Steinar, 1989, 'The Environmental North Sea Regime: A Successful Regional Approach?', forthcoming in *Ocean Yearbook,* **8**, 1989.

70. Wettestad, Jørgen, 1989, in this volume.

71. Larkin, H.A., 1988, '"The Truth, the Whole Truth, and Nothing But the Truth" (Within the 95% Confidence Interval)', in Wooster, Warren, 1988, pp. 279-83.

72. Ibid., p. 281.

73. Ibid., p. 283.

74. Wettestad, Jørgen, 1989, in this volume.

3

Scientific and technological knowledge and international cooperation in resource management

Edward L. Miles

Introduction

Among the many questions posed in the introduction of this book, three of them are of most concern to me. These are:

1. To what extent does the world have at its disposal (and how does it come by) adequate, military, legitimate and (politically) usable scientific knowledge to enable us to make complex decisions on international resource management issues?
2. At what stages in the international resource management process is scientific knowledge politically important?
3. Does scientific cooperation contribute to political cooperation in international resource management and, if so, what factors contribute to this development?

These questions struck a responsive chord in me because part of my research time since 1982 has been devoted to elaborating on the same concerns. Indeed, most of my research over the course of the last twenty years or so, and all of my involvements in real policy 'games' at national, regional and global levels have occurred at the interface between science and technology, on the one hand, and their socio political impacts on the other. While the direction of experience varied with the issue, I began to get a strong feeling of coherent patterns at work and decided to take the time to work out what these might be. The results of that exercise are contained in a monograph published by the Institute of International Studies, University of California at Berkeley.[1]

The primary objective of that work was to assess the extent to which scientific knowledge makes a difference in the negotiated solution of international resource management controversies and four case studies were chosen to represent four types of issues. The present paper is an attempt to deepen our understanding of the nexus between scientific and technical knowledge and politics and to extend the findings in the monograph beyond the concern with 'first-order' effects. I shall also include the dimension of technology as well as scientific knowledge. *First-order effects* are those which are the immediate results of the negotiations between states parties concerning the management of some international resource. However, over time these initial results produce their own effects, i.e., consequences, which may or may not have been intended by those who set the process in train. These *second-order effects,* in turn, produce effects of their own. The question which intrigues me here is what is the political significance of these second and third-order effects over time in terms of their consequences for:

a. The knowledge base?

b. Types and evolution of organizational arrangements?

c. Types of policies?

d. Types of implementation strategies?

e. Levels of international cooperation?

Levels of international cooperation are defined as points on a continuum (least to most) from:

1. Separate states coordinating action on the basis of tacit understandings.

2. Coordination of action on the basis of explicitly formulated common standards but action is implemented solely on a unilateral basis.

3. Coordinated planning combined with unilateral implementation.

4. Coordination through fully integrated planning and implementation.

I pose these questions because in my initial analysis I concluded that in two of the four cases the indirect effects over time were far more significant for management than the direct, first-order effects. Before we get to the current problem, however, I need to summarize the findings from my earlier study.

Initial findings

The management of international resources was approached as a problem of collective action in which the type of resource was characterized in terms of public goods criteria. I used John Ruggie's fourfold typology which distinguishes two polar types of collective goods and two mixed types.[2] The former consist of those which exhibit the characteristics of divisibility and appropriability (pure private goods) and those which exhibit the characteristics of joint supply and non-appropriability (pure collective goods). The latter consist of those which exhibit characteristics of either joint supply and appropriability or divisibility and non-appropriability.

The cases which I analysed covered the characteristics of divisibility and non-appropriability (high seas salmon fisheries in the North Pacific, the effects of hydrocarbons in the marine environment and radioactive waste disposal in the marine environment) and joint supply and non-appropriability (forecasting the social effects of global climate change). I chose to ignore pure private goods which, by definition, do not constitute problems of international collective action between governments and mixed collective goods which exhibit the characteristics of joint supply and appropriability because there are very few such cases in the real world and they had already been analysed by Ruggie and Miles.[3]

Each case was analysed from the perspective of the following seven questions:

1. What is the nature of the resource in question?

2. What questions do political actors typically ask about the resource?

3. What questions do scientists typically ask about the resource?

4. How do the scientific questions relate to the questions raised by the political actors, if at all?

5. Who develops the links between the concerns of the scientists and the political actors using what kinds of criteria?

6. By what criteria are initial management decisions arrived at?

7. How are later management decisions made? Do they draw on new knowledge gained on a systematic analysis of past mistakes, or are they a response to new exogenous influences having little to do with prior linking of scientists and political actors' aims?

The approach to the definition of knowledge and consensual knowledge which was utilized was adopted from Ernst Haas. Knowledge is defined as:

> the sum of technical information and of theories about that information which commands sufficient consensus at a given time among interested actors to serve as a guide to public policy . . . [4]

Consensual knowledge is knowledge which is accepted as a basis for policy by groups and individuals professing differing political ideologies. The link between knowledge and collaborative behaviour in this case lies in the perception of the possibility of joint gains by the parties in question.

Since the acquisition and use of knowledge in international resource management controversies, as elsewhere, cost money, governments typically raise benefit/cost considerations in some form. This dimension required further elaboration beyond noting whether the knowledge base was consensual or not. In each of the four cases I therefore asked:

1. Does the knowledge relate to simple descriptive processes or to complex cause/effect inferences?

2. If the latter, what are the costs of acquiring such knowledge, and what level of confidence is likely to be attached to the results?

3. If cause and effect inferences are necessary, is short-term acquisition possible, or are long-term investigations required?

4. Is the knowledge of whatever kind, linked to immediate distributive consequences?

The results of the analysis showed that the most important factor was whether the knowledge was consensual and this condition seemed to vary inversely with the presence or absence of immediate distributive or regulatory links. The other major findings of this study are:

1. . . . that indirect rather than direct links to management decisions will facilitate the emergence of consensual knowledge. Consensual knowledge can also emerge even when there are direct links to management if there is a prior consensus among the parties concerned about the nature of the regime and the decision rules within which they will play. However, this is a more unstable situation than one in which only indirect links exist. Furthermore, direct links are usually designed into the management system only if governments wish it, as in the cases of high seas salmon and the first period of radioactive waste disposal. The reasons why governments may wish to do so seem to depend exclusively on the nature of the issue and what is at stake. If direct links are not designed into the system, they can evolve only over long periods of time — i.e. a decade or more — and only if a prior consensus on the regime has emerged . . . [R]esearch results can contribute to the emergence of such a consensus . . .

2. Whether or not a system is designed to facilitate direct links to management, the factor of time is extremely important. Over the long run, the accumulation of knowledge produces unanticipated consequences for management. Direct links facilitate immediate knowledge utilization by doing — i.e., discrete acts of management. Indirect links facilitate knowledge utilization over time by thinking — i.e., changing conceptual approaches to the management problem.

This has to be realized ahead of time and adequately structured into system design. One can infer that scientific knowledge will play a larger role in management decisions if the rules of the system permit iterative decision-making and therefore learning by trial and error . . .

3. At least one organizational design criterion can be derived from our analysis: from the scientific perspective, it is preferable that the research being conducted be of sufficient concern to warrant continued government support, but that decision processes be deliberately designed to provide a buffer between research results and their utilization for regulation and — especially — for the distribution of benefits and/or apportionment of costs. Moreover, since we know that knowledge accumulation over time may facilitate indirect links to management decisions that may rival the direct links in importance, it is necessary to plan for these by designing a system which can learn cumulatively from trial and error . . .

4. That the specifics of the issue combined with the interests at stake determine the type of decision-making organization designed and the pattern of implementation chosen. These factors by themselves, however, are not sufficient to determine whether scientific knowledge plays a significant role in shaping management decisions. It seems that the pattern of politicization is far more important. The higher the level of conflict, the greater the constraints on utilizing scientific research results. Conflict over regime rules or distribution of gains and losses can be equally constraining. In addition, contamination of the issue by external political issues of high salience (exogenous influences) is a wild card in the process of knowledge utilization. Such contamination can be used to good effect, as in the case of high seas salmon, or it can produce severely adverse consequences, as in the case of radioactive waste disposal.

Some time ago, Ruggie [5] argued that:

Physical and technological parameters are important determinants of international responses to technology when those responses concern research, scanning and monitoring, and problem recognition in general — when, in a word, the issue is to *discover* or *understand* some process or situation. When, however, the issue is to *manage* some process or situation, the weight of political purposes becomes preponderant.

I think that reality cannot be so easily dichotomized between understanding and managing. I think, furthermore, that the evidence available shows that science in international policy processes is always a dependent variable and never an independent variable when we confine our vision to first-order effects. Policy variables are always dominant because the players are pursuing a range of complementary and conflicting objectives which relate to the divisibility of the stakes and the relative immediacy of international regulation which implies differential gains and looses for the parties involved.

In these situations, the importance of science and scientific expertise increases dramatically if, and only if, governments cannot get what they want any other way *and* they place a high value on getting it. Budgetary constraints then become critical. But, remember, because we are focusing on first-order effects, this is not necessarily the whole story. Indeed, experience with both the high seas salmon and hydrocarbons issues suggests that we may have to modify these findings significantly when we consider second and third-order effects.

Since the findings reported earlier suggest that international resource management or environmental protection issues exhibiting the characteristics of divisibility and non-appropriability are the most troublesome to handle, let us choose two issues which are of the same type but which are of sufficiently long duration to test for the significance of second and third-order effects. In doing so, we will be particularly concerned to probe the conditions surrounding the emergence of consensual knowledge since a considerable amount of learning is implied here. The cases we shall choose are satellite telecommunication and the regulation of the radio frequency spectrum and two of the issues impinging upon international collaboration in the civilian uses of nuclear energy, i.e., control of proliferation and disposal of radioactive waste.

Satellite telecommunication and the regulation of the radio frequency spectrum

This is not a case primarily of scientific knowledge *per se* but of technological advance. Technology is politically relevant because it can affect, sometimes profoundly, the interests that join or divide nations.[6] The mechanisms for transfer of political effects are the impacts of technological advance on the capabilities of states and the potential effects on the distribution of gains and losses *vis-à-vis* the interests and values at stake. This has considerable effect on the creation and maintenance of coalitions and the strategies which players choose to pursue their interests as they define them. The problem for the analyst is in determining exactly what the effects will be over time and in predicting how technological advance will affect the *outcomes* of existing and potential conflicts. Bound up in here as well is the question as to what extent will cooperation occur? The issue of satellite telecommunication is almost an ideal case through which to follow these concerns.

The radio frequency spectrum is a common property resource around which a regime has built up since 1865. The regulatory problem posed by the emergence of the communication satellite in the early 1960s, therefore, was one of adapting an existing regime to the demands of a revolutionary new technology. It was not, as in the case of nuclear energy to be considered later, a question of creating a regime *ab initio*.

The International Telecommunication Union (ITU) was itself the creature of technological advance, that is the telegraph. The ITU was the result of an attempt by states to establish the framework within which this recent invention would be exploited since it dealt with a medium no single state could control by itself. Institutionalization was required at the international level in order for agreement to be reached on the technical systems to be used, methods of handling messages, establishment of rates and accounting procedures. The process of international institutionalization arose out of bilateral interactions between neighbouring states, then it spread to the European continent. It was globalized by another technological advance, i.e. the invention of the radio in 1927.

Member states saw to it that organizational tasks would be restricted to providing a forum within which decisions would be made, providing for technical coordination of frequency utilization and making recommendations for technical performance standards to which equipment must conform.[7] This was the implementation strategy chosen. An operational role for the ITU was never considered and, when the idea was proposed much later, with respect to the need for supervisory and enforcement capabilities, was never welcome.

With respect to the advent of satellite telecommunication, the world did have at its disposal adequate, unitary, legitimate and politically usable scientific knowledge to facilitate management of an international resource, i.e. the radio frequency spectrum. This knowledge base had been developed historically in the twentieth century discipline of radio engineering. Managing use of the spectrum has always involved a combination of international cooperation (technical problem solving) and conflict over access to and use of the choicest frequencies.

The knowledge *per se* was never a major issue. Even the caution evident in 1959 was more the response of the ITU's organizational culture which traditionally opposes major organizational innovation than a real conflict about the adequacy of the technical and economic information base. In any event, it did not last long once the Secretary-General had grasped the implications of the opportunities he was facing.

Satellite telecommunication was always a template for the working out of pre-existing organizational issues and conflicts in the ITU at the same time that it represented a new set of demands to which the organization had to respond. Moreover, given the nature of the good and the divisibility of the spectrum in particular, technical cooperation goes hand in hand with conflict. These are constant themes in the organization's history. The political spill-over effect of technical cooperation is therefore always constrained.

Whether there will be cooperation or conflict is a function of the kind of issue defined in terms of the pay-off matrix. Whenever the aim of any party is to redistribute benefits or whenever the effect of any proposal is to threaten existing large-scale investment in system design and operation, conflict arises.

Because protagonists for major organizational change — i.e., the need for global planning in frequency allocation versus. the first-come first-served traditional approach — sought to use the advent of satellite telecommunication as the lever to induce the change they desired, this immediately raised the stakes of the struggle. Given the pattern of political control within the ITU between 1958 and 1965, there was little chance that the attempt would succeed. On the regulatory dimension, therefore, choices made with respect to organizational arrangements, policies and implementation strategies were all the traditional ones. Levels of international cooperation within the ITU did not therefore increase noticeably.

Where the conflict developed, and indeed became intense, occurred at the conjunction between issues related to organizational arrangements, types of policies and implementation strategies. These conflicts occurred on two dimensions, i.e., within the ITU with respect to regulatory approaches and between the ITU and a new organization, INTELSAT, created to exploit the commercial opportunities offered by the new technology. Let us look first at emerging second and third-order effects on the regulatory dimension before we turn our attention to INTELSAT and the operating dimension. Three second-order effects are detectable over the course of the first decade (1958-68). The first is an enormous expansion in the scope of the ITU's regulatory task. The second is a significant increase in interorganizational conflict and cooperation within the components of the ITU's task environment. And the third is a loss of regulatory initiative to INTELSAT both with respect to assigning positions in the geostationary orbit and the setting of technical standards for satellite telecommunication systems. Each deserves some elaboration.

Some appreciation for the scope of expansion in the ITU's tasks can be gained by a glance at the demands which were placed on the organization between 1958 and 1968 which are solely related to the advent of satellite telecommunication:

1. The initial demands for the allocation of frequencies for satellites including bands for telemetry, command and control facilities.

2. The necessity for determining technical standards for simultaneous channel sharing. A subsidiary part of this includes requirements for the automatic or ground command shut-off of transmitters whose batteries are recharged with solar energy.

3. The control and limitation of microwave communication over land necessitated by the requirements of transoceanic satellite communication.

4. The registration of call letters for the identification of signals.

5. Avoidance of the saturation of sections of the equatorial orbit for geostationary satellites given limitations in the resolving power of antennae.

6. Achieving coordination between existing and planned satellite communication systems. This also includes those regional and

national systems then under study.

7. Regulation of direct broadcasting by statellite.

8. Achieving better policing of the use of radio transmitters by nationals of member countries to guard against harmful interference between ground stations and orbiting satellites.

9. Expanding technical assistance programmes in the form of education and training of necessary personnel.

One would have assumed from this list of demands commensurate growth in budget and professional staff but this was not the result. As the organization grew, the professional to general staff ratio in fact increased from 64.15 per cent in 1958 to a high point of 99.27 per cent in 1960, then decreased to 71.07 per cent in 1963, slid to 46.46 per cent in 1967 and finally increased slightly to 50.87 per cent in 1969. What was happening, particularly after 1963, as the technical demands grew, was that advanced member states would second their own staff to the organization for limited periods of time. No doubt this was designed to restrict budgetary growth but it also had the effect of constraining organizational autonomy since it made the ITU more dependent on its most advanced member states. Here we see a merging of second and third-order effects.

With respect to interorganizational conflict and cooperation, as ITU's role expanded, the organization experienced a commensurate expansion of its domain. However, since other organizations were also being affected by satellite telecommunications, the number of other organizations with which ITU had to maintain relations increased as well. Some, like the WMO and the Committee on Space Research (COSPAR) of the International Council of Scientific Unions (ICSU) were allies. Others, like the UN Committee on the Peaceful Uses of Outer Space (COPUOUS) and INTELSAT were seen as antagonists. The problem with COPUOUS was accentuated by the creation of the Working Group on Direct Broadcasting by Satellites within COPUOUS as a major focus of international regulation. The difficulty arose because this Working Group was driven by lawyer/diplomats from Ministries of Foreign Affairs who knew little or nothing about ITU and national coordination appeared to be weak. Early actions of this group were therefore seen to be troublesome by ITU officials.

As a contrast, the ITU/WMO connection was a very happy one for several reasons. WMO found that it needed ITU as a result of the emergence of the weather satellite, which brought with it a corresponding need for special frequency bands for transmission of data. Since there was no conflict of jurisdictions, the relationship was symbiotic. The fact that the two organizations were located across the street from each other, which facilitated interpersonal relations, was also a help.

Demands for interaction were heavy and continuous so that the two Executive Heads agreed to institutionalize the relationship from 1960.

The content of interaction ranged over issues like avoidance and elimination of harmful interference, allocation of frequencies, organization and operation of data transmission systems and technical studies and recommendations concerning radio communication. This is therefore a clear case of a second-order effect which did increase significantly levels of interorganizational cooperation. But at the same time we should note that there are effective barriers to intersecretariat interaction concerning the allocation of frequencies. For instance, in both the WMO and the International Civil Aviation Organization (ICAO) national members decide which frequencies are particularly appropriate for transmission of meteorological and navigational data. In order to obtain these frequency allocations from the ITU, the secretariats of other organizations may not approach ITU officials directly. Of course, occasionally there are informal discussions by secretariat officials as they chance to meet, but these do not carry any weight.

The process by which IGOs decide which frequencies are needed and then lobby for them has two stages. In the first or 'internal' stage an organizational position is developed by appropriate groups within the organization participating depending upon the technical problem involved. In the WMO, for example, this stage calls for interaction between the secretariat and national representatives so that each national meteorological service is consulted about its particular needs. But even this is a delicate operation because each country jealously guards its frequency allocation rights. Once the organization chooses a position the second stage begins. At this point each national meteorological service takes up the question with its own postal, telephone and telegraph administration and tries to convince it to seek these frequencies for the WMO in the ITU. Final allocations are then worked out among national representatives in ITU meetings.

As a result of these conditions, coordinated interorganizational planning cannot go beyond a very low level — sending observers to meetings — because the effective decision-making capacity rests with governments, not secretariats. Admittedly, joint working groups sometimes go beyond the observer level but not sufficiently beyond it to have a major impact on governmental control.

Finally, ITU/INTELSAT tension and conflict are an inevitable consequence of two decisions taken by ITU member states. The first decision, not surprisingly, was to separate the regulatory from the developmental function by vesting responsibility for exploiting the commercial promise of satellite telecommunication in a novel entity (mixed public/private) called INTELSAT. The second decision was to restrict the nature of change within the ITU, particularly to constrain the IFRB and to retain the seniority rights system of allocation against demands for global planning. Therefore, given the fact that the technology would be driven by the manager of INTELSAT, the US public corporation COMSAT, there would at the least be rivalry over technical standard setting and choice of positions in the geostationary orbit. This occurred consistently in the early years but then declined from the mid-1970s.

The emergence, development and implications of INTELSAT

The INTELSAT experience differs in several important respects from that of ITU. The most important reason for this was that a choice of implementation strategies was made first by a single dominant player at the time, i.e., the United States, and this choice dictated both organizational design criteria and types of policies to be pursued. That this strategy was both unique and successful is to be explained by the compelling stream of benefits relative to costs to be derived over time by all participants in the system, not just the dominant player. This was possible as a result of the nature of the good and the promise and effects of technological advance.

Three characteristics of satellites offered significant promise of benefits over time. Relative to all other forms of communication, especially cables, the factor of distance is of no relevance when a satellite is placed in a geostationary orbit at an altitude of 35,800 km in the plane of the earth's equator. In one leap therefore, the problem of remoteness, whether faced by a single country or a region, could disappear. Moreover, satellites possess multiaccess capabilities whereas cables are only point-to-point. Over time, significant economies of scale could be achieved which would affect not only the design life of satellites but also of receiving ground stations because the more powerful the satellite, the simpler and cheaper the ground station required.

Given these characteristics and given the fact that only one of the two superpowers was then willing to exploit this technology on a commercial basis globally, a combined Executive/Congressional/Private Industry coalition in the US moved quickly to realize the promise of satellite communications. Congress passed the Communication Satellite Act in 1962 which established the Communications Satellite Corporation (COMSAT) as a profit making entity governed by public and private shareholders with no public investment.[8] The COMSAT team, at the same time, foresaw the possibility of INTELSAT because the full promise of the technology could not be realized without global application.

Accordingly, the criteria derived for the implementation strategy emphasized.

1. Urgency.

2. Commercial aspects of the venture.

3. Global sharing of the technology.

4. Avoiding the usual shortcomings of inter-governmental organizations, [i.e., fractionated authority and lack of effective control, protracted decision time, entrenched bureaucracy, etc.].

5. Achieving the broadest participation possible while avoiding purely political compromises.

6. Commitment to establish a single global entity to avoid duplication and waste.

7. The need to achieve economies of scale.[9]

This implementation strategy dictated as a first step convening of a global conference to create a regime (decision rules plus organizational arrangements). It was expected that definitive arrangements would take some time to negotiate and should have as a basis a period of experience. This called for negotiation of interim arrangements as a first step. The Interim Arrangements for a Global Commercial Communications Satellite System were concluded within six months in 1964, a historic achievement indeed; the first INTELSAT satellite was launched in 1965, and the Definitive Arrangements were concluded in 1971 and entered into force in 1973.[10] The USSR chose not to participate and dissuaded other member states of the Soviet Bloc from doing so.

In terms of organizational design, as a *global* intergovernmental agency, INTELSAT was then unique. Since that time, only a successor organization, INMARSAT, designed to provide maritime satellite communication services to member states of the International Maritime Organization (IMO) has been created. Even at that time, only two other *regional* intergovernmental organizations in Europe were of a similar design: the European Company for the Chemical Processing of Irradiated Fuels (EUROCHEMIC) and the European Company for the Financing of Railway Rolling Stock (EUROFIMA).

The structure of INTELSAT under the Interim Arrangements was very simple and reflected the clear dominance of the United States. The governing body was called the Interim Communications Satellite Committee (ICSC) and the manager was COMSAT. 'Investment shares in the organization were determined on the basis of projections of long-distance traffic likely to be carried by satellite'.[11] And shares determined voting power so that the United States had a share/vote of 61 per cent, Western Europe jointly 30 per cent and the combined shares of Australia, Canada and Japan then accounted for only 9 per cent. But the overwhelming dominance of COMSAT, in addition to its potential conflict of interest, presented disadvantages as well as advantages.

The dominance of COMSAT assured rapid development of the technology and was a major drawing card for participation by developing countries, but it stimulated concerted opposition in the European camp, to the point where this would become a sticky point in the negotiations over the Definitive Arrangements. The result was that no single state was permitted to exercise more than 40 per cent of the vote. It is worth noting that the analog for organizational arrangements under the Interim regime was the approach utilized by multinational consortia operating networks of transoceanic cables. These networks were based on two fundamental principles: a) undivided ownership of intercontinental facilities; and b) investment in cable systems in proportion to use. Control was vested in the carriers, not in governments.[12]

Membership in INTELSAT is open to any state which is at the same time a member of ITU. The structure of governance includes the Assembly of Parties where states participate directly as the principal organ. Each party has one vote and the Assembly meets biennially. In addition, there is another plenary body, this time of all shareholders including therefore corporate entities, called the Meeting of Signatories. This body meets annually and each representative has one vote. The executive oversight function is performed by the Board of Governors, consisting of 27 members from any signatory or group of signatories meeting the minimum share requirement annually established by the Meeting of Signatories.[13] In addition, up to five seats are chosen on the basis of state representation in an ITU-defined region. This accommodates the interests of developing countries irrespective of the share requirement. Voting is on a weighted basis determined by shares with a cap of 40 per cent placed on all signatories. Finally, an Executive Organ, directed by a Secretary-General responsible to the Board of Governors, provides the management function.

Conflict and compromises in the negotiation of the INTELSAT definitive arrangements

In addition to the issue of US domination and the voting majorities to be required in the Board of Governors, there were several other major issues of conflict in the negotiations for the Definitive Arrangements. The solutions arrived at generated very important long-term consequences for the organization. These consequences include quite significant second and third-order effects. The issues in conflict were: (a) R & D, procurement and patent policies; and (b) principles for avoiding competition.

The R & D issue generated quite unusual, though quite understandable alignments. The Western Europeans, Canada and Japan pointed out that COMSAT would remain the manager for six years after the entry into force of the Definitive Arrangements, then expected for 1973. Not only would this mean that COMSAT would have done all the R & D for INTELSAT III and IV but it would also have written the specifications for the contracts to be let for INTELSAT V and even VI. This would mean that in the early years of the internationalized manager, operations would still be based on decisions taken by COMSAT.[14]

The Europeans, on the other hand, were intent on developing their own technological capabilities in the field and were very much opposed to the policy of conducting R & D in-house by COMSAT. They insisted that contracts be let and that a ceiling be placed on in-house R & D by COMSAT.[15] This was opposed, not only by COMSAT, but by the developing countries whose representatives refused to subsidize the technological development of Western Europe, Canada and Japan. They had no objection to a US monopoly on R & D because this was the most efficient solution.[16]

The Europeans were therefore unsuccessful in their main objective but they did succeed in getting a larger share of contracts being let. But, even though bidders quickly formed international teams to respond to invitations by INTELSAT, and even though INTELSAT insists that a lot of effort goes into decisions to allocate work among team members from different countries, the result through INTELSAT VI is still that US companies are the prime bidders.[17]

The issue of avoidance of competition had two parts. First, draft Article XIV of the Definitive Arrangements on the Rights and Obligations of Members required any member which intended to establish, acquire or utilize space segment facilities separate from INTELSAT for domestic purposes to consult first with the Board of Governors on the issue of technical compatibility. If, however, a member intended to participate in an *international system* other than INTELSAT, the issue would again have to be considered by the Board but, in this case, the Board's findings would include judgments of economic as well as technical incompatibility.

The Europeans, Canada and Japan saw in this an implied threat, since a US agency (NASA) was the sole launcher of satellites for INTELSAT. The threat was that should the Board, which was still dominated by the US, find any system either technically or economically incompatible, NASA could and would refuse to launch the satellite.

The second part of this issue had to do with patents. COMSAT as the manager sought to prohibit the use of INTELSAT-funded inventions and data by competing systems. Consequently, COMSAT sought to have INTELSAT retain title to all inventions and data.[18] The Europeans, on the other hand, wanted INTELSAT to sell licences with the contractors retaining title. The Europeans lost this fight again. Both of these losses had long-term effects.

In the short run, the COMSAT position was seen to be inconsistent, if not hypocritical. COMSAT pressed very strongly for a global organization with universal membership but, at the same time, their insistence on control prevented this and provided incentive for competing systems to be created. France, West Germany, Italy, Canada and Japan found the technological dependency uncomfortable and therefore redoubled their efforts to develop their capabilities outside the consortium, focusing on national systems.[19] The French in particular, in 1970, saw Article. XIV as putting their plans for a joint development with the FRG of their own regional system, Project Symphonie, at risk. Since NASA could refuse to provide a launcher, this added substantially to the French incentive to develop the *Ariane.*

The longer-term effects of the COMSAT policy were twofold. First, it stimulated the proliferation of the very same competing systems they feared. Secondly, the more COMSAT insisted on control of INTELSAT, the more narrowly the scope of the organization was defined by others.

In design, therefore, it became no more than an international common carrier and it lost the chance to develop INMARSAT which then went to the Intergovernmental Maritime Consultative Organization (IMCO, later IMO). It also lost the chance of universal membership and it stimulated the creation of the competing Soviet-sponsored organization, INTERSPUTNIK. The proliferation of competitors is an issue that now haunts INTELSAT in the 1980s.

INTELSAT performance, 1965-86

Looking at the consequences of the conflict as outlined above, one would have to conclude that COMSAT's policies produced a decline in the level of cooperation observed, but this would be an incorrect judgment. The effect of COMSAT's policies certainly created the seeds of many difficulties faced by INTELSAT today but the startling successes of INTELSAT's performance under COMSAT's direction also significantly increased the level of international cooperation in utilization of the spectrum for satellite telecommunication purposes. This dimension therefore needs consideration as well.

Table 3.1 and Figure 3.2 illustrate quite clearly the thrust of the COMSAT technological strategy for the development of satellite telecommunications on a *global scale.*

Table 3.1 shows that in the twenty-one years between the launches of INTELSAT I and INTELSAT VI, the organization produced seven generations of satellites, if we count INTELSAT IV-A and V-A as separate generations. As the thrust of the launcher increased, in-orbit satellite mass increased from 38 kg in INTELSAT I to 2,231 kg in INTELSAT VI. As in-orbit mass increased, satellite capability exploded. Effective band width went from 50 MHz in INTELSAT I to 3,086 MHz in INTELSAT VI and satellite capacity measured in telephone circuits increased from 240 to 40,000. The speed of development shows in the very limited design lifetimes of INTELSAT I (1.5 years.), III (5 years.) and IV, IV-A, V and V-A (7 years.). The first significant increase in design life since 1968 has come with INTELSAT VI in 1986.

This rapid rate of technological advance is driven by a never ending search for economies of scale. The rate of decrease in the statellite utilization charge, measured in cost per telephone circuit per annum, is a measure of INTELSAT's spectacular success. This is shown in Figure 3.1.

The initial effect of this success is shown in Figure 3.2 which illustrates the dramatic increase in the growth of traffic by region. INTELSAT, as a second-order effect, has made the world a much smaller place. Remote places have been brought closer and developing countries now have access to a global communications capability at relatively low cost.

Another second order effect of this process of rapid technological advance was to stimulate equally rapid advances in cable technology. Pelton compares the increases in capacity and cost efficiency of

Table 3.1 Technological progress in INTELSAT satellites

Characteristic	I	III	IV	IV-A	V	V-A	VI
Year of first launch	1965	1968	1971	1975	1980	(1984)	(1986)
Dimensions							
Diameter (m)	0.72	1.41	2.38	2.38	2.01 x 1.98	2.01 x 1.98	3.64
Height (m)	0.60	1.01	5.28	6.93	6.4	6.4	11.82
Solar panel height (m)	–	1.14	2.82	2.82	15.6	15.6	6.12
In-orbit mass (kg) B.O.L*	38	152	700	793	1,016	1,071	2,231
Effective bandwidth (MHz)	50	450	432	720	2,137 (four 6/4 GHz)	2,137 (four 6/4 GHz)	3,086 (six 6/4 GHz)
Capacity (telephone circuits)	240 or 1 TV	1,200 or 4 TV	4,000 plus 2 TV	6,000 plus 2 TV	12,000 plus 2 TV	14,000 plus 2 TV	40,000 plus 2 TV
Design lifetime	1.5	5	7	7	7	7	10

* Beginning of life.

Source: Adapted from Pollack, L. and Weiss, H., 1984, 'Communications Satellites: Countdown for INTELSAT VI', *Science*, vol. 223 (10 February), pp. 553-9

Figure 3.1 Satellite utilization charge (telephone circuit per annum.
          Source: Colino 1984

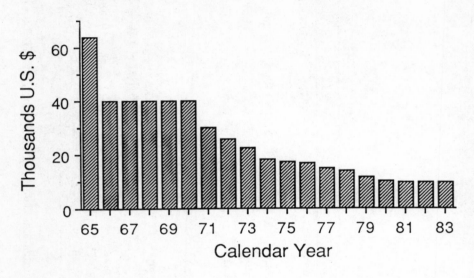

INTELSAT I and IV-A to cable systems. These are shown in Tables 3.2 and 3.3. The rates are remarkably similar. [20]

Yet another second-order effect was to modify the relationship between INTELSAT and the ITU which, as we have seen, had started out on a rather conflictual footing. If we go back to 1963 for a moment, to the Extraordinary Adminstrative Radio Conference called to allocate frequencies for space exploration, both the developing countries and the United States wished to broaden the scope of the agenda. The US in particular wished to discuss the nature of the relationship between ITU and the future INTELSAT. However, the European countries led by the UK, fearing that others might attempt to use the 1963 Conference as a vehicle to institute some radical changes in allocation and organizational structure, successfully resisted any expansion in the source of the agenda beyond frequency allocation. The eventual result, as we have seen, was that ITU was pre-empted by INTELSAT in two areas: assigning positions in the geostationary orbit and setting technical standards.

The source of the problem, particularly on the standard setting issue, was the coordination procedure stipulated in Article XIV of the INTELSAT agreement. This procedure was ' . . . completely divorced from the ITU procedure, especially as regards criteria of interference . . . '[21] INTELSAT's criteria were far more stringent than ITU's, which raised the issue of discrimination against member Administrations. Over time it was found to be simply ' . . . impractical to maintain this separation'.[22] One major source of conflict was thereby

Figure 3.2 Growth of traffic in half circuits
Source: Colino 1984

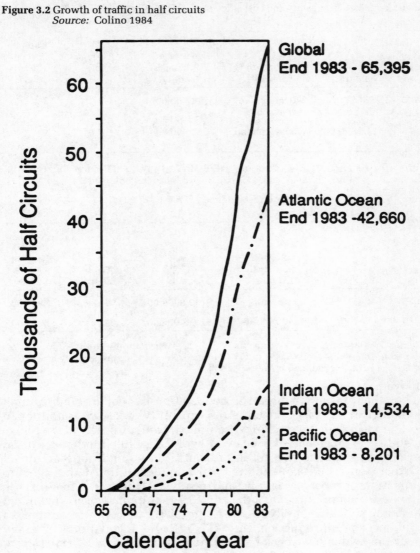

Table 3.2 Increase in capacity and cost efficiency, INTELSAT I to INTELSAT IV - A

Year	Satellite	Capacity in Circuits	Average Capital/Cost Satellite	Average Life (years)	Capital Cost per Circuit Year
1968	INTELSAT I	240 telephone circuits	$11,700,000	1.5	$32,500
1976	INTELSAT IV-A	6,000 telephone circuits	$45,000,000	7.0	$ 1,100

Source: S. Astrain, "Early Bird to INTELSAT IV-A, A Decade of Growth," *Telecommunication Journal* 42, no. 11, 1975. Reproduced in Pelton (1977)

Table 3.3 Increase in capacity and cost efficiency, TAT-1 to TAT-6

Year	Cable Facility	Capacity in Circuits	Cost of Cable	Cable Lifetime	Average Capital Cost per Circuit Year
1956	TAT-1	74 circuits	$ 49,600,000	24 years	$28,000
1976	TAT-6	4,000 circuits	$191,400,000	24 years	$ 2,000

Source: US Department of Commerce, Office of Telecommunications, *The World's Submarine Telephone Cable Systems,* OT Contractor Report 75-2, prepared by Jack S. Cole and George S. Li. Reproduced in Pelton (1977).

removed.

The other reason for increased cooperation has come about through technological advances affecting the capability to 're-use' satellites in geosationary orbit. The technical complexity and difficulty of the re-use capability is great and the need to avoid harmful interference from inappropriate spacing of satellites is acute. These conditions facilitated an expansion in the scope of the IFRB's reponsibilities with respect to application of new regulations and resolving conflicts.[23] In turn, the increased importance of the IFRB required closer technical collaboration between INTELSAT and ITU. Close interaction also facilitated the introduction into ITU's Radio Regulations of many provisions which have been based primarily on INTELSAT experience. The relationship has therefore grown closer and more cooperative with time.

Current problems which affect levels of cooperation

Pelton argues that three sets of problems relating to utilization of communications satellites are currently most serious.[24] These are:

1. Proliferaton of separate satellite systems which produces increased

competition for frequencies and geosynchronous orbital locations. This competition also threatens to produce oversupply of services and higher costs.

2. Competition at both domestic and international levels stemming from all alternative modes of communications, not just satellites. This competition fosters rapid technological advance and therefore rapid obsolescence.

3. Unclear objectives and plans for the future given an increasingly uncertain decision environment.

Pelton also questions whether the narrow technical perspective of the ITU and the IFRB, which has been quite successful to date, can '. . . survive the political and economic challenges presented by the large number of satellite systems now planned . . .'

Finally, he bemoans the facts that national policy decisions on implementation of satellite systems are made on grounds other than that of efficiency, that the economic viability of these systems will become acute in the medium term as a result of competition, and that '. . . no adequate international procedures exist to cope with this problem'.

In a way, we have come full circle to the IFRB's proposal for the ITU to replace the 'first-come, first-served' system of frequency allocation and coordination with one which provides a capability for global planning. We have shown, in fact, that the severity of the proliferation problem in satellite communication systems at this time is derived from second and third-order effects of COMSAT strategies and tactics adopted at the negotiation stage and of policies followed thereafter.

The satellite proliferation problem has produced a situation where one needs to think holistically about the resource. It is no longer just the radio frequency spectrum. It now includes the dimension of allocating orbital positions in the geostationary orbit as well. For this reason, Wihlborg and Wijkman refer to it as the orbit/spectrum resource.[25] They argue that these two dimensions should be allocated separately; that marketable, divisible and indefinite user rights for the totality of space resources should be established, along with well-defined, enforceable liability rules for interference. The alternative mechanisms for achieving allocation are defined as regimes based on either seniority rights or squatters rights, or auctions, or equitable national distribution regardless of use.

Whether what will actually happen will be as systematic as Wihlborg and Wijkman would wish is doubtful since it would demand a rather high level of international cooperation. At the moment cooperation is constrained by both existing investment in international and national systems. These appear to respond to quite different dynamics and Pelton is correct that no adequate international mechanisms or procedures currently exist for dealing with this problem.

The effect of technological advance is another wild card adding to the difficulty of making any prediction. For instance, during the preparatory phase of the World Administrative Radio Conference (WARC) held in 1979, the issue over which the most intense conflict was generated was the seniority rights question. Morever, this time, unlike 1965, the developing countries were far better organized and more experienced. And, more importantly, the structure of control within the ITU had changed so that the advanced industrial Western countries could no longer count on an automatic majority or informal veto. On that basis, one could only have predicted that the seniority rights system would have been overturned in favour of equitable national distribution regardless of use. But this did not happen.

It did not happen because the US Delegation, with very significant corporate participation, made effective use of technological advances which had come on stream since 1965 which facilitate frequency reuse and sharing. The US mounted an intense lobbying campaign in which they explained these new technologies to the Group of 77 and offered their assistance in facilitating developing country access to these technologies. This effort at persuasion won the day. It was perhaps assisted by the fact that most of the representatives at the Conference were radio engineers imbedded in the ITU subculture. It was not a primarily political confrontation among diplomats at the United Nations, where such a strategy would not have worked at all. The common knowledge base therefore provided critical support here.

The implications of the satellite telecommunications example

What lessons do we therefore draw from the foregoing? Let me suggest the following:

If there is moderate to high concentration of capabilities even if benefits are widely shared, and if the issue type is an impure collective good exhibiting the characteristics of divisibility and non-appropriability, competition over commercial stakes will still seriously constrain provision of the collective good (i.e., allocation of the orbit/spectrum resource). Conflict will arise within the group possessing capabilities over the commercial stakes and between the group with capabilities and the rest of the world over provision of the collective good. But, because benefits are widely shared, this latter dimension to conflict will be somewhat muted and the situation will allow the most advanced state to mobilize an expanded coalition from the ranks of developing countries against their competitors fighting for a larger share of the R & D pie. These developing countries will ally with the most advanced states because product costs will be seen to be lower. The effect of this pattern of coalition formation will be to increase concentration in the short run but, in the longer run, to stimulate investment and innovation by the less advanced competitors to stay in the game.

If the issue at the same time is pure, (i.e., uncontaminated by unrelated political conflicts), type of technology will become a dominant variable because prior investment in plant and equipment will not be a significant constraint on the rate of advance. Since the industry is already decentralized globally, the rate of advance will be tied to a never ending search for economies of scale and a tight feedback loop will emerge between the rate of advance, the creation of new uses and increased demand. The result will be very high availability of technological fixes to solve policy problems reinforced by a common knowledge basis which will facilitate consensus. This availability will serve as a constraint on the level of conflict.

While the efficiency of the system created to produce the collective good will be severely constrained by the commercial rivalry, the availability of technological fixes for increasing and widely sharing benefits will produce a high level of joint action (i.e., at least coordinated planning with fully integrated planning on some sub-issues) and moderate to high effectiveness. However, if the availability of technological fixes declines sharply as a result of excessive crowding of the orbit/spectrum resource, the whole system will become very unstable.

Time will inevitably produce a multitude of second and third-order effects but they do not flow in one direction. Some facilitate increased cooperation while others reinforce patterns of conflict or create new issues for conflict. Some are predictable while others are not. The examples of the effects of time which we saw in the earlier study[26] concerning high seas salmon in the North Pacific and the effects of hydrocarbons in the marine environment are not necessarily what will be experienced in other areas.

International collaboration in the civilian uses of nuclear energy

Three sets of issues are bound together here, though, in the space available, only the first two can be discussed. The first consists of the nuclear proliferation problem as it has historically been stimulated by the export policies of nuclear supplier states. Nuclear proliferation is itself a three dimensional problem since its components are diffusion of reactor technology, diffusion of the nuclear fuel cycle and diffusion of nuclear weapons capabilities. The last component is, of course, the most seriously destabilizing for the security of the international system as a whole. The second set of issues concern disposal of low-level and high-level radioactive waste, including spent fuel. The third set of issues relates to the emerging global question of nuclear power safety as a result of the Three-Mile Island incident in the US in 1979 and the Chernobyl disaster in the Soviet Union in 1986. Nuclear proliferation and waste disposal are inevitably negative externalities of human use of nuclear fission and its technologies. Safety is an inherent concern but not inevitably a negative externality.

There is a very large literature available on the nuclear proliferation problem. My concern here, though, is not to suggest solutions to the problem. It is to assess the relationship between scientific and technical knowledge and policy and the second and third-order effects, of the scientific/technical knowledge base, types of organizational arrangements, types of policies and types of implementation strategies. We particularly wish to know whether the effects increase or decrease levels of international cooperation. From this perspective, the issues of satellite telecommunication and nuclear proliferation present interesting contrasts.

What is the collective good at stake in the case of satellite technology? The answer is providing efficient and equitable regulation of the radio frequency spectrum so as to facilitate development of a radically new technology. The good is mixed because the benefits and costs of development and frequency utilization can be divided up. In the case of nuclear proliferation the good is facilitating the development of a radically new technology while minimizing the risk of nuclear conflict. Since the security of the international system is at stake, the issue is immediately one of high politics. But the scale of potential benefits which satellite technology is seen to provide makes it also a very salient issue.

The fundamental differences between the two issues are two. First, the nuclear non-proliferation issue is in a sense the reverse of satellite technology. In the latter, we have a dominant US determined on introducing and diffusing throughout the world at the fastest rate possible a compelling technological innovation which responds to real and obvious needs. In the former case, we have a dominant US trying first to prevent the spread and use of nuclear technology to others, even allies, (1945-53), by denying them access to information and equipment. When this proves futile, as it usually does, the US chooses a schizophrenic policy (Atoms for Peace, 1953) which simultaneously seeks rapid diffusion combined with safeguards to inhibit the diversion of fissionable material to weapons production. This was enormously difficult to achieve because the policy chosen made the collective good divisible and stimulated competition among the rapidly developing group of exporting countries.[27]

Moreover, the fact that the US itself embarked on the most intensive and extensive programme of technical assistance in the training of nuclear scientists and engineers and facilitating export of US reactor technology (though not the fuel cycle and certainly not weapons technology), stimulated the emergence of the very conditions the policy was designed to prevent.[28] This was clearly an unintended second-order effect of the 1953 policy. The nuclear export side of the equation worked far more effectively than the safeguards side. Safeguards were constrained both by the emerging competition over markets among the exporters and by the clear intention to limit inspections by states, like India and Israel, which were bent on developing a nuclear weapons capability.

But, to be fair, one has to admit at the same time that creating the International Atomic Energy Agency (IAEA) and institutionalizing a safeguards programme therein did represent an important achievement in increasing international cooperation. As Nye argues,[29] these were the first steps in building a global regime that ' . . . establishes a general presumption against proliferation'.

The second major difference between satellite technology and nuclear proliferation is in the knowledge base. We have argued that the principles of radiocommunication in space were already well understood by 1958. A satellite is essentially a radio relay device with the added advantage of altitude. What was not known prior to the launching of INTELSAT I in 1965 was cost, the design of the total satellite system and whether the public would find acceptable satellite telephone service with its inevitable time delay in two-way communication.[30] Consequently, INTELSAT I, with a design life of 1.5 years, was deliberately treated as an experiment.

Compare this with the non-proliferation strategy which Atoms for Peace represented. What was known was the scientific and engineering theories of controlled fission and the operational systems derived therefrom, both civilian and military. The question was how to foster the one and constrain the other. Whereas the critical decision in satellite telecommunication was a choice of implementation strategy, the critical decision with nuclear non-proliferation was choice of policy. In both cases, organizational arrangements simply followed from the critical decision. But the assumptions on which the Atoms for Peace programme was chosen were false. Not much was known about the policy process and requirements of controlling nuclear proliferation in 1953 and the issue does not appear to have been thought through. Very little was also known at the time about ' . . . the pace and cost of peaceful nuclear development'.[31] One would have to conclude, therefore, that the knowledge base was inadequate.

But the evolutionary aspects of non-proliferation policy are instructive because, here, second and third-order effects play crucial parts. Burgeoning difficulties with the effects of the Atoms for Peace policy combined with a period of detente between the US and USSR in the 1960s produced an increase in superpower collaboration to negotiate and bring into force the Nuclear Non-proliferation Treaty (NPT) in 1970. But while the NPT sought to close the loopholes in the IAEA's safeguards system, there were three major sets of problems with it. It formalized the division between nuclear-weapon states and all others and was seen by non-nuclear-weapon states to be discriminatory in its imposition of penalties. It provided no incentive for the so-called 'threshold powers' to sign the Treaty and foreswear nuclear weapons. And it did nothing to alleviate the conflict between nuclear exporters.

As Nye points out,[32] a series of third-order effects combined with totally new events in the mid-1970s (1974/75) served to usher in a crisis and to stimulate moves to increase the level of cooperation within the non-proliferation regime.

These moves were eventually successful but the catalysts included:

1. The Indian explosion of a nuclear 'device' with plutonium collected over time from a Canadian CANDU reactor using US supplied heavy-water. The whole installation in fact had been the recipient of a large share of US aid funds under the Atoms for Peace programme.

2. The OPEC-induced oil crisis of 1973 and the wildly unrealistic projections made about growth in nuclear power to satisfy electricity demand. These unrealistic projections generated a purely artificial prediction of short-falls in uranium supply which intensified the competition between states with a nuclear capability.

3. The use of portions of the nuclear fuel cycle as 'sweeteners' to ensure the sale of reactor systems as competition between exporters heated up.

One would also have to add here:

4. The emergence of 'horizontal proliferation' in which India, having become fully proficient in the Canadian CANDU technology, agreed to design and build for Argentina similar reactors which would not be subject to safeguards inspection. In turn, Argentina signed an agreement with Peru to do the same.

5. The emphasis on the Liquid Metal Fast Breeder Reactor, which produces more plutonium than it consumes, partly as a means of compensating for the predicted shortfall in uranium supplies. This threatened to bring with it all the disadvantages of a plutonium economy in the short term.

While a variety of policy initiatives were undertaken during the Ford and Carter Administrations, a few were to have very significant impacts in stopping the rapid rate of erosion of the regime. Under the prodding of the Ford Administration, a Nuclear Suppliers Group was established in London in 1976 in context of which the French agreed to accept the same restrictions on export policy as all the other suppliers did. [33]

These new guidelines were finally in place by 1978. The Carter Administration chose a suite of policies designed both to boost US credibility and to have the effect of slowing down the rate of proliferation. These included, *inter alia,* a decision to defer reprocessing of spent fuel indefinitely, to slow down the US fast breeder programme, and to try to convince others to do the same. In addition, Nye, then serving as Deputy Under-Secretary of State, was convinced that a device for focusing on the long term in a global setting was necessary.[34] The device chosen was a systematic re-evaluation, within the IAEA, of the whole fuel cycle over a two year period called the International Fuel Cycle Evaluation (INFCE). Here is a clear case where new knowledge exerted a direct impact on high-level policy choices of states.

Officially, INFCE provided a two-year period in which nations could re-examine assumptions and search for ways to reconcile their different assessments of the energy and non-proliferation risks involved in various aspects of the nuclear fuel cycle. While officially INFCE was given a predominantly technical rationale, this was a means of attracting broad participation into what was really part of a political process of stabilizing the basis for the international regime . . .

As a diplomatic device, INFCE helped to re-establish a basis for consensus on a refurbished regime for the international fuel cycle. The very process of engaging in international technology assessment helped to heighten awareness of the non-proliferation problem and the threats to the regime.[35]

The net result of the exercise was significantly to slow down the pace at which the plutonium economy was being developed. Participants agreed on a more cautious approach with respect to introducing weapons-usable fuels into the fuel cycle; that safe storage of spent fuel does not require re-processing; and that the economic advantages of plutonium recycling in thermal reactors were not compelling. These results combined to reduce the predicted pressure on uranium reserves by more than 50 per cent, thereby removing a significant source of competition and conflict.

However, it must be admitted that the events which were most powerful in curtailing the pace of development of the nuclear proliferation problem were not produced by new knowledge. Instead, they derived from the structural decline of the nuclear power industry, especially in the United States.[36] Electricity demand growth had shrunk from the 7 per cent average annual increase which it had been for almost three decades to about 3 per cent from 1974. In large part the oil crisis of 1973 accounted for this because it produced a heightened awareness of the efficiencies to be gained by conservation and therefore of price elasticities in the industry. The result was near fatal to the industry which, all of a sudden, had a catastrophic excess capacity problem.

If that were not all, the industry was seriously affected by inflation in fuel costs, construction costs and the real cost of money so that manufacturing costs rose rather than fell over time.[37] In addition, there were serious management failures in the US, the Three-Mile Island incident occurred in 1979, and growing public disenchantment with and growing opposition to nuclear power developed in Western Europe, the United States and within the fisheries sector of Japan.

All this combined to precipitate a major long-term decline in the industry and, with it, this removed fears about the urgent need to avoid the plutonium economy. This development has not stopped the continued growth of nuclear weapons capabilities among the 'threshold states', Pakistan being the latest one to join the club, but it is slow growth. The decline of the industry, plus the lessons learned from INFCE, did serve to remove diffusion of reactor technology and the fuel cycle from the critical list of urgent policy problems.

What then can we say about the dynamics of nuclear non-proliferation as an issue?

If there is high concentration of capabilities and severe skew in the distribution of benefits and if the issue type is an impure collective good exhibiting the characteristics of divisibility and non-appropriability, then competition over commercial stakes (i.e., access to and control over markets) will seriously constrain production of the collective good (i.e., global security). Conflict will arise within the group possessing capabilities over the commercial stakes and between that group and the rest of the world over provision of the collective good. Contamination of the issue by unrelated factors (i.e., the intensity of particular regional conflicts) will serve to increase the stakes and further constrain provision of the collective good.

Moreover, if the technology requires very large capital investments, heavy initial costs and infrastructure requirements will serve to reinforce concentration of capabilities but technological advance will still lead to partial diffusion of innovations. This diffusion will feed into conflict over the commercial stakes and act as a further constraint on the provision of the collective good. The particular technological characteristics combined with conflict over commercial stakes identified above will reduce the availability of technological fixes for controlling proliferation. Players will therefore be able to achieve only the lower levels of joint action (i.e., tacit understandings, or mutual coordination combined with national implementation). The overall level of effectiveness of joint action will be weak to moderate and regulations will be porous. Regulation will at best be able only to slow down the rate of proliferation, not to stop it.

Scientific and technological knowledge will have a direct impact on state behaviour only after supplier states perceive the threat of proliferation as an urgent, common problem. Before this occurs, the dynamics of commercial rivalry described above will act as a barrier to the transference of research results. Perception of threat, in turn, is precipitated primarily by external, not internal, events and cannot be relied upon routinely as a support for desired policies. Second and third order effects of policies pursued as a result of commercial rivalry will intensify the problem rather than ameliorate it.

Sea-dumping of low-level radioactive waste

Disposal of radioactive waste is a sensitive and difficult political problem wherever it arises. In most cases, this is a primarily national problem. The only cases in which it was a problem to be handled via international collaboration involved sea-dumping of low-level radioactive waste and the assessment of the scientific, technical, legal and institutional feasibility of disposing of high-level radioactive waste below the seabed beyond national jurisdiction. Both of these programmes were located in the Nuclear Energy Agency (NEA) of OECD. However, since only the sea-dumping issue carried with it an operational programme from 1964 to 1982, we shall only deal with this case here.

This issue, too, represents an impure or mixed collective good exhibiting the characteristics of divisibility and non-appropriability but with a perceived large difference between private and social costs. The resource, *per se*, is the global or regional marine environment. It is a resource to be used as well as protected; therefore, the major policy problem to be solved is the permissibility of disposing of low-level radioactive waste into the marine environment. The argument about permissibility hinged for most of the eighteen years of the life of this programme on predicted environmental and health effects of this use of the marine environment. The predictions had to rest on an extensive knowledge base relating to the conditions of disposal, standards concerning waste form, packaging, limits on component radionuclides, disposal procedures, monitoring and retrieval.

In this case organizational arrangements channelled international collaboration to respond to certain questions posed concerning low-level waste disposal in the marine environment. But it was really the choice of policy which later proved to be critical since it dictated certain implementation strategies which produced a significant stream of second and third-order effects and which maximized learning among the participants.

In 1958 the then Organization for European Economic Cooperation (OEEC) had created the European Nuclear Energy Agency (ENEA) to foster international cooperation among OEEC members in nuclear energy. (With the addition of Japan in 1972, the OEEC became the Organization for Economic Cooperation and Development (OECD) and the ENEA became the NEA). On the initiative of Norway late in 1960, ENEA took on a concern for ocean disposal of radioactive waste, though at that time the focus was only on the North Sea.

The origins of the specific ENEA role in sea-dumping operations, however, go back to 1964 when the Germans proposed to organize a collaborative, experimental dump of low-level radioactive waste in the Northeast Atlantic. The rationale for this was that the FRG and other OEEC members needed to evaluate the ocean option in comparison with the land-based option; in particular, they needed data on safety and cost in order to permit such a comparison. The argument was that since other member states had the same need, it was better to cooperate in doing the experiment than to do it separately.

At that time the UK and Norway expressed very strong interest in such an experiment and they were later joined by The Netherlands. The group of interested states fully realized that the land-based disposal option was the primary one for Germany as for others but the members recognized that in some countries demographic and geographical problems made the ocean option more attractive. The first motivation for the experiment was therefore to cooperate in order to expand the knowledge base and to share the costs of doing so.

Once decision was made by the organization formally in 1965, a critical second-order effect emerged in the form of a need for cumulative learning capability among the organizational sub-units concerned with sea-dumping operations. As plans proceeded, it became clear that a major organizational role for ENEA in these operations was required since the experiment would occur in the ocean beyond national jurisdiction. Procedures had to be developed to make it a credible as well as a legitimate exercise of high seas freedoms given the risks involved. Credibility and legitimacy would also come from the kind of oversight established by ENEA at every stage of the process.

The procedures eventually decided on included the following:

1. Clear national authorization would have to be developed in each case.

2. A risk assessment would have to be made prior to each operation.

3. The choice of disposal site would have to meet certain stipulated criteria.

4. Common standards would have to be developed and applied to: (a) design of waste package containers; (b) design of waste form; (c) limits on amounts of waste; (d) design of operating procedures aboard ship, including the design and performance characteristics of the ship itself.

5. All national plans and designs would have to be approved by the organization according to explicit criteria.

6. The organization would have to have independent observers aboard ship during disposal operations with the authority to stop the operations if necessary.

ENEA then convened three groups. One group was concerned with elaborating criteria for choosing a disposal site and then choosing such a site. This group thereafter met only when the site needed to be changed or specific questions arose. The second group was institutionalized as the Group of Specialists which developed the common standards and reviewed national plans and designs. The Secretariat ran separately the independent observer operation. The third group was an Executive Committee which provided oversight, subject to review by the Health and Safety Sub-Committee of ENEA and final approval by the Steering Committee. Successful dumps were organized in 1967, 1969, 1971 and then on a routine basis between 1973 and 1976.

Each dumping operation was reviewed in some detail by the Steering Committee. By the end of the second dump in 1969 a considerable amount of collective learning had occurred which served to increase the level of international cooperation. Several participants discovered that for them the sea-dumping option was considerably cheaper than land-based disposal and that the radiological hazards under existing IAEA standards were minimal. This realization increased support for organizing further dumps but increasing political opposition was also in the offing, triggered as a second-order effect of the dumping operations.

At the last moment before the 1967 dump, the Norwegian cabinet prohibited Norway's participation in the operation. The source of this decision seemed to be the Minister of Fisheries, reflecting concerns of his constituents plus his own preferences. Between 1967 and 1970, opposition from the costal communities in Portugal and Spain increased as a result of sensationalist reports in the French and Spanish press. Later Ireland also began to express certain fears. However, while the NEA shifted the dump site to accommodate these concerns and kept all governments fully informed at every stage, the dumping operations proceeded on schedule.

Political conflict began to increase in 1972-73 in relation to preparations for the Stockholm Conference and the negotiation of the London Dumping Convention. What was actually at stake here, as in the case of nuclear non-proliferation, was the structure of the larger regime that was being built. The components of the global regime eventually came to be:

1. Article 25(1) of the Convention on the High Seas, of 1958: Every State shall take measures to prevent pollution of the seas from dumping of radioactive wastes, taking into account any standards and regulations which may be formulated by competent international organizations (i.e., the IAEA).

2. The London Dumping Convention (LDC) of 1972, (entry into force in 1975), which defines dumping (Article III), regulates substances which may *not* be dumped (Annex I — the 'Black List') and substances which may be dumped on the basis of permits issued by national governments and under stipulated conditions (Annex II — the 'Grey List'). High-level radioactive waste is on the Black List while low-level radioactive waste is on the Grey List.

3. The IAEA, which is the primary scientific and technical advisory body to the Contracting Parties to the LDC. The IAEA officially sets global technical standards in defining the specific radioactive wastes which may *not* be dumped and in advising national authorities how to proceed with the dumping of low-level radioactive waste which Annex II permits.

4. The International Commission on Radiological Protection (ICRP), a non-governmental body which nevertheless is the most authoritative source for recommendations on principles and standards relating to radiation protection and safety for human beings. The ICRP is closely linked to the IAEA which routinely accepts its recommendations, thereby giving them intergovernmental effect.

5. While the NEA/OECD is a regional organization, over time, as another second-order effect, it assumed global prominence because it was the only international organization which had a mechanism for implementing an operational programme of waste disposal. Consequently, NEA became the source for most of the IAEA's *operational* recommendations and it participates as an observer in

the Annual Consultative Meetings of the LDC. But it is worth noting that the NEA's operational rules were in fact derived primarily from the UK since the UK Atomic Energy Authority had the widest experience with conducting disposal operations. In this way the UK rules were globalized with some amendments.

The pattern of escalation of the political conflict was in two stages: 1972-73 and 1979-82. In 1972 Norway raised the ante in the NEA Steering Committee by linking sea-dumping to the anticipated LDC and arguing the need for international legislation on sea disposal. This legislation would set out permissible levels of waste disposal as well as provide for international legislation of sea disposal operations. This proposal was not accepted but, in the meantime, public controversy was increasing. As a result, the Secretariat proposed to suspend operations until after the Stockholm Conference. The UK refused to agree to that and insisted on a 1973 dump under the existing rules. Only the UK, Belgium and The Netherlands participated in that operation.

At a later meeting of the Steering Committee, Norway formally urged suspension of operations until the IAEA could produce its first set of recommendations under the LDC. The Norwegian proposal was supported by Denmark, Portugal and Sweden but it was opposed by the UK and others and was not adopted by the Steering Committee. Between 1973 and 1976, the operations were routine but the Secretariat found itself in an increasingly awkward position given the entry-into-force of the LDC. This event required a change in policy in their view and they pushed hard for the Steering Committee to formalize the arrangement. This the Steering Committee agreed to do in 1976 and the negotiations were concluded in 1977.

The Secretariat's rationale for a change in policy was that between 1964 and 1976 NEA had provided the framework for cooperation on radioactive waste disposal and the opportunity for interested member states to share in the accumulation of practical experience. However, now that the LDC had come into force, signatories were able to dispose of radioactive waste themselves under conditions stipulated in the Treaty and according to regulations issued by the IAEA. Therefore OECD member states could now organize such dumps themselves with a consequent decrease in the scope of Secretariat involvement. The Secretariat role under the formal arrangement would be limited to giving advice and establishing a system of international surveillance supplementing national control.

Under the formal arrangement, member states would undertake to submit their sea-dumping operations (singly or jointly) to international surveillance. The NEA would be responsible for applying stipulated procedures and keeping the Steering Committee informed. No longer would it be necessary for the Steering Committee to approve every single dump ahead of time.

Without going into the details, this largely is the operational significance of the NEA Multilateral Consultation and Surveillance

Mechanism for Sea Dumping of Radioactive Waste, completed and signed in 1977. The 1977 to 1979 dumping operations were routine and the mechanism worked well but, in 1978, there was first appearance of the Greenpeace Ship, *Rainbow Warrior*, at the dump site, though no attempt at direct interference was made. After the operation was concluded, Greenpeace sent a letter of concern to the UK Secretary of State for the Environment. This signalled the beginning of another round of escalation in the conflict.

Note, however, that the previous incidents of conflict were essentially between governments which were members of the same organization. Conflict was therefore muted. The entry of Greenpeace into the fray signalled involvement of mass publics. Finding themselves at a disadvantage within NEA, the opponents of sea-dumping, i.e., Spain, Portugal and particularly Norway and Denmark took the fight to the Consultative Meetings of the LDC where non-governmental organizations had a formal role. The opposing coalition in the LDC was initially based on the countries indicated above plus the Pacific Island States led by Nauru and Kiribati plus the environmentalist organizations. Over time, as the conflict heated up, this grew to become the dominant coalition.

Between 1979 and 1982 Greenpeace attempted repeatedly to interfere with dumping operations and successfully mobilized the Spanish coastal communities. The latter, being primarily Basques, put pressure on a new Socialist Spanish Government which changed its position on the entire nuclear question for Spain and, together with Norway, became co-leaders of the anti-dumping coalition in the LDC. This coalition was successful in pushing through a vote for a two-year moratorium in 1982 over the opposition of pro-dumping NEA member states plus the US, Canada and the USSR, among others. When the UK Government insisted it would go ahead with the dump as planned, Greenpeace mobilized the Seamen and Transport Workers Union to refuse to load the ship. Since the UK Government were at that time in a major confrontation with the coal miners' union, they opted not to fight this issue as well and the dump never took place. By that time, Greenpeace had also mobilized mass publics in The Netherlands and elsewhere. This became an election issue linked to the burgeoning global anti-nuclear movement. The governmental response in turn was to keep a low profile and abandon dumping operations.

Let us now ask two questions. First, were the sea-dumping operations of NEA legal? The answer to that is a clear yes, since they were conducted pursuant to a regime which permitted ocean disposal of low-level radioactive waste under national control and according to IAEA regulations. Secondly, was ocean disposal of low-level radioactive waste as conducted by NEA a safe disposal option? Safe in this context means relative to IAEA/ICRP standards and regulations. This is essentially a scientific knowledge base question and NEA undertook coordination of two full-scale multilateral scientific investigations of its dump sites in 1980 and 1985 since all sites were required to be reviewed every five years. The 1980 review was much less sophisticated theoretically than the 1985 review. By 1985 theory and models had become far more sophisticated than they were in 1980 and available data were more plentiful and of higher quality.

The 1980 review had concluded that the site was suitable for receipt of packaged wastes during the next five years at rates comparable to the past. Only if the annual rates were to increase by more than a factor of 10 would it be desirable to reconsider the safety of the site. The 1985 review concluded that if dumping were carried on for five years, under existing regulations, *at ten times current rates*, the estimated dose equivalents to members of critical groups would be less than 2×10^{-7} Sv./yr.- This amounts to less than 0.02 per cent of the maximum criterion then suggested by the ICRP, i.e., 1 m Sv./yr.-1 when exposures were received over long periods. This finding was not overturned by a completely independent scientific review conducted by IAEA at the behest of the IMO/LDC.

On the basis of these results representatives from Australia, Canada and Ireland on the review group (Expanded Panel) which reviewed the results of the independent scientific review, proposed the following conclusion:

> No scientific or technical grounds could be found to prohibit the dumping at sea of all radioactive wastes, provided that dumping is carried out in accordance with internationally agreed procedures and controls.

Such a categorical statement was not acceptable to representatives from the anti-dumping coalition and the group could agree only on the following compromise:

> No scientific or technical grounds could be found to treat the option of sea dumping differently from other available options when applying internationally accepted principles of radioprotection to radioactive waste disposal.

What then did the NEA/OECD member states learn from the accumulated experience of the 1964-82 dumping operations? They learned:

1. That sea-dumping under current regulations was not only a safe option but also an economical one, far less costly than land-based disposal for low-level radioactive waste;

2. That each could benefit individually more by a cooperative approach than under a purely national approach;

3. That national approaches were, by themselves, less credible and therefore less legitimate than collaborative approaches; and they learned

4. How to carry out sea-dumping operations efficiently, effectively and safely.

But, on the other hand, they learned also that all of the above is not enough if mass publics turn against the nuclear option. The sources of the political objections to sea-dumping are several. The primary fears, in spite of the scientific evidence available, concern potential adverse impacts on living resources and tourism. The public here is not concerned with the degree of risk; just the possibility of danger is enough to foreclose the option. In addition, there are concerns of principle that those who choose to go nuclear should dispose of the waste in their own territories rather than in a global commons. Finally, there are those who would eliminate the nuclear power industry entirely and preventing a solution of the waste disposal problem is but a means to that end. All of these positions are impervious to scientific and technical evidence but they can all be powerful political symbols which can be used to mobilize large segments of populations.

When this happens, national authorities do not wish to buck the tide because the results of doing so can be painful at election time. They therefore can be forced to choose more costly options of waste disposal or, more frequently, seek to buy time by storing wastes for longer periods. Let us attempt a general formulation of the dynamics of the low-level radioactive waste disposal issue. If the issue is an impure collective good exhibiting characteristics of divisibility and non-appropriability, if the focus of action is on controlling or avoiding negative externalities, and if the size of the group is limited (i.e., 2-20), then joint action by those states directly affected will easily be perceived in terms of pursuing joint gain. The most important policy constraints will be monetary and interdependence costs. However, within those constraints, the level of collaboration achieved will be high enough to encompass coordinated and even fully integrated planning and effectiveness of joint action will be high.

As noted above, a precondition for effectiveness is the small size of the group. But restricted size, given the nature of the activity in a global commons, will generate increasing protests by states whose governments object to the activity on the basis of popular fears of adverse impacts to well-being. If domestic publics are mobilized on the issue, confrontations will develop and the activity can be stopped in spite of impartial scientific reviews of safety and effectiveness.

Conclusions

The stimulus for this paper was provided by three of the questions posed by the organizers of this Conference. Let me rephrase them.

1. Is the available scientific (and technical) knowledge base adequate, legitimate and usable for the resolution of international resource management issues?

2. When is the knowledge base politically important?

3. Does scientific (and technical) cooperation contribute to political cooperation in international resource management? If so, why?

Initial answers to these questions were provided in the earlier study by Miles [38] but this focused on first-order effects primarily. The present study chooses two issues with sufficient longevity to examine the emergence of second and third-order effects but, even here, I have restricted my concern to the relationship between second and third-order effects and:

1. The knowledge base.
2. The types and evolution of organizational arrangements.
3. Types of policies.
4. Types of implementation strategies.
5. Levels of international cooperation defined in terms of a continuum from tacit coordination to fully integrated planning and implementation.

Let me now summarize what I think we have learned.

Satellite telecommunication is a relatively pure issue, i.e., it is largely uncontaminated by external issues of unrelated political conflict. In fact, exogenous influences are at a minimum. The length of time is about 30 years or since 1958. The knowledge base was adequate for regulatory purposes and it was developed over time within the discipline of radio engineering. With respect to the regulatory dimension, evidence is available of three types of second and third-order effects. Between 1963 and 1975 two of these produced impacts on the scope of organizational tasks (expansion) and on the domain of ITU's interorganizational relations (expansion). The former have direct links to management decisions while the latter create only indirect links. But, in each case, the triggers are technological innovation, the demands this poses for the organization, and perceptions of the Executive Head of what opportunities are thereby created for organizational growth and development. This connection sets in motion a host of strategic and tactical decisions in a never ending stream.

The third type of effect relates to demands to change the approach to allocation of the spectrum. This struggle antedates the emergence of satellite telecommunication but is accentuated by it and the links to management decisions are direct. Two time periods must be distinguished. The first is 1959-65 when the advanced industrial countries of the West unquestionably controlled the organization and could therefore block any attempt at replacing the seniority rights system. However, as technology advanced and satellite systems proliferated, fears concerning the saturation of the geostationary orbit intensified and the issue was raised again in 1979. By this time it was the developing countries who commanded the necessary majorities but the attempt to change the system was deflected by the United States, the representatives of which make use of recent technological advances relating to frequency reuse and sharing to convince the Group of 77 to leave things as they were. This increased the level of cooperation between the two parties in which the US undertook to bear the cost of providing developing country access to this technology in return for continuation of the seniority rights system.

Changes in the operational knowledge base are important sources of second and third-order effects. The US/Group of 77 relationship is one example of this; ITU's relationships with WMO and, especially, INTELSAT are also good examples. The initial development was determined solely by whether the organizations' jurisdiction conflicted or whether their needs were complementary without the dimension of jurisdictional conflict. But even where conflict existed in the beginning, as between ITU and INTELSAT, the relationship over time became more cooperative given the technical requirements of coordination. Technical cooperation can sometimes facilitate political cooperation but only at a low level and it depends on the job to be done. Between the two organizations the level of cooperation did increase from level 1 (tacit coordination) to level 2 (coordinated action via common standards with unilateral implementation). But one cannot expect more than that since the relationship is constrained by the sectoral organization of states and their corresponding international networks.

Beyond task expansion and limited interorganizational integration, the organizational arrangements, policies and implementation strategies do not change much. The initial implementation strategy for ITU was as a forum within which technical coordination on frequency utilization could be achieved and performance standards for equipment developed. This approach became almost the organizational ideology which was deeply ingrained in the organizational subculture. It is very resistant to change and this resistance is reinforced by the political effects of divisibility. Attempts to introduce major design changes in the approach have consistently been defeated and satellite telecommunication has been accommodated within this traditional approach.

Contrast this with the commercial development and operations dimension. There the issue remained relatively pure, the time period was the same, the knowledge base with respect to principles of radio communication in space was adequate though it was non-existent with respect to operations and costs. This dictated an experimental approach merging the disciplines of radio and aerospace engineering. The critical decision was the one relating to choice of implementation strategy. After that, organizational arrangements and policies followed. The intertia of past traditions was completely absent. This was an entirely new game in which there was one dominant player (the US) who made all the rules.

Why then was it successful? It was successful because the stream of benefits provided relative to costs was and is compelling and is generally seen to be so by all concerned. States collaborate either to seek benefits which they perceive as important and which cannot be achieved through their own actions alone or to avoid/minimize the negative externalities of their own or others' actions. The US approach clearly satisfied the first condition of this rule; the combination of implementation strategies chosen together with policies pursued produced a very high level of international cooperation. In fact, this is the first of only two examples of level 4 cooperation (fully integrated planning and implementation) we have encountered here.

But all is not success. We have encountered as well five triggers of second and third-order effects which generate adverse results. The COMSAT negotiating position in 1969-71 increased political conflict, led to a limit of 40 per cent being placed on any single country's vote and eventually produced a much narrower definition of the scope of INTELSAT's programme focus than could have been achieved. It also ensured that the Soviets would not join INTELSAT and would prevent the East Europeans from doing so. This, in turn, stimulated a proliferation of satellite systems which by 1984 had become a serious problem.

In addition, the NASA monopoly on launchers combined with the effects of Art. XIV of the draft Definitive Arrangements reinforced the desire of the French and the Japanese to develop their own launchers. China adapted ICBM technology to the same purpose and a later wrong choice by the US relative to the Shuttle versus expendable launchers intensified the competition from US private companies. These effects did not produce any changes in the knowledge base beyond diffusion of launching capability. But rapid technological advance in satellites stimulated rapid advance in cable systems and the conflict over INTELSAT's procurement policy did produce some accommodation for the European view, at least in principle. No major changes have been made in organizational arrangements, policies or implementation strategies. The level of cooperation remains high and, as we have noted, an effective *modus vivendi* has been arrived at with ITU.

The proliferation dimension of the nuclear energy issue is highly contaminated which greatly complicates any attempt at control. It is the oldest issue of those considered here, having been created in 1945. With respect to controlling proliferation, the knowledge base between 1945 and 1953 was non-existent and the assumptions on which policy was based were not only wrong but counter-productive. They in fact stimulated the very phenomenon they were put in place to control and this was the first second-order effect. But at the same time, a significant decision was taken to create IAEA in order to institutionalize the twin concerns of diffusing civilian uses of nuclear energy while controlling proliferation via a focus on safeguards. Here choice of policy was the critical decision and organizational arrangements followed. The latter did succeed in increasing the level of cooperation, from level 1 to level 2.

A policy of technological denial is usually unworkable because knowledge, when it exists and is sought after, diffuses easily. The policy stimulated attempts to get around the restrictions imposed within the group of potential nuclear suppliers. These countries also participated inside and outside the IAEA programmes and between 1954 and 1974 nuclear proliferation became a serious international policy problem in spite of the NPT, and the level of cooperation within the group of supplier countries declined markedly. Competition for markets was the order of the day. This was reinforced by the second-order effects of the OPEC oil crisis of 1973 both with respect to assumed demand for electricity and to presumed shortfalls in uranium reserves. The stage was therefore set for a virtual explosion of proliferation and a rapid introduction of the plutonium economy.

But that very fact, combined with powerful ancillary events, produced a surprising third-order effect. The ancillary events were the Indian explosion of a nuclear device in 1974 and, among other things, the growing tendency by supplier states to resort to including weapons — usable components of the nuclear fuel cycle as 'sweeteners' in the sale of reactor technology. The perception of a rapidly growing threat to international stability among supplier states was the critical ingredient that facilitated acceptance of a major change in policy. Creation of the Nuclear Suppliers Group and Agreement on measures to slow down the rate of proliferation produce increased cooperation on the nuclear export issue (from level 1 to level 2) from 1976. This was reinforced by the INFCE study which significantly expanded the knowledge base. It was also reinforced by a structural change in the nuclear industry from the late 1970s. This is clearly a completely exogenous variable but both developments served to slow down the rate of proliferation. Choice of implementation strategy appears to have been the critical change here in 1976, i.e., focus on the nuclear suppliers — this brought with it an organizational innovation (the Nuclear Suppliers Group) and a change in policy.

Two time periods must also be distinguished on the radioactive waste issue. Between 1964 and 1976 the issue was relatively pure. The knowledge base was inadequate but governments decided to build it experimentally and operationally. Choice of implementation strategy was the critical decision which led to the institutionalization of a very high level of international cooperation. This is the second example of level 4 activity we have encountered. This stimulated a new arrangement within NEA which significantly expanded the organizational task and it facilitated major innovations in policy which stressed reliability of operations, stringent oversight, common standards, monitoring, and an independent role for the Secretariat.

We know now that very special circumstances must exist before level 4 activity can emerge. In the case of satellite telecommunications it was to realize as rapidly as possible the promise of the new technology which could be done only on a global basis. In the case of radioactive waste disposal the triggers were three: (a) a perceived need to solve a common problem among a small group of countries; (b) the need for legitimacy given the use of the global commons; and (c) the perceived benefit of cooperating to reduce costs. These all added up to the need for internationalizing disposal operations as the means of solution.

The second time period occured between 1979 and 1982. Here the issue became highly contaminated (no pun intended) but this contamination came in the form of the mobilization of mass publics. Governments are far more vulnerable to this kind of attack than they are to facing the direct probes of other governments. In this case one catalyst, Greenpeace, stimulated political opposition within dumping countries as well as elsewhere and then made common cause with other opposed governments in a different forum. The effect was to combine symbolic victory (the moratorium vote in the LDC) with political conflict internally in dumping states. This combination was crippling for those who wished to continue dumping.

The level of cooperation among the opponents seemed to increase to level 3 (coordinated planning/unilateral implementation) but within the Greenpeace coalition itself it attained level 4. Dumping was prohibited effectively, though not formally, even at the same time that the knowledge base was significantly expanded and it was shown to be safe as conducted under present rules and regulations. The two most important exogenous influences operative were the growth of the global anti-nuclear movement and the seriousness of the Spanish Basque problem which induced a new government to change course on this issue.

What can we say generally about the dynamics which drive international resource management issues and which therefore affect the knowledge base and the level of cooperation which can be achieved?

Big problems arise over impure collective goods exhibiting the characteristics of divisibility and non-appropriability. Skew in the distribution of capabilities, benefits and costs is also important because these always raise the commercial stakes and thereby accentuate problems of divisibility. Even moderate skew will constrain provision of the collective good because it will trigger significant rivalry over commercial stakes, but the type of technology can be an important variable here in shaping how extensive conflict will be since it affects both the size of the pie to be shared and its divisibility. The size of the group *per se* does not appear to be too important a variable on these issues since conflict is endemic and is driven by rivalry among the most capable players.

Issues can change their characteristics over time, and therefore their dynamics, if one varies the divisibility factor significantly. Increasing divisibility, for instance by adding regulatory/distributional consequences will lead to a decline in both collaboration and effectiveness. Decreasing divisibility, on the other hand, if the good is seen to be important by governments, will tend to increase collaboration and effectiveness. But, since on issues involving negative externalities, size is important for facilitating perceptions of a need to pursue joint gain, type of technology may also emerge as a significant variable here if important technological fix options exist. Bargaining over apportionment of costs will be the most difficult issue to be resolved but the difficulty may be surmountable if the players continue to focus on the pursuit of joint gain. Joint gain will permit higher levels of collaboration to emerge and in turn facilitate greater effectiveness in the regulatory exercise.

In many cases the knowledge base is adequate, legitimate and usable for the resolution of international resource management issues. Where it is not, governments have been quite flexible in supporting its production. But where the knowledge base is directly relevant for either distributive or regulatory decisions, its political salience increases. Whether or not governments interfere with it, suppress it or ignore it is a function of a prior consensus among them relating to the existence of an important joint need. Scientific and technical cooperation do not automatically facilitate political cooperation in international resource management issues. The critical variable is always the nature of the good in question and especially its divisibility. The most important decisions for the level of cooperation achieved have to do with choice of implementation strategies and/or choice of policies. Choice of organizational arrangements is secondary though flexibility is greater if one is starting from scratch, which can often happen with technological innovation.

Exogenous influences are truly wild cards in the process of international resource management. Depending on the issue and the circumstances they can go either way. They can facilitate cooperation, as in the case of nuclear proliferation, or they can inhibit it, as in the case of radioactive waste disposal. They cannot be planned for. Similarly, second and third-order effects are wild cards. Sometimes they prevent or retard international cooperation. Increasing the knowledge base over time can indeed occasionally increase cooperation and contribute directly or indirectly to management decisions. The only way one can plan for this is to design management systems which can learn from trial and error.

Notes

1. Miles, Edward L., 1987, *Science, Politics, and International Ocean Management: The Uses of Scientific Knowledge in International Negotiations, (Policy Papers in International Affairs*, no 33,) Institute of International Studies, University of California, Berkeley.

2. Ruggie, John Gerard, 1972, 'Collective Goods and Future International Collaboration', *American Political Science Review*, vol. 66, pp. 874-93.

3. Ruggie, John Gerard, 1972, and Miles, Edward L., 1983, 'On the Roles of International Organizations in the New Ocean Regime', in Choon-ho Park (ed.), *The Law of the Sea in the 1980's*, Law of the Sea Institute, Honolulu, pp. 383-445, and Miles, Edward L., 1983 (2), 'IOC Data and Information Exchange: Implications of the Law of the Sea Convention', *Marine Policy*, vol.7, no. 2, April 1983, pp. 75-89.

4. Haas, Ernst B., 1980, 'Why Collaborate? Issue Linkage and International Regimes', *World Politics*, vol. 32, no. 3, pp. 357-405.

5. Ruggie, John Gerard, 1975, 'International Responses to Technology: Concepts and Trends', *International Organization*, vol. 29, no. 3 Summer, p. 558.

6. Wohlstetter, Albert, 'Strength, Interest and New Technologies', *ADELPHI PAPERS*, September 1968.

7. Codding, George A. and Rutowski, Anthony M, 1982, *The International Telecommunication Union: An Experiment in International Cooperation*, Artech House, Dedham, MA, and Jacobson, Harold, 1973, 'The International Telecommunication Union', in Robert Cox and Harold Jacobson (eds.), *Decision-Making in International Organizations: The Anatomy of Influence*, Yale University Press, New Haven, pp. 59-101.

8. Colino, Richard R, 1984, 'The INTELSAT System: An Overview', in Joel Alper and Joseph N. Pelton (eds.), *The INTELSAT Global System*, American Institute of Aeronautics and Astronautics, Inc., New York, vol. 93, Progress in Astronautics and Aeronautics, pp. 55-94.

9. Colino, Richard, R, 1984.

10. Colino, Richard R, 1984.

11. Colino, Richard R, 1984.

12. Levy, Stephen A., 1975. 'INTELSAT: Technology, Politics, and the Transformation of a Regime', *International Organization*, vol. 29, no. 3 (Summer), pp. 655-80.

13. Colino, Richard R. 1984.

14. Miles, Edward, 1970-71, *International Administration of Space Exploration and Exploitation*, Graduate School of International Studies, University of Denver, Denver, CO, Monograph Series in World Affairs, vol. 8, no. 4; see also Levy, Stephen A., 1975, and Colino, Richard R., 1984.

15. Levy, Stephen A. 1975.

16. Miles, Edward, 1970-71, and Colino, Richard R., 1984.

17. Colino, Richard R., 1984.

18. Levy, Stephen A., 1975.

19. Levy, Stephen A., 1975.

20. Pelton, Joseph N., 1977, 'Key Problems in Satellite Communications: Proliferation, Competition and Planning in an Uncertain Environment', in Joseph N. Pelton and Marcellus S. Snow (eds.), *Economic and Policy Problems in Satellite Communications*, Praeger Publishers, New York pp.

93-123.

21. Withers, David and Weiss, Hans J., 1984, 'INTELSAT and the ITU', in Joel Alper and Joseph N. Pelton (eds.), *The INTELSAT Global Satellite System*, American Institute of Aeronautics and Astronautics, Inc., New York pp. 270-310.

22. Withers, David and Weiss, Hans J., 1984.

23. Withers, David and Weiss, Hans J., 1984.

24. Pelton, Joseph N., 1977.

25. Wihlborg, Clas G. and Wijkman, Hans Per, 1981, 'Outer Space Resources in Efficient and Equitable Use: New Frontiers for Old Principles', *Journal of Law and Economics*, vol. 24, no. 1 (April), pp. 23-43.

26. Miles, Edward, 1987.

27. Goldschmidt, Bertrand., 1977, 'A Historical Survey of Nonproliferation Policies', *International Security*, vol. 2, no. 1 (Summer), pp. 69-87.

28. Long, Clarence, D., 1977, 'Nuclear Proliferation: Can Congress Act in Time', *International Security*, vol 1, no. 4 (Spring), pp. 52-76.

29. Nye, Joseph S., 1981, 'Maintaining a Non-Proliferation Regime', *International Organization*, vol. 35, no. 1 (Winter), pp. 15-38.

30. Colino, Richard R., 1984.

31. Nye, Joseph S., 1981.

32. Nye, Joseph S., 1981.

33. Nye, Joseph S., 1981, and Goldsmith, Bertrand, 1977.

34. Nye, Joseph S., 1981.

35. Nye, Joseph S., 1981.

36. Bupp, Irvin C., 1981. 'The Actual Growth and Probable Future of the Worldwide Nuclear Industry', *International Organization*, vol. 35, no. 1 (Winter), pp. 59-76, and Cook, James, 'Nuclear Follies', FORBES, 11 February 1985, pp. 82-100.

37. Bupp, Irvin C., 1981.

38. Miles, Edward, 1987.

4

Polar science and politics: close twins or opposite poles in international cooperation?

Willy Østreng

It is common to refer to the Antarctic as 'the continent of science and cooperation' and to the Arctic as 'the region of politics and conflict'. These formulations would seem to indicate that science promotes cooperation, whereas politics serves to create conflict. To some degree, such attitudes have taken root in the thinking about the polar regions. It has for instance been maintained that cooperation in the Antarctic came about because 'governments stood down for a while, pushed aside (disputes), and allowed their scientists to cooperate'.[1] The attitude is that 'Science and scientists have a kind of objectivity which is congenial to cooperation. The nature of science is not only conducive to cooperation, but indeed demands it, for no man, no nation, has a monopoly of science'.[2] To put it in a nutshell: the implication is that scientists administer transnational research values which promote international cooperation in areas where no threat to national interests exist; under favourable circumstances, these values can also become relevant to cooperation at the political level. Thus, strengthening the science component in the polar regions also means improving the conditions for international cooperation. This would apply not least in the highly politicized Arctic, where scientists are at best playing second fiddle in relation to their governments.

In this article we shall consider the interaction between science and politics in the light of such attitudes. The aim is to elucidate the relationship of research to national interests, and the ability of science — if indeed any — to influence and initiate political processes. Furthermore, we shall make use of experience gained from cooperation in the Antarctic to shed light on the problem of establishing more permanent forms of research cooperation in the North.

'The nature of science demands cooperation!'

The first question to be clarified is how science in general relates to national interests, and which conditions for cooperation this provides. Here it may prove useful to distinguish between three forms of research: (1) practical-instrumental, (2) symbolic-instrumental, (3) knowledge-instrumental.[3]

The first type — *practical-instrumental* — aims at solving current problems for immediate application, be they military, economic or of another kind. Clients are to be found in public administration, in private organizations and in industry. They have basically two objectives in mind with such research: in addition to finding answers to the problems impeding the achievement of their interests, they also wish to gain a comparative advantage in relation to their competitors. Thus, these clients will have a definite inclination to keep secret the results of the research. And secrecy fails either to attract, stimulate or invite cooperation. To the extent that any cooperation takes place, it will be restricted to a small number of 'reliable' contract partners; it will be strictly time limited; it will be exclusive. For these reasons, practical-instrumental research is ill suited as a point of departure for long-term cooperation, be it scientific or political, within nations or between them.

Symbolic-instrumental research serves primarily political ends. It is initiated in order to demonstrate that the party in question possesses scientific capacity capable, should the need arise, of being used as a basis for influence also in non-scientific fields. Here the client aims to ensure the presence of researchers in a region where he wishes to assert himself. Such presence will signal two things: first, the state's interest in and attachment to the area, and second, the government's political will to play an active part in the development of the area. In the eyes of the government, the scientific component is of secondary importance in relation to the symbolic function. This in turn means that as long as the content and organization of the research represent no threat to primary interests, researchers will be given complete freedom of choice as to topics as well as to collaborators on the basis of purely scientific criteria and priorities. The conditions for cooperation will worsen, however, if such choices should make it more difficult to maintain primary interests. Thus, symbolic-instrumental research provides both conditionally good and conditionally poor ground for scientific cooperation.

The very *raison d'être* of basic research is *knowledge-instrumental*, that is, to generate insight into how our complex, composite reality functions. It makes no attempt to solve immediate problems as such, nor to support political goals. Its motive force is scientific curiosity, and the goal is to increase knowledge and insight. When governments support this type of research, they do so because it may prove useful, whether in the near or the distant future. However, considerable uncertainty exists as to the exact utility of such research — which in addition is highly resource-consuming. Authorities will therefore naturally tend to keep expenditure down, but without falling out with their own researchers. International cooperation, to some extent, serves both these considerations. Much can be saved and little concealed. In this way governments may become vital supporting players and, indeed, major agents in bringing scientists together. Therefore, research of the knowledge-instrumental type is particularly well suited for cooperation across national borders.

The general conclusion to be drawn from all this is that the lower the practical utility of research, the better will be the conditions for establishing international scientific cooperation. Or in other words, the more that research has to do with ensuring non-scientific national interests, the more control governments will exert over cooperation possibilities. Considered against this backdrop, statements like 'science demands cooperation' or 'no nation has a monopoly of science' would seem to be of scant interest. As long as governments, by means of their policies on grants and allocations, can maintain a monopoly on the use of research results, and as long as they have differing priorities as to the type of research they wish to support, they in reality largely control the conditions for cooperation, whether it be scientific or political. Or, put somewhat differently, 'the nature of knowledge-instrumental science demands international cooperation whilst the nature of politics in general demands national control'. Just how these partly conflicting demands interact in the polar regions will form the subject of our discussion here.

The three categories of research link science with politics by means of national interests. In order to understand the potential for cooperation in the polar regions, therefore, we shall have to clarify the composition of the interest structure in each region.

The Antarctic — 'a continent of science and cooperation?'

The interest structure

In the post-war period, the interest structure in the Antarctic has been two-dimensional, related solely to economy and sovereignty. The former aspect is largely historical, connected mainly with whaling and, at present, minor krill and fish harvesting. As yet the mainland is not an object of exploitation for economic ends. Indeed, the sole interest keeping governments perpetually on their toes relates to the issue of sovereignty in the region.

Especially since World War II, sovereignty in the Antarctic has been a disputed and unresolved issue. Britain, France, Australia, New Zealand, Norway, Argentina and Chile have all claimed sovereignty rights over parts of the Antarctic. Neither the US nor the USSR — the major powers in this area — have recognized these claims. Indeed, both have reserved for themselves the right to lodge similar claims. Nor has the rest of the world *de jure* accepted these claims — which have been recognized only amongst those claimants having no overlapping territorial claims. The sovereignty claims put forward by Chile, Argentina and Britain overlap each other — a fact which has at times unleashed considerable diplomatic activity and, on one occasion, even resort to arms.

A new conflict topic appeared on the horizon in the 1980s. In the wake of the United Nations Third Conference on the Law of the Sea (UNCLOS 3), the initiative was taken within the UN to declare the Antarctic, like the deep sea-bed, 'the common heritage of mankind'. According to the Prime Minister of Malaysia, who raised the question, the uninhabited lands of Antarctica 'do not legally belong to the colonial powers. Like the sea and the seabeds, these uninhabited lands belong to the international community. The countries presently claiming them must give them up so that either the United Nations administer these lands or the present occupants act as trustees for the nations of the world.'[4] This initiative was followed by a Non-Aligned Movement communiqué of 11 March 1983, calling for a General Assembly study on Antarctica 'with a view to widening international cooperation in the area.'[5] The Antarctic powers have warily responded that they do not oppose UN consideration of Antarctica, but that they will not accept a major overhaul of the system or its replacement. This development is a most important reminder that the issue of sovereignty over Southern territories has become a global affair where more and more nations demand a say.

In the mid-1960s, sovereignty problems prompted this expert opinion: 'The Antarctic was not a promising area for any sort of international cooperation.'[6] As of this day and age, the question is rather if cooperation in the South may survive the present challenges. Both observations will be discussed here.

National interests, research and cooperation

The history of exploration and cooperation in the Antarctic has been divided into three phases: (1) national exploration (up to 1950); (2) international cooperation on coordinating the national exploration programmes (1950-88); (3) international cooperation on all levels and in all fields, scientific and political (1988-).[7]

The first phase, also called the heroic or nationalistic era, culminated in the late 1940s. Research was then carried out by expeditions organized by private or state interests which ' . . . tended to proceed in splendid isolation, even rivalry, with each other'.[8] The race for the South Pole was a dramatic illustration of this. Competition and national prestige ruled the day, rather than cooperation and communication to meet shared challenges. National flags fluttered in solitude, not in clusters.[9] This was the period of establishment on the Antarctic, and

Figure 4.1 Antarctic sovereignty claims

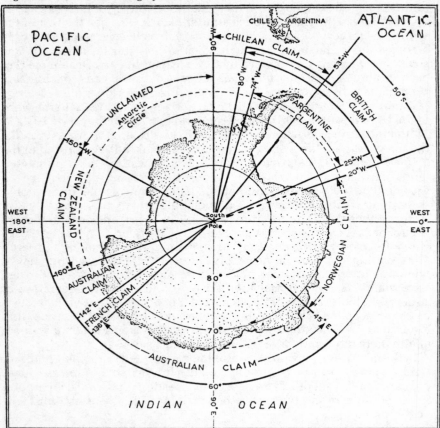

scientists were ' . . . interpreted basically as political instruments, who were exploited either to support and reinforce sovereignty claims, or to enhance national prestige; thus the intrinsic scientific merit of either a project or location was less important than politico-legal considerations.'[10] In other words, research served symbolic-instrumental ends. As to content, this was largely a matter for researchers to determine on the basis of their own scientific priorities. This was to lay a good foundation for future cooperation in the region.

The first signs of cooperation (phase 2) came in the early 1950s, a period designated the breakthrough decade in modern polar research.[11] Cooperation began with the Norwegian-British-Swedish Maudheim expedition, 1949-52; it was continued and expanded with the International Geophysical Year (IGY), 1957/58, and formalized through the Antarctic Treaty of 1959. In the course of these years, the experience gained from previous efforts was expanded and further developed. This was to result in a unique system of cooperation set out in the Antarctic

Treaty, whose main provisions are as follows: the Southern continent may be utilized solely for peaceful purposes; military activity of any kind is prohibited, including the establishment of military bases and fortifications, military manoeuvres and the testing of nuclear weapons (Article 1); furthermore, storage of radioactive waste is prohibited in the area (Article 5). The Treaty goes on to state that freedom of scientific investigation in the region, as applied during IGY, shall continue (Article 2). In Article 3 the parties agree that, to the greatest extent possible and practicable, information regarding plans for scientific programs shall be exchanged to permit maximum economy and efficiency of operations and to enable exchange of personnel between expeditions and stations to take place. Scientific observations and results shall be exchanged and made freely available. The parties may also send observers to undertake unannounced inspections at any time and anywhere in the Antarctic. In this way all parties should feel secure in the knowledge that the provisions of the Treaty are being complied with in practice (Articles 7 and 8).

The Treaty also defines the framework and organs for political cooperation in the region. As the Treaty has no secretariat of its own, the parties interact formally by means of the Consultative Meetings held every second year to discuss ' ... matters of common interests pertaining to Antarctica'. A scientific organization for the region has also been established, the Scientific Committee on Antarctic Research (SCAR). Although no formal linkage exists between the Treaty system and SCAR, from the very beginning the Consultative Meetings have used SCAR as an advisory body. In this process SCAR has had considerable influence. Among other things it has been stated, ' ... although SCAR (has) kept strictly to its scientific role, the scientific influence on the political processes of the Treaty system has been strong'.[12] Or put somewhat differently, 'While it is not clear ... that SCAR needs the Treaty, it is very clear that the treaty mechanism would be very much poorer if it did not have SCAR to turn to.'[13] In other words, an informal but real system of Antarctic cooperation has been established which clearly illustrates the linkage between science and politics.

In the course of a decade, Antarctic research moved from national rivalry to an unsurpassed system of international scientific/political cooperation. Some maintain that it is the scientists who deserve the credit here. It was they who realized the need for such cooperation, they who took the initiative and got the process under way. Moreover, they participated in the political processes, where they managed 'to turn the tables upon governments, and to exploit politics for the advancement of science.'[14]

However, the weakness of this reasoning is that it ignores the importance of the governments in question and their own motives for supporting researchers in their cooperative efforts. The symbolic-instrumental approach to research was the choice of governments, not of researchers. And indeed, from the research side it has been stressed: 'The great support given by the 12 nations to the IGY Programme in the

Antarctic was no doubt based upon other interests also than the love for polar science'.[15] For instance, it was hardly a coincidence that the USA, who recognizes none of the sovereignty claims, chose to build its Amundsen-Scott Base right on the South Pole at the very intersection of all sector claims. Other states too established research bases on political rather than purely scientific grounds, as suggested by the tendency for claimants to site their bases within their 'own' sectors.[16] On the other hand, the Soviet Union chose to establish all its bases within the Australian sector. This caused unrest in Canberra, and in March 1957 the Australian government informed the US Secretary of State that one feared that ' . . . posts originally established under the sheep's clothing of scientific research may subsequently be revealed in their wolf reality of political and military gains'.[17] In other words, politics seemed to be choosing many unorthodox bedfellows in those years, a tendency that has continued also after IGY.

Some have maintained that the political results of IGY were more important than the scientific side.[18] The Soviet Union, who previously had not been active in the Antarctic, now displayed intentions to establish a permanent presence in the region. Several of the traditional Antarctic states wished, in line with Cold War thinking, to find ' . . . a way of containing Soviet moves'.[19] The feeling was 'that unless an international solution for the Antarctic could be found, a confrontation might easily have erupted in the area. On this argument, the primary motivation for negotiating the Treaty was a negative political one — fear of chaos at the southern ends of the Earth — not a positive reason to facilitate scientific research, which seems to have been secondary.'[20] In other words, superpower considerations underlay the efforts to continue the IGY collaboration in binding legal forms. Thus the politicians now managed to turn the tables upon the scientific communities and to exploit science for the advancement of politics. This was possible because research was symbolic-instrumental, utilized as 'currency of Antarctic politics'.[21]

However, this is not to say that research was of no importance for the establishment and development of the Treaty cooperation. The services and contributions rendered by researchers have in fact been numerous. Firstly, researchers were extensively used as advisors for governments — a natural course to follow, since the objective of the regulation and cooperation in question concerned precisely research. Furthermore, they helped to spur on governments who may have hesitated to expand their involvement in the region. Gradually there arose among researchers what might be called 'science politicians', who in addition to carrying out active research themselves also took part in the political processes, both as members of delegations to the Consultative Meetings, advisors to governments and lobbyists for the scientific community.[22] In this way, science and its premises became a part of the political decision-making basis. Among other things, researchers had a central role in the definition and implementation of the cooperation philosophy which follows naturally from symbolic-instrumental research: that scientific cooperation must not harm political goals. This was to develop from a gentleman's agreement before and during IGY, into a legal obligation as set out in the Antarctic Treaty: 'No acts or activities taking place while the present Treaty is in force shall constitute a basis for asserting, supporting or denying a claim to territorial sovereignty in Antarctica or create any rights of sovereignty in Antarctica' (Article IV).

Researchers carried the intentions in this provision a stage further by initiating cooperation in various non-controversial fields. Examples here include exchange of scientific programmes, personnel and data, exchange of information on logistical conditions, preservation and registration of historical sites, conservation of fauna and flora and assistance in emergencies. None of these areas could reasonably be interpreted as impinging on sovereignty interests. Gradually, as confidence and trust grew between the parties, the limits to cooperation were extended. In 1960 only non-controversial fields were included; today we may note cooperation in such sensitive areas as the administration of living and mineral resources. Here 'SCAR (has) helped the Treaty system to develop smoothly, even to broadening the original purpose of the Treaty.'[23] There exists broad general agreement that 'None of these milestones could have been achieved were it not for the matrix of less controversial agreements (Recommendations) in which they were set and from which they developed. The driving force behind this exploration of the limits of agreement and the conclusion of the agreements before the subject matter of them became highly politically charged was again . . . fear of the chaos that might engulf the system. The price to be paid for maintaining order was a series of exercises in foresight.'[24]

Thus, researchers have influenced both the shape and the content of cooperation in Antarctica. The foundations were laid that had been drawn up between the knowledge-instrumental interests of researchers and the symbolic-instrumental interests of their governments. However, the overarching framework remained political throughout. Seen in this way, it is justifiable to stress the linkage between research and politics as being the very reason why such cooperation was established to begin with. As Ingemar Bohlin has expressed it, 'Science in the Antarctic has definitely been shaped to a far greater extent by political cycles than paved the way for political solutions.'[25]

In the early 1970s the question of exploiting the resources of the Antarctic — living and mineral resources — was raised among the consultative parties. In the course of sixteen years, three resource conventions saw the light of day: the *Convention for the Conservation of Antarctic Seals* in 1972 and the *Convention for Conservation of Antarctic Living Resources* in 1980, both of which have now entered into force. On 25 November 1988, after many years of hard negotiations, the ultimate jewel in the crown was signed, namely the *Convention on the Regulation of Antarctic Mineral Activities*.

Thus, the system of cooperation has gradually been expanded to include a fully developed regime for the conservation and exploitation of resources without conflicts of sovereignty flaring up. This is in itself a remarkable political achievement, not least in view of the fact that the entire issue of resources was deliberately set aside for fear that the 1958 Washington negotiations on the Antarctic Treaty might break down. We may here note how a long-term international cooperative relationship has extended the limits of tolerance as to how sensitive issues may be, and yet still be raised between and among the parties. Indeed, the cost of refusing to deal with such issues increases the longer such cooperation lasts. This is why the governments involved now consider the new mineral convention not only as a triumph for current collaboration and cooperation, but also as a decisive milestone in efforts to ensure future cooperation as well. In line with this, it has been suggested that the need for a review conference to modify/amend the text of the Antarctic Treaty in 1991, as provided for in Article XII, may have been reduced by this achievement. Such optimism does not necessarily mean that the road ahead will be free of problems.

The question of exploitation of resources has naturally influenced the content of research programmes. While research previously tended to be primarily knowledge-instrumental, a turn in the direction of more practical-instrumental research took place in the 1980s. The Soviet Union, for instance, has had expeditions to the Ronne and Filchner Ice Shelves to investigate the economic geology of those regions. British, Chilean and Argentine scientists are conducting economic assessments of areas of the Antarctic Peninsula. This presents challenges on several levels. For one thing, scientists have expressed concern that this development ' . . . will seriously compromise Article III of the Antarctic Treaty calling for full and free exchange of scientific information. If there is to be serious exploration, the information obtained must be privileged — especially if private industry is to participate, as it must. Thus confidentiality will replace openness in Antarctica, and difficult questions will arise as to what data can be exchanged and what withheld.'[26] Such a development may also shift research funds from knowledge-instrumental to practical-instrumental research. And unless total allocations are also increased, this will mean that the scope of basic research will be reduced, thereby also reducing the basis for international cooperation.

This new development has also brought new actors on stage: the various environmental protection organizations. Primarily they wish to have the Antarctic made into a 'world nature park', permanently protected against any encroachment. Such a goal can bring conservation interests into direct conflict also with basic researchers, who may occasionally need to modify or destroy certain elements in the natural surroundings in order to carry out their experiments. For instance, biologists have to kill seals or penguins for their studies; geophysicists have to carry out blasting with explosives — bases need to be built, etc. These are examples of interference in nature which are necessary also for conservation interests, but which, on ideological grounds, are still unacceptable to the more extreme organizations. In this way even knowledge-instrumental research, which normally serves to promote international cooperation, can itself become a source of conflict. There is every reason to assume that practical-instrumental research will be confronted with this problem to an even greater degree than basic research.

The cooperative relationship between researchers and government representatives has also changed in recent years. In particular, there seems to be increasing frustration among some scientists, as shown by this complaint: 'the Consultative Meetings are setting up their own groups of experts, subject to political and other pressures and relying less on SCAR advice, which is separated from, and largely independent of, political pressure. Political and legal matters are the concern of the Treaty and so lawyers and diplomats predominate the Consultative Meetings. These are characterized by horse trading and lobbying in the corridors, rather than open debates in meetings. The few scientists present have second-class status, although almost invariably they represent the only practical experience there.'[27]

This rather colourful description strikes home on one vital point: governments are strengthening their own political involvement and keeping a tighter rein on controlling developments in the region. Among other things, there is the insistence on a clearer division of functions between politics and science. What is being demanded is the use of the decision-making model originally set for the Antarctic. According to this model, SCAR is to have purely advisory functions, the Consultative Meetings are to negotiate, and the governments are to take decisions.[28] In this way, then, the issue of resources has slightly restricted researchers in their freedom to choose their research topics for themselves, and has reduced the extent of their functions and participation in political processes.

This politicization does not, however, mean that the basic symbiosis between science and politics is about to cease. Politicians will still need scientists to ensure the presence of their nation, and scientists will still need politicians to fund their research. The difference is rather that in the future more serious 'marital problems' may arise between the two sets of interests. The director of the British Antarctic Survey, David J. Drewry, has expressed it this way: 'Science in Antarctica is now at a threshold. Behind are the solid contributions of 40 to 50 years of undisputed, basic research; ahead lies a period of increased politicization and economic aspirations woven through with legal, environmental and conservation issues.'[29] The 'continent of science and cooperation' is in the process of becoming a continent of increasing politics. Whether that means more conflict remains to be seen.

Some factors behind the success of cooperation in Antarctica

Four points about the cooperation established in Antarctica deserve our attention:

1. *Conflict in one issue area (conflict of sovereignty) did not preclude cooperation in another (science).*
   This observation is a direct result of the fact that symbolic-instrumental research in the Antarctic throughout the post-war period has served interests in two areas, in part closely connected and in part clearly separated. These areas were connected in the sense that the one was used to promote the other: science served as a political instrument for promoting sovereignty interests. And the two areas were separate in that it was a precondition that activity within the one issue area should not influence the content of the other: no matter how reseachers might organize themselves, or which research topics they chose to focus on, these decisions were not to have negative political consequences for the interests of sovereignty in the region. Even before IGY there was a gentleman's agreement in the form of a political guarantee that research was not to influence sovereignty issues. Next followed the Antarctic Treaty, which turned this consensual agreement into a legally binding obligation in terms of international law. Parallel with these developments, the parties also decided to initiate cooperation in non-controversial issue areas. In other words, every effort was made to keep the two areas separate. At the same time the governments in question established a structure of political cooperation which could be activated if research cooperation should prove to be developing in an unfortunate political direction.

2. *Political distrust (sovereignty and East/West politics) did not impede political cooperation (the Antarctic Treaty).*
   This is especially well illustrated by the fact that Chile, Argentina and Great Britain — all of whom have overlapping sovereignty claims — were able to work together during IGY, and afterwards supported the idea of formalizing such cooperation in treaty form. Similar conditions were found to apply for relations between claimant and non-claimant nations. The distrust between the Soviet Union and the 'old' Antarctic powers during and after IGY had superpower overtones. In this case, such distrust was itself to act as a factor promoting cooperation: the Soviet Union had to be controlled. Given the enormous size of the Antarctic continent, this could best be arranged through a 'lasting', formalized framework capable of bringing together all the actors. Political cooperation was, however, developed primarily as a superstructure to, and a result of, scientific cooperation. In order to participate in the Consultative Meetings, each of the parties was to 'demonstrate its interests in Antarctica by conducting substantial scientific research there' (Article IX). Thus, scientific activity is considered as providing political status and influence, which in turn will be utilized to promote cooperation on the solution of shared scientific problems. Science becomes both the object and the subject of political cooperation. The object of distrust is the issue of sovereignty, which is rendered passive during the

period of cooperation. In this way the parties have made any distrust inactive in their political cooperation.

3. *Cooperation began in non-controversial issue areas (knowledge-instrumental and practical problem areas) and was gradually expanded to include issues impinging on the foundation of political conflict and distrust (questions of sovereignty).*
This is reflected both in topics for cooperation and in research types. In 1960 the parties were working together on the registration of historical sites; by 1988, on the conditions for utilization of mineral resources. In 1960 research was knowledge-instrumental in content; by 1988 we note a considerable element of practical-instrumental research. In other words, long-term cooperation appears to increase and extend the limits of tolerance as to how sensitive issues may be and still be taken up by the parties. The actual area of conflict gradually diminishes and narrows over time. What happens in this process is that the range of shared activities is extended without the parties feeling that this threatens their basic national interests. Cooperation promotes mutual interests rather than threatening particular national ones. This in turn increases the trust between participants so that growth in trust leads to growth in cooperation. Or in the words of Edward Miles, 'When there are mutual or overlapping interests or when states in an indefinitely iterative relationship perceive that the rewards from cooperation will be great, they alter the strategies by which they pursue their interests. In this way cooperation is learned.'[30]

4. *External pressure (from the UN and from environmentalist organizations) helped to link the Antarctic states in their efforts to administer shared resources (Antarctic resources and science) that touched the very foundation of their internal conflict (the sovereignty issue).*
The Antarctic states have always closed ranks in the face of external pressure. In the 1960s and 1970s it was India who brought up the question of administrative arrangements in the Antarctic. Since then this issue has been taken up by the UN and various environmentalist organizations. The problem, however, has remained the same: can a small handful of nations administer an entire continent on behalf of the world society without ever having been granted the mandate to do so? The Antarctic states answer this in the affirmative and automatically impose upon themselves the obligation to carry out such administration in a result-oriented manner. Any regime which is challenged and cannot produce results soon loses legitimacy. Pressure from the outside thus contributes both to cooperation and to results. And this in turn benefits scientific and political cooperation alike.

The Arctic — 'a region of politics and conflicts?'

At regular intervals the question is asked whether experience gained from the Antarctic can be put to use in the Arctic so as to reduce the level of tension in this conflict-ridden region. Ever since IGY, the frequent reply has been that people conceive of the two polar regions ' . . . in terms of their similarities, and yet they are better understood on the basis of their contrasts'.[31]

In the present context there are two contrasts of particular interest. The one concerns the structure of interests, which is uni-dimensional in the Antarctic and multi-dimensional in the Arctic. The second concerns the form of research, which is mainly symbolic-instrumental in the Antarctic and practical-instrumental in the Arctic.

The interest structure

The structure of interests in the Arctic includes strategic, military, economic, jurisdictional, social and cultural issues. In military-strategic terms, the northern regions are among the most important in the world. Air space over the Arctic Ocean, which represents the shortest distance between the two superpowers, was singled out immediately after World War II as an attack route for strategic bombers and intercontinental ballistic missiles. Today the Arctic has a vital role in the space activities of the superpowers as well as in their efforts at controlling the oceans. Of the four fleets of the Soviet Union, the Northern Fleet, based on the Kola Peninsula, ranks second to none with regard to strategic retaliatory capability.[32] This fleet reflects the global involvement of the USSR and is a part of the superpower balance of terror. Strategic nuclear submarines with long-range nuclear warheads are now permanently operating in northern waters and under the ice of the Arctic Ocean.[33] This circumstance has led the USA in recent years to introduce military countermeasures against the Soviet Northern Fleet in the same waters. In this way, the Arctic has gradually changed from a distinct military flank to a front between the blocs.

In economic terms, the Arctic is a region of growing global importance. Today there is exploration for oil and gas along the entire Arctic periphery, including offshore areas. In 1987 oil production in Western Siberia comprised 66 per cent of total Soviet oil production; for gas the corresponding figure was 63 per cent.[34] The Prudhoe Bay oilfields in Alaska are estimated to contain approximately one-third of the known oil reserves of the USA.[35] In Northwest Russia and Siberia, considerable quantities of copper, gold, nickel, tin, phosphate, diamonds, iron, zinc and coal are mined.[36] The region is also rich in living resources. Each year almost 4 per cent of total world fish catches comes from the Barents Sea; 50 per cent of Norway's total catch and 12 per cent of the Soviet catch is fished here.[37] Fishing off the coast of Alaska comprises approximately 3.5 per cent of total world catch, and 70-80 per cent of the

US catch. Furthermore, economic interests also attach to mercantile shipping in the Northeast and Northwest Passages.

Figure 4.2 Arctic sector claims

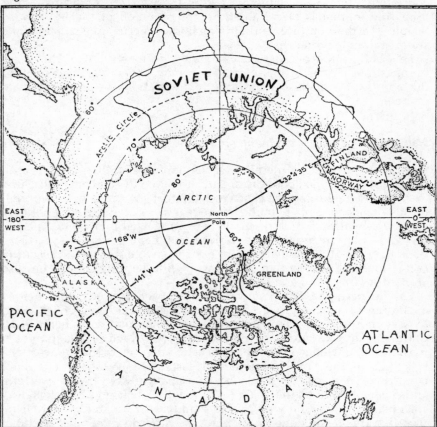

Utilization of these economic resources has accentuated the need to solve remaining legal issues concerning the oceans and seas. To date, an accepted boundary line has been drawn between Canada and Greenland. The rest of the region is still open to dispute, despite years of negotiations. The basic problem here is that Canada and the Soviet Union maintain the sector principle as the foundation for sovereignty over islands to the north of their respective Arctic coasts. Sector lines have been drawn between the North Pole and the outermost extremes of the coasts of the two nations, lines which especially the Soviet Union has maintained must be used when drawing up boundary limits at sea. However, the US, Denmark and Norway have contested the status of this sector principle in international law and do not accept the sector lines as having any relevance in determining continental shelf and economic zone boundaries between adjacent states. All recognize that if one of the parties concedes in the sector limit issue, this can later be claimed as a precedent for solving problems elsewhere in the region. In consequence, all negotiations have come to a deadlock, and the boundaries remain contested.[38] Increased economic and military pressure on this region from the South has also influenced the situation of the indigenous people and their culture, both of which are experiencing considerable strain and undergoing change.

This collocation of interests is among the most vital of the states in question. Some of these interests may indeed be decisive for the ability of a state to handle critical situations in an appropriate manner.

National interests, research and cooperation

The Cold War gave to the Northern region a geopolitical importance which has influenced both the organization and the content of research to a considerable degree. East-West distrust, coupled with the vital military and economic potential of the region, created a narrow political framework within which researchers were obliged to operate. The few non-Canadian scientists who carried out field studies in northern Canada in the 1950s and 1960s, for example, were subjected to security regulations in the execution of their work. Similar restrictions were also applied in Greenland and in Alaska.[39]

For its part, the Soviet government carried this even further by excluding foreign researchers from its northern territories. This applied to Eastern European scientists as well as Western ones. In this respect, the description provided by Professor Trevor Lloyd is illustrative: 'It must be acknowledged that there has been a definite barrier between the scientists of the Soviet Union, and associated countries and other countries. There has been no easy interchange between the 'western' group members and the rest . . . Although Polish and Czechoslovak scientists have worked with Soviet scientists in Antarctica there is no record of this being done in the north, whether in the Soviet Arctic or elsewhere. The Soviet Arctic has not yet been opened to western scientists, although a few individuals have made short visits there.'[40] The policy of exclusion applied not only to Soviet land but also to her sea territories. When on 5 August 1960 the Soviet Union expanded the limits of its territorial waters to 12 n.m. it was clearly stated that non-Soviet vessels were 'prohibited from carrying out hydrographic work and research in Soviet territorial and internal sea waters under penalty of detention by the border guard.'[41] In addition, Soviet authorities, long before the Third UN Convention on the Law of the Sea was signed in 1982, were demanding that foreign scientists wishing to work within the country's 200-mile zone apply for permission.[42]

Early on, Soviet authorities forbade their own scientists to participate in international organizations concerned with Arctic studies. They declined, for example, to participate in fora such as the Committee for

High Arctic Scientific Research, Liaison and Information Exchange, Comité Arctique and the Arctic Ocean Sciences Board.[43]

Therefore Arctic research was rapidly developing in a nationalistic and practical-instrumental direction. It was organized mainly under the auspices of national regimes, only rarely binationally and even more rarely multinationally. Prior to IGY, most US research was initiated and funded by the military authorities. After IGY the element of research for civil purposes increased.[44] At all times, military-strategic interests weighed heavily. The same most likely applied to the Soviet Union. To avoid stirring up Cold War political and military sensibilities, the smaller Arctic states decided to concentrate their research efforts to projects mainly on their own territory.[45] The superpowers also exhibited a certain restraint in involvement outside their own spheres. And in order to counteract the opponent's presumed attempts at subversion, research results were largely stamped secret. This was particularly true of the USSR. For a long time, therefore, any scientific cooperation across the East/West divide seemed unthinkable.

The exclusiveness of Arctic research is also clearly visible in what has been considered the region's success story in multilateral cooperation: the 1973 Convention on the Polar Bear signed by the US, Canada, Denmark, the USSR and Norway. The implementation of this accord confirms rather than refutes traditional Soviet attitudes. Among other things, the exchange of information among Western delegates has been extensive and true to the letter and spirit of the agreement. The Soviet contribution, on the other hand, has been so scanty as to inspire the following Western comment: 'Whether only little research has been carried out in the Soviet Union, or whether the data exchange is being hampered by governmental red tape it is difficult to tell.'[46] Nor have Soviet scientists taken part in joint field studies or invited Western scientists to participate in field work on Soviet territory — both of which activities are provided for in the agreement.

Furthermore, the convention has had no positive effects on Norwegian-Soviet cooperation on studying the stock of polar bears which both countries share in the northeastern part of the Barents Sea. Norway has long wished joint studies of the polar bear, both on Svalbard, Franz Josef Land and in the northern Barents Sea. Soviet negotiators have, on their part, insisted that the area of study be restricted to Svalbard and to the waters west of the Soviet sector line, i.e. solely to what is Norwegian territory. Norway has refused this on both scientific and political grounds.[47]

The only Arctic area where researchers have, throughout the entire post-war period, been able to enjoy some of the same freedom as in the Antarctic, is on Svalbard. Here it has been Norway's policy, in the spirit of the Svalbard Treaty, to offer researchers from countries of all political colourations unimpeded access and equal working conditions.[48]

Despite such problems, hope has remained that it might one day be possible to succeed in establishing Pan-Arctic research cooperation in the region. Politicians too expressed such ideas. As early as 1944, the US

Vice President, Henry A. Wallace, proposed that the US should lead the way in such work by establishing an 'Arctic Treaty' for *inter alia* scientific exploration and cooperation between the Arctic states. However, the Cold War was to prevent this proposal from materializing.

Nevertheless, developments in the Antarctic became a lasting source of inspiration for the desire for cooperation — for both Western and Soviet scientists alike. However, the key to success was to be found with the governments. In the shelter of 'thaw' periods in the Cold War, cooperative ideas won increased support in Western capitals, but it was not until quite recently that the Soviet government signalled its interest in breaking with its previous policy of isolationism.

In a speech held in Murmansk on 1 October 1987, General Secretary Mikhail Gorbachev presented the general outline of a new Arctic research policy. Here he stressed the importance of international cooperation and the need to exchange scientific experience gained in the Arctic. He further proposed that the adjacent states should meet for an international conference for purposes of coordinating future research and to discuss the establishment of a council for Arctic research. Here the break with the past is clear: secrecy is to be reduced through the exchange of information on Arctic experiences; the line of national self-reliance is to be supplemented by international cooperation and coordination; national organization is to be supplemented by an international research council. There are several indications that Mr Gorbachev is serious in his intentions here.

To the surprise of many observers, the Soviet Union endorsed the 1986 SCAR initiative on discussing the possibilities of future scientific cooperation in the North. The report presented on this occasion proposes the establishment of a non-governmental International Arctic Science Committee (IASC) to 'promote international cooperation in scientific research in arctic areas'. The report further proposes that 'Representatives of governments of Arctic nations should discuss the feasibility of establishing a system of regular, structured discussions and liaison on Arctic science matters. Such discussions, comprising what might be called an Intergovernmental Forum on Arctic Science Issues, would supplement but in no way interfere with the several bilateral science arrangements presently in existence between Arctic countries.'[49] In other words, scientific cooperation should be established, with a political superstructure. These proposals have been supported by the Soviet authorities, who additionally gave the all clear for an international conference on coordinating Arctic research which was held in Leningrad in December 1988. This conference was in fact proposed by Mr Gorbachev in his Murmansk speech.

The Kremlin would also seem to have modified its policy on not permitting Western researchers to work on Soviet territory. In the *Canada-USSR Arctic Science Exchange Programme* of 1984 and in the *Norwegian-Soviet Agreement on Technical-Scientific Cooperation on the Exploration of the Arctic and the Northern Regions* of 1988, the intention is that such cooperation is to be balanced in terms of content and geography, and that the parties are to participate in field studies on the territory of both parties.

These changes are of course particularly interesting because they come at a time when the Kremlin would in fact appear to have more to conceal from Western eyes than ever before, not least in connection with the rear-deployment strategy of Soviet strategic submarines (SSBNs).[50] In the 1988 agreement with Norway the USSR has, among other things, accepted that joint oceanographic studies be carried out in the waters between Franz Josef Land and Svalbard, and between Greenland and Svalbard. As early as in the 1960s these areas were designated by Soviet media as sea routes for submarines from the Soviet Northern Fleet *en route* from their Kola Peninsula bases to the Arctic Ocean, or vice versa.[51] When in addition it is borne in mind that 'Oceanography and its contribution to the knowledge of the environment are more important to undersea warfare than to any other warfare area',[52] it seems reasonable to interpret Soviet research cooperation with Norway as detrimental to Soviet security interests in the Far North.

However, this is a hasty conclusion, not least as concerns the waters between Franz Josef Land and Svalbard. Here depths are shallow, with appreciable numbers of deep-reaching icebergs and an uneven sea-bed marked by depressions lacking any outlet to deep sea waters. Under such natural conditions, submarines risk getting trapped between the ice and the sea floor with no means of escape — the so-called 'valley of death' problem. Only small attack submarines, like those used on an irregular basis by the Northern Fleet in the early 1960s, could use such a passage. The modern SSBNs of today measure up to 170 m in length and 28 m in height, and require totally different operating conditions.[53] Thus, oceanographic study in this area has in fact more the character of knowledge-instrumental than practical-instrumental research.

On the other hand, the Fram strait — between Svalbard and Greenland — remains one of the main sea lanes for Soviet SSBNs *en route* northwards to the Arctic Ocean and southwards to the Norwegian Sea. Oceanographic research cooperation across the East/West divide in this area can therefore be more risky, in military terms. However, there is also a military point in getting to know what the adversary knows and is thinking in areas where there are great strategic interests at stake. Seen in this perspective, cooperation becomes a means of obtaining access to the knowledge and insight of the adversary — if you can't beat him, join him. In this way practical-instrumental interests may, in special cases, provide a conditional foundation for international scientific cooperation. Or another explanation may be that the Kremlin is deliberately extending the range of its themes for scientific collaboration in order to achieve political credibility for its new *rapprochement* policies towards the rest of the world. Thus cooperation is considered acceptable since the political advantages are seen as outweighing the military disadvantages.

No matter what the explanation, we may safely say that the Kremlin has here taken a step in the direction of expanding its framework for scientific collaboration with Western countries. This shows that political will and changes in political circumstances can in themselves provide the preconditions for international scientific cooperation, even in areas previously considered suitable solely for practical-instrumental research under national control.

The cooperation potential in the Arctic can also be influenced by the research activities carried out in recent years by such countries as West Germany, Great Britain, Japan and Sweden. These nations possess no territory in the region, so it is reasonable to assume that their research efforts will primarily serve symbolic-instrumental goals: to 'show the flag' through the presence of scientists. This is not to underestimate the motivating power of knowledge-instrumental utility on the part of these countries, but rather to underline that symbolic-instrumental research can both provide knowledge and further political interests at the one and same time. In the long run, such extra-territorial states can gain lasting influence over developments in the Arctic only through the establishment of a formalized system of cooperation similar to that already existing for Antarctica. And indeed, Sweden has been an active supporter of efforts to establish an IASC.

Changes in Soviet policy together with the symbolic-instrumental research of the extra-territorial states can work together to give added impetus to cooperative efforts. This is not to say that there are no stumbling blocks ahead. A whole host of problems may easily reverse the present process. To highlight the challenges, something might be learned from the Antarctic experience with regard to the general relationship between national interests and the content of research.

Arctic reality in light of Antarctic experiences

Four factors were identified to explain at least part of the cooperative success achieved in the Antarctic:

1. *Conflict in one issue area did not preclude cooperation in another.*
   In the Arctic, the norm has rather been the reverse: conflict in one issue-area (politics) has led to non-cooperation in the other field (science). There are several reasons for this.
   In the Arctic, research has been largely practical-instrumental, whereas in the Antarctic it has been symbolic-instrumental. Thus, science has mainly served one goal in the North, to solve practical problems for immediate application, whereas it has served two goals in Antarctica — political as well as knowledge-instrumental. This difference has made it possible in Antarctica to isolate the two fields from each other, so that scientific cooperation would not have negative consequences for political interests. In the Arctic, research served only the one goal, that of politics, so research and politics were but two sides of the same coin. Thereby, political conflict became scientific conflict as well. This tendency was further intensified

through the differences in interest structure and conflict type between the two polar regions.

In the Arctic, the conflict has remained hegemonic, i.e. it has taken place between two competing political systems, ideologically and materially; and it has developed cumulatively through conflict in one issue area, automatically leading into the other. With a multi-dimensional interest structure like that in the Arctic, the result will thus often be a deadlocked conflict pattern. By contrast, in the Antarctic, conflict has been issue-specific, restricted to one field only, and the structure of interests has for extended periods been uni-dimensional.

In times of crisis, hegemonial conflicts appear to demand unambiguous national answers to what is interpreted as challenges from the adversary. No segment of society can free itself totally from conflicts of this type. Everything is included — state, sectors, individuals. The requirement of loyalty is close to absolute. Scientists and researchers have to follow political instructions, which in turn means that the governments take over controlling and coordinating national efforts — more so in totalitarian than in democratic states. This has, to some noticeable degree, long been the situation for the Arctic, and it most likely will continue to affect the development of cooperative efforts between East and West.

2. *Political distrust did not impede political cooperation.*
Here too the picture in the Arctic is the reverse of the Antarctic situation: political distrust has blocked cooperation, both political and scientific, throughout most of the post-war period. The reason is to be found in different types of conflict and research in the two regions. However, we are currently witnessing internal changes both within the USSR and in relations between Arctic states — changes that may pave the way for cooperation. This indicates that political will and changes in political circumstances are equally important for the establishment of international cooperation, as is choice of research form. It follows as a result of what has been said above that although the research form will always place limits on what is suitable for cooperation, politicians can adjust these limits in a more liberal or a more restrictive direction. What is now taking place is a more liberal adjustment — as indeed indicated by Mr Gorbachev in his Murmansk speech where he proposed practical-instrumental cooperation between the USSR, Canada and Norway with regard to the extraction of oil and gas on the Soviet shelf.

3. *Cooperation began in non-controversial issue-areas and was gradually expanded to include issues impinging on the foundations of political conflict.*
The first part of this statement holds true for the situation in the North and is supported by experience in the Antarctic. Scientific cooperation is to promote, not harm, national interests. This acknowledgement is fundamental to current efforts at establishing an IASC. The SCAR group report states, *inter alia* 'the new

developments should support national policies of Arctic nations
with regard to Arctic science, and at the same time should help to
increase international cooperation and communication, and
facilitate growth and exchange of scientific knowledge on a non-
national basis.'[54] This means that the parties will have to find
research topics that can meet both these requirements. In his
Murmansk speech, Mr Gorbachev identified indigenous culture as
one research topic suitable for cooperative efforts. In the agreement
between Canada and the USSR, the parties have decided upon five
main areas for cooperation: geosciences and Arctic petroleum,
northern environment, northern construction, ethnography and
education.

The Norway/USSR agreement defines biology, geology, geophysics
and oceanography as fields for cooperation. With the exception of
oceanography, these are all 'safe' topics. Also, US scientists have
found that it is possible to collaborate with Soviet colleagues on such
non-controversial topics as anthropology, archaeology, health,
environmental protection, geophysics, permafrost and wildlife.[55] All
of these are subject areas suitable for a cautious development of pan-
Arctic cooperation in the years to come.

4. *External pressure helped to link the states in their efforts to
administer shared resources that touched on the very foundation of
their internal conflict.*

It is difficult to evaluate the relevance of this observation in relation
to Arctic politics because it is unclear just which states are to be
seen as subject to pressure and which as exerting the pressure. In
the Antarctic the constellation was clear enough: the treaty parties
versus the rest of the world. In the Arctic, however, we have at least
three categories of states: the rim states, the Polar Circle states and
extra-territorial states. Today, representatives of all three groups are
involved in research in the region. This heterogeneous group appears
at present to include most — if not all — of the states which
have shown an interest in the region. In other words, no external
group has crystallized to exert pressure on developments. The
only pressure being exerted today comes from members of the group
itself.

Polar politics and science: close twins or opposite poles?

Both in the Arctic and in the Antarctic, science and politics are close, if
not identical, twins. This means that science is utilized for and is
governed by political interests. In both regions science is utilized as a
political means: in the Arctic it serves military-economic interests
through practical-instrumental research, while in the Antarctic it serves
political interests through symbolic-instrumental research. It is the
character of the national interests in question that determines the
content of the research.

There is, however, a difference between the two regions. In the Arctic, science by and large serves solely as a political means; in the Antarctic scientific cooperation seems to have assumed the additional status of a political objective on its own merits. This dualism works because the two purposes are served by different parts of scientific activity. The means-need is taken care of in the traditional manner by the presence of scientists on Antarctic soil, whilst the preservation of cooperation is the political objective. This is an illustration of how first-order effects of scientific cooperation, as discussed by Edward Miles, have produced second order effects in terms of science policy.[56]

Political and scientific cooperation alike are most easily promoted through knowledge-instrumental research, whether in its pure form or in the symbolic-instrumental version. However, it is important to stress that political factors, both in cooperation with and independent of knowledge-instrumental research, have contributed to the establishment of cooperation in the Antarctic.

In the Arctic we may observe indications that political decisions can expand the space available for limited cooperation also in fields formerly subject to practical-instrumental research under national control. This in turn indicates a division of functions between politics and science in defining the framework of international cooperation in the polar regions: the form of science shows which frameworks exist under stable political conditions, whereas politics adjusts and determines these frameworks in relation to changing political priorities and conditions. In the Antarctic, the political reins of cooperation are being tightened somewhat at present; in the Arctic they are being loosened slightly to improve the conditions for establishing cooperation.

Six different motives for polar research have been distinguished: basic research, political, economic, military, administrative and environmental motives. In this connection, it is stressed that there is no such thing as 'research spurred on by solely one motive. In practice, various motives will always interact — and counteract — each other.'[57] This is an important observation. It tells us more about the conditions for cooperation and the problems in the polar regions than do uni-dimensional explanations that single out research as the one and only catalyst for establishing and developing international political and scientific cooperation.

Notes

1. Beck, Peter J., 1986, *The International Politics of Antarctica*, Croom Helm, London and Sydney, p.48.

2. Odishaw, Hugh, 'International Cooperation', in *International Science and Technology*, unnumbered and undated, in the archives of the Fridtjof Nansen Institute, p.28.

3. Concepts I and II are developed in a very thorough and interesting study by Bohlin, Ingemar, 1988, *Modern Polarforskning*, Första årsrapport in FRN-prosjektet, 'Ett vetenskapsteoretiskt perspektiv på polarforskning', Institutionen før vetenskapsteori, Gothenburg University, p.19.

4. Statement by the Prime Minister of Malaysia, Records of the 37th UNGA, 29 September 1982, UN Document no. A/37/PV.10 (1982), pp.17-18.

5. UN Document no. A/9/132-S/15675, 1983.

6. Rowley, G.W., 1966, 'International Scientific Relations in the Arctic' in R.St. MacDonald (ed.), *The Arctic Frontier*, University of Toronto Press, Toronto, p.286.

7. Smith, Phillip M., 1969, 'Prospects for International Cooperation on the Moon: The Antarctic Analogy' in *Bulletin of the Atomic Scientists*, vol. XXV, bn. 7, p. 36. See also Johnson, Rodney W., and Smith, Philip M., 1969, 'Antarctic Research and Lunar Exploration' in *Advances in Space Science and Technology*, vol. 10, Academic Press Inc., New York.

8. Beck, Peter J., 1986.

9. Gjelsvik, Tore, 1983, 'Scientific Research and Cooperation in Antarctica' in Rudiger Wolfrum (ed.), *Antarctic Challenge: Conflicting Interests, Cooperation, Environmental Protection, Economic Development*, Duncker & Humbolt, Berlin, p.41.

10. Beck, Peter J., 1986.

11. Bohlin, Ingemar, 1988, p. 3.

12. Gjelsvik, Tore, 1985, 'Science and Politics in Polar Areas', mimeographed article, pp.3-4, archives of the Fridtjof Nansen Institute.

13. Heap, John A., 1987, 'The Role of Scientific Advice for the Decision-Making Process in the Antarctic Treaty System' in Rudiger Wolfrum, (ed.), *Antarctic Challenges III: Conflicting Interests, Cooperation, Environmental Protection, Economic Development*, Duncker & Humbolt, Berlin, pp.21-8.

14. Beck, Peter J., 1986.

15. Gjelsvik, Tore, 1983, p.41.

16. Crary, Albert, 1982, 'International Geophysical Year: Its Evolution and US Participation', in *Antarctic Journal*, vol. XVII, no. 4, pp. 1-4.

17. Goldie, L.F., 1958, 'International Relations in Antarctica', *Australian Quarterly*, vol. 30, p. 26.

18. Auburn, F.M, 1982, *Antarctic Law and Politics*, C. Hurst & Co. Publishers, London, p. 89.

19. Beck, Peter J., 1986, p. 51.

20. Laws, R.M., 1987, 'Cooperation or Confrontation?' in D. W. H. Walton, (ed.), *Antarctic Science*, Cambridge University Press, Cambridge, p. 250.

21. Auburn, F.M., 1982, p. 93.

22. 'Science politicians' are also dealt with in Timberlake, Lloyd, 1989, 'The Role of Scientific Knowledge in Drawing up the Brundtland Report', and Fløistad, Brit, 1989, 'Scientific Knowledge in the Management of Fish and Whale; Global or Regional Organizations, Single and Multi-species Approach', both articles in this volume.

23. Gjelsvik, Tore, 1985, p. 5.

24. Heap, John A, 1983, 'Cooperation in Antarctica: A Quarter of a Century's Experience' in Francisco Orrego Vicuna (ed.), 1983, *Antarctic Resources Policy: Scientific, Legal and Political Issues*, Cambridge University Press, Cambridge, p.107.

25. Bohlin, Ingemar, 1988, p. 5.

26. Quigg, Philip W., 1983, *A Pole Apart: The Emerging Issue of Antarctica*, McGraw-Hill, New York, p. 200.

27. Laws, R.M., 1987, p. 261.

28. Heap, John A., 1987

29. Dewry, David J., 1988, 'The Challenge of Antarctic Science' in *Oceanus*, vol. 31, no. 2, p. 5.

30. Miles, Edward L., 1989, 'Scientific and Technological Knowledge and International Cooperation in Resource Management', in this volume.

31. Gould, Laurence M., 1957, 'Antarctic Prospects' in *The Geographical Review*, vol. XLVII, no. 1, p. 1.

32. Ries, Thomas, 1987, *The Soviet Military Operational Command Structure and its Application to Fenno-Scandia*, Report NUPI, Oslo, 20 August, pp. 61-2.

33. Østreng, Willy, 1987, *The Soviet Union in Arctic Waters: Security Implications for the Northern Flank of NATO*, Occasional paper no. 36, The Law of the Sea Institute, University of Hawaii, Honolulu, p. 39.

34. Sagers, Matthew J., 1988, 'New Notes' in *Soviet Geography, April*, pp. 423-57.

35. Østreng, Willy, 1983, 'Det varme Arktis' in Håkon Børde (ed.), *Svalbard og havområdene*, Gyldendal Norsk Forlag, Oslo, 1983, p. 179.

36. See also Østreng, Willy, 1978, *Polhavet i internasjonal politikk*, publication AA:H012 in the study series of the Fridtjof Nansen Institute, Chapter 5, pp. 178-209.

37. Østreng, Willy, 1984, 'Soviet-Norwegian Relations in the Arctic' in *International Journal*, vol. XXXIX, no. 4, Autumn, p. 868.

38. Østreng, Willy, 1986, 'Delimitation Arrangements in Arctic Seas: Cases of Precedence or Securing of Strategic/Economic Interests?' in *Marine Policy*, vol. 10, no. 2, April, pp. 132-55.

39. Lloyd, Trevor, 1969, 'International Cooperation in Arctic Science and Disarmament', mimeographed article in the library of The Canadian Institute of International Affairs, Toronto.

40. Lloyd, Trevor, 1969.

41. Butler, William E., 1971, *The Soviet Union and the Law of the Sea*, Johns Hopkins Press, Baltimore, p. 83.

42. Gjelsvik, Tore, 1985, pp. 6-7.

43. Gjelsvik, Tore, 1985, pp. 7-10.

44. Jones, T.O., 1973, 'Coordinating Federal Arctic Research' in *Arctic Bulletin*, vol. 1, no. 1.

45. Østreng, Willy, 1973, *De skandinaviske land i Arktis: Forutsetninger og muligheter for samarbeid*, Study AA:H007 in the publication series of the Fridtjof Nansen Institute.

46. Gjelsvik, Tore, 1985, p. 7.

47. Gjelsvik, Tore, 1987, p. 7.

48. Østreng, Willy, 1978, *Politics in High Latitudes: The Svalbard Archipelago*, C. Hurst, London.

49. Roots, E.F., Rogne, O. and Taagholt, J., *International Communication and Coordination in Arctic Science: A Proposal for Action*, Oslo, 17 November 1987, p. 2.

50. Østreng, Willy, 1988/89, 'The Barents Sea in Soviet Rear-Deployment Strategy', forthcoming article in *Naval Forces. International Forum for Maritime Power*.

51. Østreng, Willy, 1978, chapter 3, pp. 70-121.

52. Bishop, Charles, 1959, 'Oceanography in Naval Warfare' in *US Naval Institute Proceedings*, vol. 85, no. 5, p. 82.

53. Bergesen, Helge Ole, Moe, Arild and Østreng, Willy, 1987, *Soviet Oil and Security Interests in the Barents Sea*, Frances Pinter, London, chapter 3, pp. 79-83.

54. Roots, E.F., Rogne, O. and Taaghold, J, 1987, p. 15.

55. Washburn, A.L. and Weller, Gunther, 'Arctic Research in the National Interest' in *Science*, 8 August 1986, vol. 233, p. 637.

56. Miles, Edward L., 1989, in this volume.

57. Bohlin, Ingemar, 1988, p. 8.

SECTION 2:
Science, Environment and Development

5

The role of scientific knowledge in drawing up the Brundtland Report

Lloyd Timberlake

'The most important questions that Man must answer are questions on which Science has nothing to say', according to the historian Arnold Toynbee.

This perhaps sums up the view of science which guided the World Commission on Environment and Development during the three years over which it worked on its report, *Our Common Future*. The Commission had been asked by the UN General Assembly not to report back on the physical realities of the present natural world, but to seek paths toward a better, more secure, more equitable human world. Thus the Commission was most concerned with values — what resources, what livelihoods, had value and how these could be preserved and enhanced. And as the psychologist R.D. Laing said about science: 'All natural science can say about values is that they do not come within its domain of investigative competence'.

Commissioner William Ruckelshaus of the United States, twice head of the US Environmental Protection Agency (EPA), summed up many of the Commissioners' scepticism of science — and brought a laugh at the same time — when he said during a Commission debate: 'I don't want to give too much credence to the scientists. When I was head of EPA, I would have a bunch of them in my office in the morning telling me that some substance was so good for me I ought to put it on my breakfast cereal. Then I'd have another bunch through in the afternoon telling me that the same stuff was so dangerous I should not be in the same country with it'.

But Ruckelshaus said this while he was actually calling for more scientific data to back up a specific area of the report. He felt that the Commission should not call for certain expensive activities unless science had documented that a serious problem existed.

Thus science and scientists were not the driving force and the initiator in the Commission's conclusions. They acted more as a referee. Some Commissioners referred to science when they wanted to call for action, others when they were making the case that such calls were at worst ill founded, at best premature.

Science got into the Commission from several sources, virtually the same sources which bring science into the deliberations of parliaments and cabinets. In the Commission's public hearings on five continents, scientists were among those who testified. I found it interesting, however, that when toward the end of its work the Commissioners referred back to what was said at various hearings, they almost inevitably spoke of the testimony of common people: youth, farmers, rubber tappers. The testimony of these people was almost always more dramatic, memorable and easier to comprehend than the testimony of the technocrats.

The Commission Secretariat commissioned countless reports from scientists on special issues. Many of the people listed in the twenty pages of acknowledgements in the back of the report are scientists; many scientists served on the advisory panels on energy, industry and food security.

And of course, some of the Commissioners themselves were distinguished scientists and academicians, including Saleh Abdulrahman Al-Athel of Saudi Arabia, president of the King Abdulaziz City for Science and Technology; Istvan Lang of Hungary, secretary general of the Hungarian Academy of Sciences; Man Shijun of China, director of the Research Centre of Ecology, Academica Sinica; and Vladimir Sokolov of the USSR, director of the Institute of Evolutionary Animal Morphology and Ecology, Academy of Sciences. Each of these, and many of the other Commissioners, also had scientific advisers working with them personally, or were submitting draft chapters to advisers back home, or both.

All of this raises the question of the *type* of scientists upon which the Commission relied. By and large these were not the primary researchers doing pure science in the field but the *policy researchers* who take pure research and try to turn it into policies which governments and organizations can follow.[1] The International Institute for Environment and Development (IIED) does this work in such fields as energy, agriculture, Third World urban development and marine resources; it advised the Commission in these fields. The World Resources Institute in Washington played a similar role.

Perhaps the hottest scientific debate in the Commission arose over the chapter on species and ecosystems, specifically on the rates of extinction of species. This is a very young field of research, and the Commission in seeking a safe consensus finally turned to the International Union for the Conservation of Nature and Natural Resources (IUCN), which has access to the work of myriad primary field researchers. IUCN offered the latest and soundest statistics and commented on the Commission's recommendations.

The most emotional general debate occurred on the issue of nuclear energy. Yet this debate, on a highly scientific subject, was strangely 'unscientific'. By this I mean it was all about values and questions of how this form of energy affected societies and what sort of society the Commissioners wanted to live in. Thus the key concluding sentence, which took months of debate, is nothing more than a Commission opinion: 'The generation of nuclear power is only justifiable if there are solid solutions to the presently unsolved problems to which it gives rise'. And the following sentence is the sort of compromise one always gets in reports where science and values jostle uneasily: a call for further research. Gordon Goodman of the Beijer Institute advised the Commission on the scientific and data parameters of the energy chapter, but his work was in the nature of making sure that the recommendations were consistent with energy realities. Again, he acted as a referee, but his advice lacked the final decision-making power of a football referee.

One of the Commission's key conclusions was that rapid economic growth is required to reduce mass poverty and narrow the gap between the developing and the industrialized nations, and that this growth is achievable by means which will not degrade the environment. Both clauses of this conclusion have been very controversial. But the point here is that the Commission in this conclusion was not being led by science, but was instead setting a task — or even an agenda —[2]for science. Most present forms of economic development do degrade the environment. Science is being asked to develop forms of agriculture, industry and energy production which are both economically and environmentally sound.

The Commission was healthily aware of the fact that science — or more specifically the ways in which science is interpreted by decision-makers — can be as much a part of the problem as of the solutions. Much of the Commission's report is concerned with very controversial scientific issues such as global warming, ozone depletion, species loss, and ecosystem degradation. Scientists cannot answer the hard questions about the future course of these syndromes because the only experiment being carried out in these fields is in changing this planet. We lack other planets upon which to alter the variables in different ways. We have no way to find out whether the burning of large amounts of fossil fuels will alter the climate other than to wait and see.

And given the plethora of Ph.D.s churned out annually in the industrialized North, scientists can always be found who will testify to decision-makers on behalf of optimism and inaction. Scientists, because a large part of their livelihood involves doing research, tend to testify that more research is required before there is a basis for action. Successful politicians, because they got where they were by successfully manipulating the system — whatever system might operate — tend to want to put off making major changes in that system. Those leaders who do not want to rock their various boats join the scientists in demanding more data.

The thinking of many of the Commissioners along these lines was guided by a seminal paper commissioned by the WCED secretariat from Dr Brian Wynne, University of Lancaster, UK, entitled 'Characterising Uncertainties in Energy Policy Analysis'.[3] Wynne pointed out that most people have the naive view that science focuses on uncertainty and tries to clear it up. In fact, science artificially excludes uncertainty by erecting basic structures which all assume are correct. If the uncertainties crowd too violently in upon this basic structure, it changes. For instance, models of such phenomena as global warming admit uncertainty but systematically exclude that uncertainty. Policy-makers trying to base policy on these models may not understand this.

A more basic problem, even less well understood, is that while scientific research may decrease *ignorance*, it may increase uncertainty. We were much more certain about the structure of matter last century when we saw ball-like atoms as the smallest units, than we are today with our hazy notions of quarks. The study of atomic structure has actually led physics to proclaim an 'uncertainty principle'. And it was much easier to develop policy upon the use of chlorofluorocarbons — before we became aware of their poorly understood effects upon the ozone layer.

Wynne maintained that uncertainty 'has rapidly shifted from the margins of policy and decision making to the core', and 'attempts to reduce it by throwing science into the gap under urgent timetables frequently only generates worse uncertainties'. But these uncertainties are not so much the result of experts disagreeing as the result of uncertainties within institutions and conflict among them. Wynne notes that in many cases uncertainties thus become 'concrete resources' for institutions wishing to manipulate decisions one way or another.

Commission Chairman Gro Harlem Brundtland's own frustration with policy-makers' response to such syndromes can be seen in her foreword to the report: 'The present decade has been marked by a retreat from social concerns. Scientists bring to our attention urgent but complex problems bearing on our very survival . . . We respond by demanding more details, and by assigning the problems to institutions ill-equipped to cope with them.'

Though science is theoretically value-free, scientists are not.[4] Scientists speaking for the West German government early in this decade emphasized the lack of proven connections between acid rain and forest death. Then surveys revealed mass German forest loss. Then German government policy changed. But the scientific data on the connections between acid pollution and tree death had *not* changed. Scientists in the pay of the British government have also emphasized the lack of 'proof' in this issue, right up to the present. But as data comes in about damage to British crops and forests and monuments, there are signs of a British policy change. Yet we still do not know precisely how acid emissions kill trees, any more than we know precisely how cigarette smoke causes lung cancer.

Another difficulty in communicating with scientists, besides being aware of their hidden biases, is that scientists do not communicate well with non-scientists. Those producing scientific PhDs are not merely encouraged but required to write in a style which the general population finds extremely difficult to interpret. An analysis of the historical reasons for this odd state of affairs would make an excellent PhD thesis. But historical reasons aside, it is clear that today scientists advance in their chosen fields by communicating only with other scientists. (Bertolt Brecht wrote: 'Science knows but one commandment: contribute to science'.) Those who attempt to talk to the general public, that is to 'popularize' their findings, are viewed with grave suspicion by their peers. Thus scientists will continue to be interpreted for the general public by two different craftsmen perhaps not best suited for the purpose: journalists, whose basic job is to sell newspapers; and political leaders, whose basic job is to convince the voters that they are being well looked after.

The Commission also dared to grapple with one of science's more self-serving areas. It notes in *Our Common Future* that half a million of the world's scientists are working on weapons research, and that this work accounts for about half of the world's research and development expenditure. Thus it does not take a cynic to predict that a great many scientists are going to resist bitterly the Commission's call for a new definition of 'security' not based on 'the arms' culture'.

Thus the relationship between scientific data and the Commission's conclusions were confused and messy, as are most relationships in human activities. But then science has always had a peculiar relationship with the environmental movement. Little of the real pioneer work was done by scientists. Rachel Carson, whose book *Silent Spring* is often hailed as the beginning of the modern environmental movement, is a journalist, and her descriptions of bird species' extinctions due to pesticides are now seen to have been exaggerated. The truth she offered was not a scientific truth. Barbara Ward, author of such seminal books as *Only. One Earth*, was an economist. But she offered a vision that inspired many politicians and decision-makers. Canadian earth scientist J. Tuzo Wilson wrote in describing the revolution in thinking which led to the theory of plate tectonics: 'For the most part it was not experts but rebels, outsiders and interlopers from other fields of science who suggested the need for a revolution and produced the evidence supporting it'. Such has been true in the environment field, and has been true of most 'scientific' revolutions. 'Experts' tend to have too much invested in the status quo to make revolutionary break-throughs.

But straight science may have a more significant and straightforward role in the follow-up to the Commission's work, for some very depressing reasons. The Brundtland Report was launched in April 1987. Since then, scientists have learned, and announced, that the periodic hole in the stratospheric ozone layer over the Antarctic is bigger than previously thought; further, there has been a dramatic thinning over the Northern hemisphere, which will doubtless increase the number of skin cancer cases in that region of the globe. The data on global warming have also become better documented and substantiated since the Report was published. And the documentation of extinction rates continues to improve. The International Council of Scientific Unions (ICSU) expects to coordinate an 'International Geosphere-Biosphere Programme' in the near future, which should also add data on the disruption of various natural global systems.

In short, fears which were vague when the Commission was drafting its report are now becoming more firmly based in scientific fact. All those concerned with keeping the momentum of the Report alive will have to keep abreast of these rapid scientific advances and bring them to the attention of the public, the media and policy-makers by all means available. This process will be aided by the fact that many of the non-governmental organisations (NGOs) involved in the follow-up are scientific in nature — bodies such as IIED, WRI, IUCN, etc.

But the trick is to get this data out of the hands of scientists and into the public domain. The great problem with much of the Brundtland agenda — improved aid, increased international cooperation, increased international equity, making all governmental agencies environmentally responsible — is that it lacks a political constituency. Candidates for public office in the North rarely mention these issues in their campaign speeches. But serious threats of increased skin cancers, disrupted northern agriculture, and the flooding of major national seaports such as New York, London and Oslo can become political issues. UNEP has been arranging briefings for law-makers on climate change, and is finding a growing demand for such presentations.

The physicist Werner Heisenberg wrote that 'natural science does not simply describe and explain nature, it is part of the interplay between nature and ourselves'. Being a scientist, he probably meant that as a compliment to natural science. But science in general has a lot to answer for in this 'interplay'. It has invented the weapons that can destroy nature as we know it; it has produced the chemicals which pollute our water systems and our atmosphere. It is, in the democracies, up to the electorate and those they elect to harness and direct science to make that interplay between nature and ourselves more supportive of both nature and ourselves. If we can make this venture fashionable enough, even the scientists might join in.

Conclusion

Science was not the driving force in the making of the Brundtland Report. Although some premisses were delivered by scientists, generally they were not attributed much weight. Nor were the main conclusions scientifically founded. The claim that we can have economic growth without damaging the environment is a sheer statement of opinion. The report is a *political* document, not a *scientific* one. In the hearings that were carried out in connection with the making of the report, testimonials made by 'ordinary' people were given much weight by the Commission. Generally, it appears that public opinion and fears are stronger driving forces for politicians than scientific reports.

One reason for the rather peripheral role played by scientists in this connection has been their lacking of ability and/or will to convey their results in an understandable manner. There is a need for *policy researchers* whose task it should be to formulate the results in such a way that they can be used in the political decision-making process. Scientists may be in a better position to play a more important role in following up the Report.

Notes

1. The concept 'policy researchers' as used here is similar to the concept 'science politicians' used by Østreng, Willy, 1989, 'Polar Science and Politics: Close Twins or Opposite Poles in International Cooperation', and Fløistad, Brit, 1989, 'Scientific Knowledge in the Management of Fish and Whale: Global or Regional Organizations, Single and Multi-species Approach', both articles in this volume.

2. See Young, Oran, 1989, 'Science and Social Institutions: Lessons for International Resource Regimes', in this volume.

3. Wynne, Brian, 1985, 'Characterising Uncertainties in Energy Policy Analysis', paper commissioned by World Commission on Environment and Development, Geneva.

4. See Young, Oran, 1989, and Andresen, Steinar, 1989, 'Increased Public Attention: Communication and Polarization', both in this volume.

6

The credibility of science in international resource management

Helge Ole Bergesen

The role of science in policy-making both nationally and internationally has become confused by two general tendencies running counter to each other: the simultaneous over and underestimation of science.

The former arises from the sometimes rather naive belief in modern industrialized society that the human brain through scientific methods can find solutions to most of our problems, whether technical, medical or social. In short, whenever there is a problem, there must be a scientific answer to it; if only we commit enough resources, our bright scientists will find the answer. They will identify the causes of the problem and point to the remedies. On this basis appropriate political action can be taken and the problem is solved.

   On the other hand we have the tendency to underestimate the role of science, which is often the result of initial overestimation: as any scientist knows, devoting resources to a scientific problem does not necessarily lead to a clear answer. At best the scientists involved will come up with a lot of new questions, at worst with contradictory answers. This creates opportunities for shrewd politicians who have discovered how science can be twisted and used in different ways and for different purposes — so why not use it for one's own? This way of thinking easily leads to an 'unholy alliance' between politicians wanting to postpone difficult decisions, and scientists — or rather administrators of scientific institutions — preoccupied with fund-raising for their institutes. [1]

   It is my contention that this unholy alliance is the rule not the exception in the relationship between public policy-making and research institutions working on issues of political importance to governments. As I will demonstrate below, the agenda opened up by the World Commission on Environment and Development (the Brundtland Commission) has created excellent opportunities for new alliances of this kind.

The purpose of this article is to provide some thoughts on how such unholy alliances can be broken up — in other words how to prevent science from becoming a tool in the hands of governments or other political actors. This discussion will be applied to the issue area of energy and environment, as defined in the report of the Brundtland Commission.

If we want to prevent such a development, the first thing to do is to define the proper role for science in international resource management. There are no doubt some problems which can be fruitfully studied by scientists, but others which cannot. Let us start with the latter: science can never tell us whether we should base our future on nuclear energy or not. Science cannot tell us whether man has the right to extinguish certain natural species. Science cannot tell us how large a risk we, that is humanity, should run with regard to the global environmental problems, such as global warming and depletion of the ozone layer.

The right questions

In order for scientific knowledge to play a constructive role in resource management, we must formulate the right questions to which scientific answers can be found, and then allocate the resources necessary for such inquiries.

First of all we have the apparently simple 'What' questions: What is happening to endangered species? What is the state of desertification in the Third World? How rapidly is deforestation taking place?

Secondly we have the more difficult 'Why' questions: Which are the causes of the death of the forests in Europe and the degradation of the natural environment in our rivers and the oceans?

And thirdly we have the equally difficult 'How' questions: Which are the best remedies to various environmental problems? Which are most cost effective?

Defining the questions for research and assigning priority among them is a very difficult and controversial process in which politicians, bureaucracies and interest groups will actively participate. It is the prerogative of governments and parliaments to make such decisions including the allocation of funds, but scientists should give them advice as to the priority of research and in addition point to the questions which cannot be answered through scientific inquiry. Politicians and bureaucrats will certainly be aware that scientists and their institutions will have a natural tendency to point to their own field of work as the most important. There is nothing wrong with scientists asking for more funds for their own discipline but they should not in bargaining with the political system compromise on their most precious assets, their independence and their professional norms.

This is where in my opinion the key to the proper role of science lies, that is in the best traditions of academic life. Ideally, scientific independence means that the research process should proceed according to prescribed methods in search for the truth regardless of political or social priorities. However, as is all too well known, this attitude often leads scientists into the pleasant, quiet and often irrelevant world of the ivory tower. So independence in attitude and funding must be combined with concern, which implies that scientists have an obligation to their community. On the other hand, they should not become ordinary participants in the political game if they want to maintain a role as scientists. In other words, social concern must be tempered by the professional norms of science.

In dealing with international problems, independence must be coupled with transnationality if science is to acquire credibility in the world community. All too often we have seen in the area of resource management that scientific results produced by institutions in one particular country involved in the political process are not recognized as valid by other countries. So transnationality, in the sense that the scientific process is carried out in close professional cooperation among scientists across political and cultural cleavages, is a prerequisite for international credibility.

Energy and development

I shall now apply these general views on the role of science to the issue area of energy and development as described by the Brundtland Commission. As pointed out by Timberlake[2] in his contribution to this volume, we have numerous unanswered, critical questions in this area: which are the climatic effects of different kinds of energy used, in particular the burning of fossil fuels? What is the impact of variations in temperature and climate on different regions of the world? And which are the most efficient remedies to the global environmental problems connected with energy use?

The problems described above concerning the role of science are particularly acute in this context: the issue area is marked by a high degree of politicization, strong interest groups — such as the oil and nuclear industry — and considerable uncertainty as to the nature of the problems and the causal relationship between different factors. In other words, the odds are strongly against a constructive and independent role for science in this area. Nevertheless, if these problems are to be solved, before it is too late, it is essential that independent scientists play a prominent role as watchdogs for the global environment. This should be done primarily by monitoring and reporting on the development of critical variables relevant to this issue area ranging from climatic change to development issues.

In more concrete terms, the reporting could encompass indicators of climatic change, desertification, deforestation, energy efficiency and hydrocarbon use in different countries and regions, the use of non-renewable energy, in addition to key development indicators related to basic needs, such as infant mortality and malnutrition. Factual development on such variables should be reported openly and objectively by independent transnational research teams, preferably related to scientific NGOs. In this way science could serve as the alarm bell for the global environment. What I have in mind is a kind of 'ecology amnesty' revealing the facts to the world in order to increase the pressure on governments and intergovernmental organizations.[3]

Sustainable development — conceptual consensus?

In theory, this idea looks fairly simple — in reality it would be much more complex and encounter severe political difficulties. The first question to be raised is: what is the basis for international scientific fact-finding? which are the concrete matters to be investigated and along what dimensions are they to be measured or evaluated? In other words, we need yardsticks which are generally accepted, as the basis for such scientific efforts, if they are to have any political impact.

Without such underlying consensus science may easily be turned into political instruments in the hands of the most powerful governments.[4]

The World Commission on Environment and Development set out to define such a consensus on the principal issues facing the world community in this field. The key instrument in its efforts to build a new political coalition for international action is the concept of sustainable development. This seems to be the core in what is considered a new approach to this complex of problems, but to what extent can international consensus be established around it?

A problematic concept

In spite of its importance, the Commission fails to give a precise and operational definition of this concept, but underlines two key elements in its use of the term:

- the satisfaction of basic material needs for the poorest parts of the world population, and
- the ecological constraints on future economic activity imposed by various environmental considerations.

(The possible contradiction between the two is solved by emphasizing the need to reorient economic growth.)

In addition, the Commission includes the notion of equality in its development concept, both at a national and international level: popular participation and 'equitable opportunities for all' (p.44) are seen both as an objective in itself and as a means for economic development.[5]

On the world scale this notion is introduced rather cautiously and indirectly, but still with noticeable force: 'Living standards that go beyond the basic minimum are sustainable only if consumption standards everywhere have regard for long-term sustainability. Yet many of us live beyond the world's ecological means, for instance in our patterns of energy use . . . sustainable development requires the promotion of values that encourage consumption standards that are within the bounds of the ecological possible and to which all can reasonably aspire.' (p.44)

The concept of sustainability in fact embraces all the key trends in the international development debate since the 1960s:

- The traditional, neo-classical growth theories are reflected in the emphasis on economic growth in the third world, measured by conventional standards, such as GNP per capita. Proponents of 'trickle down' theories can easily find support for their position in the report.
- The basic needs approach — the dominating trend in the 1970s — is, as indicated above, wholeheartedly supported by the Commission.
- By stressing equality and grassroot participation the Commission takes account of the radical or social-democratic criticism of foreign aid of the late 1970s.
- The ecological message in the report echoes the warnings of the first environmental movement in the West in the late 1960s and early 1970s.

So, there is something for everybody in *Our Common Future* — which should be no surprise since the report is primarily a political document. Politicians need to build coalitions for their causes, and adopting diverse and partly contradictory ideas in the same policy platform often suits that purpose very well. However, the price of such compromises is ambiguity and uncertainty.

Energy and sustainable development

In Chapter 7 on energy, environment and development the Commission defines the 'key elements of sustainability' in the following manner: sufficient growth of energy supplies to meet human needs, energy efficiency and conservation, protection of public health and of the biosphere (p.169). Even if 'a generally acceptable pathway to a safe and sustainable energy future has not yet been found' (p.169),[6] the Commission clearly leans towards 'a low energy path' as the only 'realistic option open to the world for the 21st century' (p.174). In principle, its conclusion is unequivocal on this point: 'a low energy path is the best way towards a sustainable future' (p.201). However, the operative implications of such statements of principle are not clearly or explicitly spelled out. The Commision undoubtedly advocates a change — perhaps a radical change — away from present patterns of energy use, which are considered unsustainable, but the recommendations are often vague and almost invariably open to interpretation. Let me give a few examples of such ambiguity.[7]

Nuclear energy

It is well known that the commissioners held different opinions on this issue. The controversy was resolved by the ingenuous statement: 'The generation of nuclear power is only justifiable if there are solid solutions to the presently unsolved problems to which it gives rise [proliferation and waste disposal]. The highest priority must be accorded to research and development on environmentally sound and economically viable alternatives, as well as means of increasing the safety of nuclear energy' (p 189). The last sentence highlights the problem of ambiguity: what kind of government action will *not* be consistent with that recommendation? How can one give 'the highest priority' to both of these objectives?

Energy use in industrialized countries

As the Commission regards the 'low energy path' as the key to the solution of the global environmental problems, it emphasizes the need for improved energy efficiency and conservation in the industrialized countries, where the potential for saving is largest (p.196). It even stresses that 'the process (of energy efficiency) must be accelerated **to reduce per capita consumption**' (p.59, emphasis added), but this position is not spelled out in the energy analysis — apparently because it is too controversial. To avoid criticism, the Commission simply refers to the study by Goldemberg et al., which concluded that a reduction of 50 per cent in per capita energy consumption in the rich countries is possible — and desirable. The Commission itself simply states that 'properly managed, efficiency measures could allow industrial nations to stabilize their primary energy consumption by the turn of the century'. This is basically a technical statement (which may be disputed by technical experts) and not necessarily any guideline for policy.

Fossil fuels

The Commission underlines the environmental problems caused by the combustion of fossil fuels: global warming, urban pollution and acidification. It stresses the need for more research on climate change and close monitoring of future developments, but apart from that fails to give any concrete policy recommendations. This could be taken to mean that the Commission is not opposed to expansion of coal use, provided it is energy efficient. Another reasonable inference would be to advocate a shift from coal or oil to gas — on the basis of this part of the report. A third — and more radical possibility — is to say that this sector must be given lower priority than renewable alternatives. Hence, fossil fuels must be replaced by the latter, whenever feasible.

The role of science

These three examples demonstrate the difficulties the Commission has encountered in trying to give operational contents to the concept of 'sustainable development'. In most of the controversial cases the problems have been solved by ambiguous and contradictory statements,which was necessary — and legitimate — for the Commission itself. However, the remaining ambiguity creates severe difficulties for the follow-up process, in particular for the relationship between science and politics.

As indicated above, science can only play a constructive role in the international resource management under the following conditions:

- It must be independent in funding and transnational in organization.
- It must have financial resources for the tasks assigned to it.
- Its role *vis-à-vis* the political actors must be carefully defined and adequately protected.

Under such circumstances science can gain credibility as an independent participant in the policy-making process, but still clearly distinguished from the participating governments and interest groups. The latter two are there to promote their interests, the former should not take its self-interests into account, but advocate 'good' solutions according to specified criteria.

Is this possible in the area of energy, environment and development? It follows from my interpretation of the message from the Brundtland Commission that it is very difficult to define a clear-cut role for science here. This does not mean, however, that it has no contribution to make. As indicated above, independent scientific reporting wil be crucial in several ways in the follow-up process.

But the problem is how to relate the scientific findings to intergovernmental discussions and policy-making *in the absence of generally agreed standards of behaviour*. As long as the politicians cannot agree on operational concepts of development — not to speak of guidelines for action — scientific results may be irrelevant or very difficult to use. As a result science can either be excluded from the policy-making process or deliberately used by the actors with the resources to do so. For example, the international nuclear power lobby will probably present research results underlining the need to limit CO_2 emmissions. Countries with large hydrocarbon reserves — and consumption — will sponsor research on the need to protect tropical forests.

So, the scene may be set for two possible roles for sciences in this area:

1. increasing political (ab)use of scientific resources and research results in the political bargaining process, or
2. new 'unholy alliances' of the kind mentioned above, between politicians eager to postpone difficult decisions and research institutions equally eager to increase their funding. In both cases, the independence of science will be compromised — or corrupted. It is up to the scientific community itself to avert these dangers and to define for itself a credible, transnational role as an independent 'watchdog' for the global environment.

Notes

1. Lloyd Timberlake had formulated this very clearly in his article in this volume: 'Scientists, because a large part of their livelihood is doing research, tend to testify that more research is required before there is a basis for action. Successful politicians, because they got where they are by successfully manipulating the system — whatever system might operate — tend to want to put off making major changes in that system. Those leaders who do not want to rock their various boats join the scientists in demanding more data.' Cf. Timberlake, Lloyd, 1989, 'The Role of Scientific Knowledge in Drawing up The Brundtland Report', in this volume.

2. Ibid.

3. Ibid.

4 .In other words, the scientific inquiries in question will fail to produce 'consensual knowledge', cf. Miles' (1989) use of that term in his article in this volume.

5. All quotations are taken from the report of the Commission, *Our Common Future*, Oxford University Press, Oxford, 1987.

6. It is tempting to ask whether it will ever happen.

7. This discussion is based on the report itself. It would have been possible to take into account the analyses underlying its work, such as *Energy 2000*, a report to the Commission (Zed Books, London, 1987), and J. Goldemberg, T. Johansen et al., *Energy for a Sustainable World*, World Resources Institute, 1987. However, this will increase the problem of interpretation, since the number of viewpoints and positions is proportionate to the number of analysts.

7

Global environmental monitoring and information systems — an operational perspective

Leif E. Christoffersen

Introduction

Over the last two decades, the rapidly growing awareness and public debate about global environmental issues have taken place during a period when two major technological revolutions have occurred. The first involves computers capable of examining and storing vast amounts of detailed information. The second arises from satellite-based remote sensing able to obtain images of any area of the world on a frequent basis and in considerable detail. Science has provided these powerful technological tools which seem well suited to advance our knowledge of how development and environment interrelate on global, regional, national and local scales. The question is — can they be put to good use in enhancing global environment?

A recognition is emerging that major environmental issues have to be understood in an integrated global developmental context. This point was forcefully made by the recent Brundtland Commission's report. Environmentalists and other scientists as well as policy-makers and economic decision-makers need to speak the same language, and also need to refer to data bases that have common credibility in order for this interaction to take place. Today, this is rarely the case, although many efforts are under way to try and make it come true in the near future.

Operational tools

Within the UN system, United Nations Environmental Program (UNEP) took a bold step in 1974 to set up the global environmental monitoring system, known as GEMS. Its basic purpose was to 'keep track of environmental trends, to be able to predict events and to provide decision-makers with sound information upon which to base environmental action plans'.[1] At the outset GEMS gave priority to monitoring pollution and its effect on human health. Subsequently this was broadened to five environmental features — the climate; long-range transport of pollutants; land-based (terrestrial) renewable natural resources; the oceans; and human health.

GEMS set out to be an overall coordinator of various environmental monitoring systems undertaken by many other organizations. It soon became clear that the lack of a common global data base was a major bottle-neck in making such monitoring meaningful to expected users. In the early 1980s, the global resources information data-base (GRID) was set up within GEMS. It was to be a system for channelling key environmental data from as many sources as possible to any potential user. Who were the main categories of intended users? The first UNEP report on GRID reported that they were expected to be 'scientists trying to understand the functioning and behavior of our global environment, or planners making important management decisions about the regions under their jurisdiction'.[2]

The gaps in our scientific knowledge regarding the various processes that determine natural resource uses in the global economy are still enormous. 'If I was asked to identify the greatest single scientific advance of the 1980's', noted Michael Gwynne, the senior official at UNEP handling GEMS and GRID, 'I would say that it is the realization among scientists that the world's environment must be looked upon as a *complex entity* which can only be understood through a comprehensive global approach. Increasingly it is being realized that such a global approach to understanding environmental change is better than responding individually to, for example, such apparent recent problems as *acid* deposition, *carbon dioxide* increase and *stratospheric* ozone depletion'.[3]

Such a realization among scientists may seem long overdue in light of the gravity of environmental problems facing the world. Single efforts rather than team efforts have been the traditional norm among scientists. Indeed the concept of environmental sciences is not yet well established in the scientific community. This is particularly so with respect to issues relating to developing countries, where rapid use and destruction of many natural resources cause major threats to their own long-term future as well as to the global environment.[4]

Many major environmental concerns monitored by UNEP or other bodies arose from popular science, journalism or from environmental groups, rather than from well-established scientific research findings.[5] Those concerning the African continent arose primarily from individuals or groups outside rather than inside Africa.

However, since global environmental monitoring is still at a preliminary stage, we must be careful not to judge it as a final product. Most of its proponents agree it is incomplete — in coverage, selection of priority and data quality. One has to understand that any new system needs time to develop and cannot be expected to be complete at the outset. In building stepping stones towards a more comprehensive system, we mainly need to be certain that we are moving in the right direction, and that in so doing we are encouraging the development of an effective and cost-efficient overall system.

The Brundtland Report and Africa

One of the questions raised against the present information systems, including GRID, is whether they monitor the effects of environmental degradation rather than its root causes. As the Brundtland Commission's report spells out, in Africa, for example, the main causes of such degradation are poverty, excessive population growth, fragile soils, inappropriate agricultural technology and a policy environment that does not easily foster solutions to the above. We concentrate considerable resources on monitoring the disappearance of forests and wildlife areas, the apparent expansion of desert areas, and other forms of land degradation. But the most basic problems that need more urgent focus have more to do with alleviating low levels of income, overcoming insufficient economic and social advancement and strengthening national policy frameworks that can encourage long-term sustainable development. We try to monitor changes in physical characteristics but spend far less attention and resources on factors which determine individual and community behaviour with regard to the environment.

The influence of most popular writings, which have not been careful in sorting out fact from fiction, has caused the spread of considerable misinformation in this field. At the same time scientists themselves seem to have had problems communicating with people outside academic circles. During the 1970s and particularly in the early 1980s, when severe drought hit many areas of Africa, it became popular to highlight attention on an apparent 'natural' expansion of desert areas, especially the Sahara. During the drought years, there was plenty of evidence regarding lands turned into sand, depopulated villages and people on the move away from desert areas. A wide variety of different estimates were made about the rates of desertification, many of which indicated a gloomy long-term forecast of a continuous expansion of desert areas. But opinion makers were less well educated about countervailing trends, such as a rather remarkable capacity for vegetation regrowth in many desert or semi-desert areas when more normal climatic conditions return. In a recent UNEP publication, two of the best known scientific experts on arid lands and deserts, Dregni and Tucker, concluded there is no scientific basis for assuming there has been a long-term physical expansion of deserts such as the Sahara. They note that meteorological satellite observations have demonstrated the large international shifts in green biomass production levels possible on the south side of the Sahara. These observations have thrown doubt on the validity of statements claiming that 'permanent shifts in vegetation zones have occurred in that part of the Sahara as a result of desertification'.[6] Hence the idea of an 'encroaching Sahara' has not been established firmly on basis of available and accepted scientific evidence.

However, it is widely recognized that poor people suffer greatly in dry land areas of Africa, especially in periods of change, whether temporary or long-term. Most serious are the many man-made problems of land-degradation arising within traditional agricultural and livestock areas and also on new farm land that has been cleared from forests. In other words, the changing nature of many agricultural practices, in part due to fast growing population density, is causing permanent damage to soils that no longer can remain productive at available technological levels. As noted by Dr Adedeji, executive director of the UN Economic Commission for Africa, 'At the root of Africa's economic backwardness, stagnation, and decline, lies the poor performance of the agricultural sector and . . . the low level of technology and the very limited application of science to agricultural development in Africa.'[7]

From an operational viewpoint, I have had many occasions to wonder about the lack of strong scientific underpinning of many environmental issues. In a recent communication with a professor of environmental sciences at the University of California, I asked why this was so. The response was: 'There are human and scientific reasons why scientists do not involve themselves more in these issues. The answer in simplest terms has to do with status, fame, fads, money and facilities . . . Little status is generally attached to environmental sciences. These are part of applied sciences, which have low status in academic life, and, are of an *interdisciplinary* nature, which has even lower status. The very interdisciplinary and applied aspects of these complex problems discourage most scientists.'[8]

Status apparently is interlinked with fame, which stimulates research funding and provides research facilities. A fad implies an issue that captures broad interest for a short period of time. It may not yet be substantiated by solid scientific evidence. A fad issue can open up research fundings for researchers, but it has a high risk, since the needed continuing long-term funding commitment may be elusive.

Science and technology in Africa

In Africa, the role of science and technology at the national level was given relatively low priority after countries achieved their independence. As a former long-term adviser to an African president recently told me, the focus during and after independence was on finding appropriate political solutions on the assumption that the resolution of economic and technological problems would then easily follow. He noted that this assumption turned out to be incorrect. Today most national economies and scientific communities in Africa are weak and many are deteriorating. Africa is the only continent in the world where per capita incomes are falling in most countries, and this is occurring at a time when the volume of private capital flows are negative and when the level of official development assistance to the continent is stagnating. In addition, the national scientific research capabilities have deteriorated in most African countries despite major efforts to educate and train scientists. Nowhere is this more evident than in agriculture, which is the dominant economic sector in Africa in terms of both income and employment. A continent that twenty years ago could feed itself is now forced to import food in ever increasing volumes. Dr Nana-Sinkam, a senior official of the UN Economic Commission for Africa, recently stated that 'Sub-Saharan Africa's systems for the generation and dissemination of agricultural research and technology are ill-equipped and poorly focused and, in their present state, cannot meet the requirements of the present crisis'.[9]

Over the last two decades the policy pursued at national levels in most of Africa, to tax heavily, directly or indirectly, peasants and other rural producers to provide funds for urban, industrial and public sectors, have not only had a devastating effect on the agricultural sectors themselves, but also on the associated national research capabilities. More reliance was put on immediate use of imported technology than on adapting technology from elsewhere to African conditions or generating new technology for Africa.

Only recently have there been encouraging indications of change. National agricultural research programmes are now receiving more attention from African decision-makers. New bodies, such as the African Academy of Sciences, under the leadership of the internationally respected Thomas Odhiambo, of the International Center for Insect Physiology and Ecology (ICIPE), in Nairobi, are encouraging and fostering serious African scientific research. These hold some hope for the future, but there is a long way to go to compensate for past neglect. In order to reduce the growing technological dependency on Western countries, it is more important than ever to establish world class research programmes at African universities and research institutes. A recent study on African education noted: 'Ironically, no African nation can afford to have such programmes in the short run, yet none can afford not to have them in the long run.'[10] What is of special significance is that among both African and international scientists, there is strong emphasis on the need to take environmental factors into account. Dr Nyle C. Brady, former director of the International Rice Research Institute and now a senior official in USAID, expressed this emerging consensus as follows: 'As technology is developed and harnessed for use in Africa, preference must be given to technology that protects the natural environment. In fragile regions, agriculture can become a battle ground between ecology and technology. Costs and benefits of new production technology must be fully assessed in terms of impact on natural resources.'[11]

In Africa, it is particularly at the national level that large obstacles exist for the generation of new technology and also for effective use of the GEMS and GRID frameworks. The gap is vast between present global environmental assessments and key national management actions and scientific research. There are many reasons for this situation. Besides deteriorating science and technology systems in Africa over the last decades, and within this, few opportunities for environmental-related sciences, there have been other contributing causes:

- Weak data bases exist for most economic and social development planning. Within each sector a multiplicity of data series exist, even within the same ministry.
- New environmental data, and information on broader natural resource management issues, are virtually never interlinked with data systems used by national economic decision-makers.
- The fragmentation of donor assistance in Africa is acute and pervasive in most sectors and often acts as a disincentive to more focused and integrated data systems at the national level.
- Declining budgets due to deteriorating economic conditions.
- The agenda setting for issues to be monitored is often dominated by advocacy groups outside Africa rather than inside the continent. The high degree of political and media influences of environmental advocacy groups in industrialized countries, as compared with the relatively low level of influence of local environmental groups in Africa, have often brought about a disproportionately high degree of external influence on national debates on environmental priorities in Africa.
- The lack of scientific emphasis on human behavioural patterns influencing individual or community decision-making on environmental and developmental issues. Let me mention three examples: (a) little is still known about the real reason for Africa's exceptionally high population growth rates and how to reduce the high fertility levels projected for the future; (b) inadequate understanding exists about how to deal with resettlement of people, as in the case of nomadic tribes whose migratory routes are being made inaccessible; and (c) long-term agricultural sustainability issues, so central to environmental policy, need to be better understood in the context of how poor peasants perceive the degree of risk involved. Hence, clearly a much closer link between natural sciences and behavioural sciences is needed.[12]

Furthermore, GEMS and GRID focus on high technology — computers and satellite-base remote sensing — which can be inhibiting for national level users, unless there is a clear idea of priority setting, and careful selectivity of which aspects of such technology are appropriate for local use.

A sense of selectivity is important in determining which aspects of the high-technology menu are most appropriate in a given national context in light of economic costs, compatibility with local cultures, and use of local skills and resources. Better priority-setting means that a central focal point is needed to decide on national issues of foremost significance to that country so that data systems can be designed accordingly. Gathering data without such clear focus has often meant costly and useless activities. The dilemma of finding an appropriate technology in this context was noted by John Parry of McGill University, Canada as follows: 'There is no easy solution to the problem of selecting appropriate sensors and sensor parameters for the developing world. However, it is ironic that at a time when there is intense rivalry among technologically advanced nations to produce more sophisticated sensors capable of finer resolution — 30M for the thematic mapper on Landsat 4, 10M for the panachromatic mode in spot image — most of the countries of the developing world have no means of using precision digital data, and in any case really need *more general resource information*, than pixel by pixel detail.'[13]

The lack of focus and priorities is also reflected in the UN system, among other international donor organizations, and regional institutions. In the UN system alone there are over 130 major environmental networks and major data banks. Most are unrelated to each other. Hence, although the basic overall concepts behind GEMS and GRID are laudable — namely to create order and systematic approaches to a complex field of increasing importance to global development and security, much remains to be done to make these systems effective in serving data needs of national level decision-makers as well as the science community.

Concluding remarks

The many obstacles mentioned may lead some to draw negative conclusions and despair regarding the eventual usefulness of these systems. That is not my intention. Rather, I want to conclude on a note of some optimism — which is so essential in order to foster action. As noted many years ago by the distinguished Norwegian scientist and internationalist Fridtjof Nansen: 'Let it be fully understood that melancholy and pessimism — however attractive they may be — are sins, in as much as they lead to inactivity, which is as serious a sin as any in the world.'[14] Considerable action is being taken — and much more can also be done.

At international levels there are major efforts under way to begin to rationalize and systematize the vast array of environmental networks and data bases, particularly since the Oslo meeting of July 1988 of UN agency heads. In parallel, major 'building block' efforts at the national level are being pursued; hence over time international systems can be expected to serve more effectively various operational and scientific users. Much can be done to encourage and foster local and national scientific research in developing countries, including multidisciplinary environmental sciences. More international recognition, including funding, must be given to environmental scientists, and even more so to teams of environmental scientists, particularly in developing countries. This should help to foster the needed capacity in each country to internalize the resolution of national environmental problems and integrate them into developmental decision-making. Also, this would help foster better priority-setting among issues, and hence better data base systems, which then can respond to an agenda determined primarily by national perspectives but also taking into account regional and international dimensions of the problems.

Furthermore, natural sciences need to work more closely with behavioural sciences in order to provide a stronger scientific underpinning for global environmental monitoring systems. Both sides need to caution opinion-makers on differences between short-term, temporary environmental phenomena versus the real long-term issues. Understanding what motivates human behaviour in this context is of key importance to all such knowledge. More effort can be made to foster stronger national monitoring systems. From this can emerge better direction and operational focus in the gradually evolving international monitoring and information systems for the global environment. The two major technological tools mentioned at the beginning of my presentation, which open up vast, new opportunities for global environmental monitoring, also have a promising potential for encouraging more interdisciplinary scientific research as well as for stronger international cooperation.

But, as mentioned above, a lot of resources is spent on monitoring changes in physical characteristics in sub-Saharan Africa. Important as they may be, these physical symptoms do have very limited explanatory value. More attention should, therefore, be paid to the underlying processes explaining the patterns of land use documented by remote sensing data. In other words, it has become increasingly important to include social and behavioural sciences in order to be able to identify why changes are taking place.[15] This also seems to be critical for strong and operationally useful national research systems.

Since enclaves of sophisticated technology can easily become out of touch with local needs, more emphasis should be put on 'connecting' remote sensing and environmental monitoring to other sciences involved in resource management. This issue must be addressed up front if remote sensing is to play a positive role in the strengthening of national research systems in African countries.

Notes

1. UNEP, 1982, Report on GEMS.

2. UNEP, 1985, Report on GRID.

3. Gwynne, Michael, *Global Monitoring: Needs, Principles, Practices*, paper presented at the Twentieth International Symposium on Remote Sensing of Environment, Nairobi, Kenya, 4-10 December 1986.

4. See Bergesen, Helge Ole, 1989, 'The Credibility of Science in International Resource Management', in this volume.

5. Timberlake, Lloyd, 1989, 'The Role of Scientific Knowledge in Drawing up the Brundtland Report', in this volume.

6. UNEP, *Desertification Control Bulletin*, 16 November 1987.

7. Keynote presentation, December 1986, to the Twentieth International Symposium on Remote Sensing of Environment, Nairobi, Kenya.

8. Letter from Professor Daniel Botkin, University of California, dated 14 September 1988.

9. Nana-Sinkam, S.C., Director, Joint ECA-FAO Agricultural Division, Addis Ababa; presentation to the high level meeting on African Agricultural Research and Technological Development, Feldafing, Federal Republic of Germany, September 1987.

10. *Education in sub-Saharan Africa*, World Bank Policy Study, 1988.

11. Brady, Nyle C., 'Creating and Sustaining a Green Revolution in Africa' in *International Agriculture Update*, June 1988, University of Illinois.

12. Young, Oran, 1989, in this volume.

13. Parry, John T., 'Perspective and Issues for Remote Sensing in the Tropics' in M.J. Eden and J.T. Parry (eds.), *Remote Sensing and Tropical Land Management*, John Wiley and Sons.

14. Quoted in Hygen, Johan B., 'Fridtjof Nansen's views of Civilization and Ethics' in Per Vogt, *Fridtjof Nansen, Explorer-Scientist-Humanitarian*, Dreyer, Oslo.

15. See Young, Oran, 1989, in this volume.

SECTION 3:
Science and International Pollution

SECTION 3
Catchment and river modelling (7 chapters)

8

The role of science in the international regulation of pollution

Sonja Boehmer-Christiansen

Introduction

Direr visions, worse foreboding
Glare upon me through the gloom,
Britain's smoke-cloud sinks corroding
On the land in noisome fume . . . (Henrik Ibsen,1866)

. . . matters are generally divided into air pollution, land pollution and water pollution. In fact there is only one pollution because every single thing, every chemical . . . will end up in the ocean. (Jacques-Yves Cousteau)

Cousteau, we now know, is partially wrong and Ibsen has to some extent been proven right on the basis of scientific evidence painstakingly collected one century later. Testable and agreed knowledge about the physical world and mankind's effects is beginning to persuade enough people to accept such knowledge as truth. We now know what earlier generations or far-sighted individuals only suspected, namely that pollutants from many countries may not only circle the whole globe, but may finish up in and chemically react with the upper atmosphere. We also know that chemicals undergo complex transformations on their way through natural cycles, that poisons released into air or water may either be rendered harmless or changed to become more toxic and that their eventual incorporation into geologic deposits is decided in geologic, not human, time.

Pollution control, on the other hand, relates to human experiences and perceptions of environmental damage. It involves continuous learning by social institutions and reflects a new dimension in economic, commercial and technology policy: the taking into account, during the making of current decisions, of 'nature' and its fate at the hands of mankind.

International society is only beginning to learn how to deal with the effects of human activities on the quality and quantity of shared natural resources.[1] Our growing, if still patchy and incomplete, knowledge of the natural world, its processes and interactions with man-made introductions, determines our ability to assess correctly and to predict. What is done in practice, however, is determined by politics and must be based as much on what is known, as on what we suspect on the basis of ignorance and intuition.

This contribution first discusses why pollution control involves a complex process of public policy-making influenced by a very broad range of factors. The identification of a scientific-political complex at the international level oversimplifies the analysis of decisions taken at this level.[2] A number of case studies of international regulatory efforts then provide some empirical evidence for the general discussion of the role of science. A brief summary of British environmental policy and the impact of harmonization within the supranational context of the European Community complete the chapter. Without such a broad approach, the complex and often ambivalent role of science cannot be isolated.

The multi-faceted nature of pollution control

Pollution control, or environmental protection, at any level is a multi-faceted activity because it has far-reaching and often very unequal economic impacts on society. The environmental consequences of human activities need to be understood and the direction of scientific research itself influenced accordingly. The economic and technological consequences of proposed environmental regulations, as well as the capacity and willingness of political institutions to respond to these concerns, all contribute to the making of environmental policy at the national level and thus affect international decisions as well. Governments are rarely fully in control of the issues raised and domestic politics thus becomes a part of intergovernnmental negotiations. If we want to understand and improve the role played by science in this often long and frustrating process, an understanding of the underlying processes of policy-formation and implementation at the national level is required.

This means that factors other than objective knowledge about pollutants, their fate and effects in the environment must be isolated before the role of science can be assessed. These factors include the political priorities and ideological commitments of specific governments, their political stability, especially with regard to pressures from environmental and industrial lobbies, their isolation or otherwise from environmental learning processes; as well as the perceived economic and technological consequences of specific abatement proposals. Because environmental regulations often have significant effects on international trade, e.g. as non-tariff trade barriers and thus as tools of competition, they tend to affect the rate and direction of technological innovation and usually impinge on the distribution of welfare and wealth. These factors are therefore also likely to enter international negotiations, either explicitly or implicitly. When environmental concern or awareness differ between nations, as is the norm rather than the exception, they tend to become decisive.

The fundamental question to be explored therefore is not what contribution science can or should make to global pollution control, but rather what, on the basis of empirical studies, has persuaded governments and industry to enter such alliances with environmental lobbies and to commit political and financial resources to pollution control, i.e. to the abatement, enforcement of strict standards and public acceptance of such measures? As shown by Oran Young, such persuasion is the task of numerous social institutions engaged in political processes.[3] Both the inputs to and outcomes of such persuasive processes are conditioned by society and, for environmental protection, must result either in technological innovation producing more benign processes and products, or change individual behaviour, such as changes in attitude to particular parts of the natural environment, in consumption patterns and expectations of the future. Because these factors may differ signicantly between societies, international agreement will not come easily if at all.

Pollution control as a process in public policy-making

This process can be broken down into three consecutive stages:

- awareness and understanding
- selection of policy response
- implementation and enforcement

In each of these steps, scientific evidence and research can and usually do play a major role, especially if we define science sufficiently widely to include the research and development underpinning technological innovation. Here only the first two steps, the development of awareness and understanding and the formation of policy, will be discussed in any detail. Without an understanding of causal relationships, the detailed measurement of flows, distributions and accumulations of pollutants, as well as the identification of their sources, more efficient and cost-effective policy options cannot be identified. However, more than one policy option may achieve similar outcomes. Technological competition is quickly involved and thus struggle for consumer appeal and market shares.

As we move away from the first step, where science narrowly defined may indeed be a major source of information, there is a growing need for information — factual data and understanding — not from the natural sciences but from the social sciences, especially economics, politics and social psychology. These sources of knowledge are not discussed here, but it should be stressed that virtually no provision has so far been made for their explicit incorporation into international agreements.[4] This is a major weakness because it means that scientific evidence and argument are necessarily overemphasized in international negotiations, especially in the official justification of policy preferences.[5] This in turn helps to explain why 'science' is so often treated by politics as the exclusive legitimizing criterion in its justification of policy, a point to which I shall return below.

There can, however, be no scientific or ecological need for abating or preventing pollution, although scientific information may well persuade us to try to prevent changes in ecological relationships. Who is to do the persuasion? What forms of justification persuade most effectively? Often it is indeed the communication of scientific and other knowledge, as well as its subsequent assessment and interpretation, which will determine whether or not society perceives a need for policy revision; at other times it is the mere suspicion of danger and intuition, or the immediate experience of major accidents, like Chernobyl, *Amoco Cadiz*, or Soveso, all of which had almost immediate effects on international relations and regulations. Damage or risk assessment arising from all these forms of knowledge will then have to be evaluated in relation to other national and international priorities.

Pollution control is usually justified with reference to one or any combination of the following three objectives:

1. An *economic* objective: to limit or prevent resource deterioration, damage or depletion below some optimal level, so that benefits at the margin outweigh the costs;
2. A *selfish* objective: to limit or prevent negative effects on individual or public human health, i.e. to protect the human species and its individual parts, with emphasis usually on the latter.
3. A *moral* or 'green' objective: to preserve and protect nature for its own sake or in its own right, including the conservation of its beauty and independence from human intervention.

International efforts to limit pollution have so far been concentrated in the realm of resource management, probably because here the existence of common interests is most readily demonstrated. This does not mean, however, that the other dimensions are absent or can be ignored. If they could, then the role of science (provided the link between damage and damage costs can be quantified) would indeed be less ambivalent and the resolution of intergovernmental conflict, at least in principle, somewhat simpler. This role can be examined more closely by looking at each of the above objectives separately.

Resource management

International efforts to limit pollution in the interest of resource management tend to be simplified and the role of science enhanced, but not necessarily made very much easier, by two factors.

First, a policy which is restricted to the definition of objectives rather than to the identification of technological or other solutions, i.e. which defines the ends but not the means, means that the allocation and distribution of compliance costs and enforcement costs are left to individual states. This simplifies bargaining on the surface, but often delays international agreement because answers to these questions will have to emerge at the domestic level before genuine international commitment is possible. In finding solutions to these social and economic 'side-effects' of international regulation, the state is only one among many actors, and often a weak one. Such agreements are rarely satisfactory, however. The powers of the international community to ensure compliance are virtually nil and the onus of achieving the agreed objectives falls almost entirely on the domestic political system, (which may, however, be strengthened by advisory international inputs).

Second, international pollution control agreements in their conception have tended to place too much hope on the ability of science rather than economics or moral values to legitimize action. Science can never arbitrate over conflicts of resource use or priorities of social policy.[6] Yet the definition of pollution as adopted, for example, by most international conventions protecting the marine environment, implies that pollution can be judged on the basis of scientific knowledge alone. This perception follows directly from the widely accepted definition of marine pollution as effects in the environment caused by introductions which result in harm, hinderance or impairment.

Human health

Pollution experienced as threat to individual human health is of course also a moral imperative, but one which excludes effects on the natural world. Human health may be achieved at the expense of environmental wholeness, as population growth in conditions of severe poverty demonstrates only too well. Emissions and discharges into oceans and the higher atmosphere can and have been justified on the grounds of protecting the health of people employed or living near the emitting sources. Appeals to human health are, however, a most powerful threat with a very direct impact on political structures.[7]

Yet even safety and health standards can never be purely 'scientific'; judgements need to be made at many stages of the decision-making process and these include evaluations of individual claims and rights, which may conflict with community interests and goals as seen by government. Human health is a policy area where science has the greatest difficulties of 'proving' causal relationships conclusively,[8] and where policy-makers from different nations are immediately confronted with differences in policy priority. Some societies are undoubtedly more given to health worries than others, and those with the greatest fear of ill health and shortened life-spans, for whatever reason, are probably more readily prepared to act 'with precaution' than those which are either less risk averse or more concerned with more immediate problems, such as obtaining enough to eat or changing political structures. A government very worried about individual health risks is rarely poor.

Ultimately, protecting individual human health may have little to do with protecting natural resources from overexploitation by the human species. To 'shrink' environmental protection into this issue of individual human health is not likely to offer much help to international resource managers unless 'science' can prove that pollutants harming natural resources are also likely to have serious transfrontier or even global health effects (as appears to be case for the ozone depletion).

Nature protection

In the absence of immediate economic or health justifications for pollution control, there remains a moral dimension which may be labelled 'greenness'. It is not a new phenomenon, but has affected Western societies (and probably others) repeatedly during past centuries.[9] In recent decades it has probably been weakest in the years during and immediately following World War II and is likely to remain weak in societies preoccupied with economic growth. Even this may now be changing fast, both in practice and normative theory.[10] Economic growth, with its negative effects on both land and the diminishing marginal utility of income, may explain why both industrial societies and agricultural communities are becoming increasingly concerned about the loss of wilderness and species variety. This new concern may be justified with reference to religion or the non-economic value attached to 'wilderness' and the aesthetic pleasures of the biosphere.[11] Economic justifications based on the calculations of long-term effects of pollution damage may also be devised, but they are unlikely to persuade the practical businessman and the politician.

The supporters of 'green' values may, however, come into serious conflict with resource managers, as this volume itself may illustrate. My research experience suggests that the balance of power between the various groups involved in the final decision made at the national level will tend to tip against environmental protection measures justifiable on purely long-term economic grounds, until alliances are formed between green groups and a sufficiently large number of offical interests. In other words, until significant parts of the domestic political system see the environmental lobby as an ally rather than an irrational opponent. The point at which the balance tips will vary between countries. It is likely to be reached later in countries like Britain, where political stability tends to weaken the need for such alliances.

The function of science in pollution control

Science is valued as ammunition for their respective causes by the supporters of all three objectives, but effective action against pollution need not be dependent on new or even scientific proven knowledge. In many cases, human perceptions and intuition provide sufficient knowledge to serve as justification. If human beings experience pollution as a threat, then scientific argument and evidence that these perceptions are erroneous is unlikely to have much effect, as is well illustrated by the nuclear debate in several countries.

It can be concluded from the argument above that even if the science base identifying damage effects were fully agreed, an effective abatement technology were available, the legal-administrative institutions for implementation and enforcement of control measures at the national level were in place and a polluter able to pay had been identified, intergovernmental agreement on international pollution regulations is still not assured, even for cases of common resource management. In the real world, governments must respond to much more than 'facts'. Their own survival may depend on being seen to respond to what is felt to be most urgent or morally right.

Underlying this challenge to the view that science can determine, strongly influence or even initiate pollution control strategies, are two assumptions which need restating. First, the basis of pollution control is often ethical and not scientific, and therefore inherently conflictual within societies and between societies. Second, science itself, because of its own internal propensity for conflict, can only make a limited contribution to the resolution of international conflicts over public choices.[12]

None the less, there remains one fundamental common interest between governments with respect to science, that of funding cooperative research. To learn more about pollutants and their effects in the environment is a truly common interest. Scientific cooperation rests on this and tends to persist even in highly competitive situations. It may be encouraged by them. On the other hand, official perceptions that knowledge gained by international cooperation is still largely related to national efforts and thus adds status and influence to a particular nation state, should not be discouraged.[13]

For national scientific communities to survive in situations hostile to the funding of environmental research, it may even be the best way to persuade government that an 'independent' national knowledge base is required in order to defend national interests. Science clearly has its own interest in the pollution control game.

Science as an independent interest

Organised science consists of powerful, often competing institutions dependent upon public or industrial funding. It has a direct and powerful interest in the study of pollution, but very little in its control. Since the control of pollution relies only in part on science to play the role of handmaiden or justification, 'power' and influence in the regulatory process may soon pass to other professional groups such as lawyers and engineers unless, of course, the scientific community itself can ensure that control strategies are adopted which depend on its continuous advice. This is more likely to be the case when control rests on the use of environmental quality standards (as is preferred by Britain with its system of a scientific civil service interlocking at all levels with administrative structures) than, at least in the shorter term, for regulation by uniform emission or discharge standards with their more intrinsic appeal to lawyers and engineers.

Science also has an interest in uncertainty, in the promise of its own ability to create certainty, as well as in restricting the access of other 'professionals' to policy-makers. The most basic interest of scientists, to be acknowledged by their peers as honest researchers, may create conflict with policy-makers, who have a very urgent need for clear answers, simple strategies, certainty in forecasting and persuasiveness *vis-a-vis* the general public.[14]

Facing conflicts within its own ranks (in competition for resources and truth) and with its major consumers, simply means that scientists, once organised into institutions giving policy advice, are no more 'trust-worthy' than most other respectable pressure groups.[15] They too will make use of fashionable arguments in order to further their own interests and concerns.[16] The making of final judgements about what needs to be done or what can remain as it is thus remains the responsibility of the 'competent authority', which may or may not act in the best interest of society, itself or the planet.

Scientists and science may be threatened by too close an identification with government. The role of science in the justification of policy preferred on other grounds, i.e., as a legimatizing fig-leaf, may mean that science is misused by politicians who are trying to cover their own preferences with appeals to the imperative of true or objective knowledge. This may also lead to 'politics' trying to transfer to 'science' (and unaccountable scientists) the responsibility for their decisions, a most harmful outcome for the scientific community.

In theory, scientists themselves should be very aware of the politics associated with pollution negotiations and to ensure that only agreed knowledge and good science is widely communicated. This is increasingly more difficult in modern society and raises the issues of scientific independence and credibility. Different types of science are being produced for different markets, with scientists coming under growing pressure to deliver certain answers, measure unknown risks, as well as act like lawyers in providing persuasive arguments to conflicting parties.[17] This in turn may have serious impacts on policy itself. Given this situation, two normative questions can now be asked about the role of science. Should scientists do more than advise policy-makers, and if so, can policy proposals made by scientific organisations be trusted any more than those made by other interested parties? In order to answer these questions, a general look at the legitimate place of science in policy-making for pollution control is required.

Any assessment of the role of science in policy is also influenced by philosophical assumptions, in particular in the degree of faith an observer places in the capacity of science as a method of creating objective knowledge and in the rationality of decision-making processes in the real world. In a highly rational model of society, science and human preferences alone might lead directly to 'good' policy, but this view is now seriously disputed even on theoretical grounds.[18]

If it is agreed that political will is created less by preferences based on objective knowledge than by justifiable choices based on such knowledge viewed through cultural filters and interpreted by values, emotions, wishful thinking, fears as well as expectations, then the conclusion drawn from empirical studies that the role of science is ambiguous and often indeterminate should not come as a surprise. This does not mean that the ideas of rationality and rational resource management, or of science as a major factor in the justification of action, should be discarded, but rather that the role of science in resource management and especially pollution control should not be exaggerated. This is particularly true for international regulatory efforts, which may require a supranational legal framework permitting redistributive mechanisms before they can become effective.

The role of science in international regulation

The process of reaching agreement beyond the question of whether or not there is a widespread pollution problem in the first place, but about what is to be done at the intergovernmental level, is not only complicated by the multi-faceted nature of pollution control discussed above. It becomes even more problematical in cases where political systems perceive the cause of pollution in terms of polluters and pollution victims. Cases like this become particularly dependent on an agreed knowledge base. Even reaching agreement on the objective facts of where the pollutants originate and what their effects are on whom in a specific pollution case, may be impossible or, at least, very time consuming.

The attribution of blame is therefore a factor of major importance in international negotiations. Especially in cases of alleged common property or transfrontier pollution by one or more states acting against the interests of others, little progress is likely until the 'facts' are agreed. The discovery of the facts then becomes part of the political process, an observation which fully supports the view put forward elsewhere in this book, namely that science is a dependent variable.[19] In such cases, the reaching scientific agreement in itself requires a prior degree of international commitment to common action and responsibility.

Once this commitment exists, it stands to reason (and empirical work supports this) that the suspected polluter is more interested in learning the 'entire scientific' truth of the allegation than the state which considers itself to be a victim, if only to gain time for adjustment at the domestic policy level. The polluter thus has an interest in gaining more knowledge, but also in delaying its accumulation or at least policy impact. The first country to adopt tougher, expensive measures, on the other hand, possesses a strong additional domestic political interest to act internationally, namely to spread the burden more widely in order to 'equalize' the terms of competition.

Even if there is no allocation of blame, pollution control, because of its domestic political and economic implications, may still become an issue of intergovernmental conflict. Indeed, the observer of international pollution conflicts cannot avoid noting that knowledge based on international cooperative efforts does not always mean the same thing to different political systems, and that conflict often arises because of secondary effects of pollution control. For example, different societies may come up with different solutions to the same problem, which in turn may, or are expected to, produce international problems.

Time in itself may become an international problem, because different institutions and groups learn at different rates. Some may be convinced that they know the 'truth' long before others, others again may resist learning in order to defend existing commitments or habits. This in turn points to the important role played by credible, scientifically respected non-governmental organizations.[20] Persuasion, conveying new information and therefore learning, is (or ought to be) an integral part of international as well as the national policy-making process. A question requiring further exploration is whether the application of bargaining theory encourages such learning.

Therefore, while it is indeed possible to identify, at the international level, a scientific-political complex where administrators and politicians, together with their lawyers and scientific advisors, are engaged in bargaining (and hopefully learning), the factors and forces which shape national positions adopted need also to be investigated, especially if learning is to be made possible and international bargaining to be improved. Looking at such bargaining from within nation states soon reveals that we are dealing with much more than disputes over science and politics (narrowly defined), but with a scientific-political-economic-cultural complex.

The international response to ozone depletion has been interpreted elsewhere in this book[21] as illustrating the success of 'science' in mobilizing international politics effectively, while 'science', being 'moderate', appears to have failed to produce more than moderate policy responses for the North Sea.[22] Are scientific inputs (both objective and political) to each case comparable? How many other, especially economic and cultural, factors or considerations have influenced the negotiations implicitly? I shall come back to these particular cases below.

Here my initial question, about what persuades governments to act against pollution, transforms itself into whether the identification of a scientific-political complex is a paradigm sensitive enough for the understanding of international decisions. I am arguing that pollution control, because it involves the social control of technology and behaviour, is not easily dealt with effectively by international regulation. Too often the lowest common denominator outcomes are produced and successful cases of regulation more readily explained with reference to commercial and domestic political interests rather than a shared environmental concern based on agreed scientific knowledge. Harmonization of environmental standards may instead turn into the harmonization of national expenditure on a specific environmental problem.

International case studies

International responses to pollution problems may be somewhat arbitrarily divided into more successful and less successful ones on the basis of the degree of conflict they have produced and the extent and nature of intergovernmental regulatory agreements eventually achieved. A regime which gives rise to less stringent regulation and much unresolved conflict is considered less successful than one which produces more stringent regulation. This is not, it must be pointed out, an entirely satisfactory way of assessment, but no other criterion of measuring success appears to be available at this stage.

One can then ask to what extent science can be considered responsible for this differentiation, or whether other factors offer a better explanation.

More successful agreements: the cases of ozone depletion by CFCs, oil pollution and nuclear waste dumping — did science play the decisive role?

All the agreements included here deal with a single pollutant or a small number of pollutants transported or discharged together (i.e. a small number of sources and therefore fewer targets of regulation). They were negotiated among a relatively small number of directly interested parties. Scientific evidence for serious damage, i.e. the threat perception created by science among government officials (but not necessarily NGOs) ranged from very serious for ozone, moderate and variable for oil pollution to insignificant for nuclear waste disposal at sea. Science appears to have played a different role in each case.

Chloroflurocarbons

The relative absence of prolonged intergovernmental conflict was the immediate reason for agreement being reached in Vienna and Montreal. This agreement has initiated developments which will lead to the complete phasing out the production and use of a group of pollutants within a specific time period for the entire globe. Only Japan still has serious reservations about giving up some uses, and substitution will be very costly for countries like China which now produce CFCs as refrigerants. Japan has promised, however, to prevent the escape of CFCs into the atmosphere by means of containment and recycling. The European Community (EC) has already used this global agreement to allocate quotas on the production, supply and import of CFCs among its members. What were the factors and conditions which encouraged such a decisive agreement?

Science clearly put before mankind a potential threat (or risk) which was immediate, serious and convincing enough to mobilize the political systems of dominant international actors. They were representing the people likely to be affected most: white-skinned people spending much time outdoors and living in higher latitudes. The effects predicted from ozone depletion (but not yet validated by experiment) were expressed in terms of millions of human cancer deaths as well as widespread damage to crops.

A more persuasive argument for a global political response is hard to imagine, especially as this risk appeared not to be balanced by any military benefit accruing to any one major party. The threat itself was brought to the attention of international society by respected non-governmental actors, the organized scientific community in alliance with some governments and the environmental lobby, also well organized internationally. Scientists were not expressing themselves as individuals, but through influential professional lobbies such as NASA (USA) and the British Antarctic Survey supported by international scientific bodies. This alliance alone may well have carried with it a greater credibility than any pronouncements made by governmental actors acting alone.[23]

Scientific knowledge, even though still largely theoretical and not yet fully explanatory, thus created a powerful (but not unthinkable!) threat perception with immediate and widespread effects on human health and property. This lends itself well to social engineering (or manipulation) through fear and as such to the creation of powerful societal responses.[24]

Non-scientific factors appeared to have played a lesser role, largely because they encouraged rather than discouraged international regulation. Apart from a generally supportive international climate, substitutes for CFCs were becoming available and more stringent regulation thus became a part of the lucrative international game of commercial competition for market shares and new products. CFCs are produced by a handful of large chemical companies not likely to go out of business even if CFC production is banned, and the market for substitutes is likely to be a growing one. Governments could identify wealthy corporate polluters able to pay without significant costs to the public purse. They were also able to rely on environmental activists who were keen to encourage implementation through the market by appeals to both green consumerism and industry's responsibility.

Oil lost at sea

Oil pollution from vessels as well as the dumping of nuclear wastes into the deep ocean came to be strictly regulated internationally during the 1970s.[25] In the former case, rapidly growing scientific information about the effects of oil, a natural product which is broken down by bacterial activity in the sea, actually weakened initial fears about the harmfulness of marine oil spills and releases to marine resources. This enabled somewhat more relaxed negotiations, concentrating on genuine trouble spots and the compensation of injured human parties. For humans, economic damage from oil pollution meant damage to coastal amenities and harm to some offshore resources. Individual sea birds also suffered, but were not threatened by extinction.

Since coastal areas, ports and offshore areas are very much subject to national controls, international concern became concentrated on the regulation of large oil tankers owned or hired by oil companies and already subject to a considerable amount of international legislation. Once the problems of enforcing additional environmental controls on foreign vessels had been resolved, effective regulation through port state enforcement, supplemented by other measures such as coastal state rights supplementing the duties of states of registry, was achieved.

Technological solutions to the problem existed or became quickly available, e.g. in the form of onshore reception facilities, better on-ship storage of waste oils, improved ways of loading oil and ways of washing out tanks. Technological solutions usually do exist, at a price, and industry responds once new markets beckon and government is prepared to share the R & D costs with industry and research organizations.

Once again, and most importantly, the governments concerned about oil pollution were able to identify two corporate polluters able and willing to pay that price. Oil is not a waste product and its value was rising steeply at that time. Both the international oil companies and ship owners much preferred international regulation to a variety of national measures. International bargaining was concerned with timetables, the stringency and zonal variation of standards and the enforcement powers of governments. When finally adopted in 1982, the Law of the Sea Treaty did little more than codify and generalize existing treaty law and practice developed during the 1960s and 1970s.

Both oil pollution control and phasing out of CFCs demonstrate the importance of both the position adopted by industry and its ability to pay the compliance costs without involving governments. This may well have been the decisive condition for effective and speedy international agreement. In contrast, the negotiation of regulatory measures under comprehensive treaties covering large numbers of pollutants and even more sources, as well as involving a growing number of governments, is clearly more troublesome and may become a negotiator's nightmare. A small number of the parties probably assist international negotiations because not only are 'transaction costs' reduced, but also the allocation of compliance costs can become part of the control negotiations.

The above cases demonstrate that the resolution of disputes over liability, the technological consequences of regulation and costs of different control strategies form as much a part of international negotiations as scientific evidence for damage and its causation. The case of nuclear waste dumping demonstrates a rather different set of conditions, however, with science being in fact overruled altogether.

Nuclear waste dumping at sea

Forces other than scientific knowledge, such as power-politics, moral objections and commercial considerations — as well as generalized fears about environmental effects which science could or would not sustain — were at work when the dumping of nuclear waste finally ceased in the early 1980s. Britain was the last country to do so.[26]

During the relevant negotiations under the London Dumping Convention, no convincing scientific case for the harmfulness of low-level dumping was made and the decision to recommend the cessation of this practice had to be justified rather lamely on economic and social grounds. Even without scientific support, international opposition clearly proved to be powerful and insistent. Britain, however, which faced domestic political and economic problems from the use of alternative land disposal options, succeeded in resisting this pressure for almost a decade, and did so on 'scientific grounds'.

Many other governments, however, either disbelieved the scientific evidence of 'harmlessness' or allowed other factors to overrule this, such as generalized anti-nuclear or environmental pressures. A bias by the scientific community advising governments in favour of the cheapest disposal option (at least for reactors along the coast), was widely and probably correctly assumed.

Less successful agreements: acid rain and marine pollution from land-based sources — did science fail?

Scientific predictions about harmful, long-term effects arising from the chronic pollution of resources which are economically exploited in different ways by a large number of parties, are not only notoriously difficult and expensive to make. They also invite cost-benefit calculations biased towards current practices, as well as official protection of corporate interests. The effects tend to be widely dispersed in time and space, the pollution sources numerous and firmly under national jurisdiction. Both acid rain and the North Sea pollution are examples of this most complex case. Effective international agreement here must be considered a genuine achievement demonstrating human capacity to learn and to act, in the end, responsibly.

Acid rain

Research on acid rain policy in Europe and North America shows that meaningful international agreements involving increasingly stricter standards and genuine national abatement efforts, proved to be very difficult indeed. Negotiations began in the early 1970s but were not concluded, even within the EC, until mid-1988 and thus took approximately a decade longer than international agreements for the control of vessel-source pollution in the oceans. This happened in spite of the scientific basis for air pollution control probably having developed at an earlier date and with evidence of real problems being considerably larger. If science had been the decisive factor, then global air pollution issues should have been resolved first.

Reaching international agreement about air pollution required long time-spans so that domestic policies, especially energy policies, could be adjusted to take new threat perceptions and technological developments into account. Domestic policy implications were clearly much larger than for vessel related marine issues. Countries with the largest overall abatement costs actively resisted international policy developments in the meantime and may thereby have initiated a process for widely traded goods such as cars, which achieves the harmonization of environmental abatement costs rather than environmental quality or standards.

Many motives other than dedication to environmental protection encouraged governments either to adopt or to resist more stringent control measures. The Government of the Federal Republic of Germany, for example, began taking 'acid rain' very seriously once forest damage had received much publicity and did so in spite of considerable scientific uncertainty. It was in fact also engaged in protecting and expanding not only the jurisdictional role in pollution control of central government *vis-à-vis* the provinces (Lander).[27] Political parties were engaged in bitter battles for electoral support at both the Lander and federal levels. In addition, some federal ministries and some regional governments also used the acid rain issue to safeguard cherished (but by then threatened) commitments to and investments in nuclear power. 'Southern' (nuclear) Lander saw themselves as victims of 'Northern' coal burning ones.

In West Germany many parties were therefore quickly persuaded by the SO_2 theory of forest decline. Once the clean up or closure of coal-fired power stations had been decided, at enormous cost, Bonn very quickly became active internationally in support of much tougher controls. Instead of a 30 per cent reduction of national emissions, it demanded 60 per cent.

In order to fend off this potentially more threatening international onslaught from within the European Community, Britain looked to its scientists for help, and did with considerable success. Decisions were delayed until the 'evidence' was available. And in the end and according to official statements, it was science which persuaded the British Cabinet that a nationalized industry (the CEGB, but to be privatized), was indeed partially responsible for acid rain damage in Scandinavia. The same science could have been available to the British government much earlier, but perhaps from different, less trusted sources. Evidence that there is more damage at home than initially suspected is now gradually accumulating.[28]

While many German power stations were old and their replacement by larger units desired by federal government, the reverse was true in Britain with its large and relatively new (if dirty) plants. German utilities, largely in private hands and very wealthy, could be made to pay without serious effects on the public purse or other public policies. Again, the reverse was true in Britain.[29] Here government was not only devoted to deregulation, but deeply concerned with reducing public expenditure. Only Britain also possessed the political stability to pursue anti-environmental priorities without needing the electoral support of the environmental lobby.

Policy convergence between environmental regulation and other objectives encouraged German responses after an initial period of resistance dominated by the supporters of German coal mining. For Britain the process of adjustment to international demands over 'acid rain' was both more costly and politically difficult. The impact of proposed international environmental regulations on the existing policy network was such that these were opposed with considerable determination and success.

The grounds on which a government may defend itself against international demands may vary, but reference to insufficient scientific evidence is clearly attractive and useful, as well as offering an eventual answer. Scientific knowledge is often unclear or indefinite enough to justify delay for those who are willing to accept higher risks or need time for adjustment. Decisions may be delayed by other processes as well, e.g. the industries affected may first have to battle with each over the allocation of compliance costs and thus the chosen control technology. For example, in the control of vehicle emissions oil companies, the producers of lead additives for petrol and car manufacturers all share compliance costs rather differently among themselves depending on the technological solution (lean-burn engines, add-on catalytic converters or both) that is adopted.

Awareness of the costs of pollution abatement to industry both encouraged and directed scientific research in both countries, but for some time, the objective of this research differed. Governments cannot, however, determine the outcome of scientific research based on international cooperation and thus, when using this strategy, leave themselves open to persuasion and pressure. This would appear to be happening to Britain in the acid rain case.

North Sea pollution

In this case environmental protection might be thought to involve little more than the consideration of economic self-interest because the objective is to prevent the depletion of living resources and the lowering of environmental quality for specific uses. In the case of North Sea pollution control arguments about the balance of costs and benefits of stricter regulation have tended to dominate the debate, certainly in Great Britain. In addition, there is continuing uncertainty about the 'real' causes of environmental deterioration, especially about the role played by pollution in reducing fish stocks and the spread of certain diseases in marine animals.

In Britain the use of the North Sea for the disposal of a whole range of wastes has long been considered the 'best practicable' or even 'environmental option'. This has created disagreement with other nations also using this marginal and highly exploited sea, but with different waste management systems and threat perceptions. Science was to be the judge but has so far been unable to come up with clear answers favouring either side.

This failure of the preventive approach may be explained by the fact that depletion or degradation of the same resource (e.g. fish stocks, water quality, forests) may be of different value to different actors, and the level of what is acceptable quality very much a consequence of resource use, which may differ (e.g. tourism versus waste disposal). International outcomes were therefore necessarily based on bargaining,[30] with a tendency for 'lowest common denominator' solutions. Because the costs and benefits are fairly unequally distributed in cases of different waste management regimes, a clear division between polluters and pollution victims tended to emerge at the conference table, which discourages agreement. If the cause even of the agreed damage is genuinely disputed or uncertain (pollution or overfishing, man-made depletion versus changes due to natural cycles), progress will be slowed down further.

In such situations, science tends to become a tool of politics rather than being an instrument of rational intergovernmental decision-making. This rather ambiguous role of science appears to be typical of regional seas agreements set up to deal with land-based sources, as well as international regulatory attempts for the prevention of 'upstream-downstream' transfrontier pollution. Progress in such cases is very much dependent on an agreed science base, even though this will not be sufficient for the achievement of controls stricter than those acceptable to the 'dirtiest' member. More research to improve the common knowledge base would clearly be the best strategy for common action. Nations have a tendency to blame foreigners before looking at their own responsibility, and only more objective knowledge gathered cooperatively can help to dispel any unfounded allegations.

It is therefore concluded that in less successful international regimes science has tended to act as a political tool in the bargaining process over the distribution of blame and thus compliance costs. Economic strategies to resolve such disputes exist of course, but there is little evidence that they have been used so far even by environmentally aware nations.[31]

However, Britain's resistance to international demands for more stringent air and North Sea pollution control measures was not overcome at the global level. It took place within the much tougher bargaining and legislative framework of the EC. A closer look at both this regime and British domestic policy developments is required for the full understanding of both cases.

Harmonized regulation within the European Community

Once a state joins a supranational body like the EC, a regime change takes place and the political and legal pressures for harmonized regulation may come to dominate over national preferences. This has allowed Britain and Germany, as representatives of divergent positions in both cases here discussed, to face each other across the conference table and become involved in serious bargaining over common emission standards, national percentage reductions (or bubbles) and common environmental quality as well as product norms. Within the EC, environmental regulation may now proceed taking into account technological, social, as well as commercial considerations.

In more voluntary regimes, it is more difficult to see changes taking place towards more preventive approaches unless major polluters give up their demands for 'reasonable' scientific certainty before accepting the political and economic costs of compliance. This is but one aspect of two much larger moral issues. How much should a particular society (or mankind) be prepared to pay now for risks engendered, or likely to engendered, in the future? To what an extent, if at all, should richer nations impose extra costs on the poor in the 'common interest'?

British policy developments

Until the late 1970s the British policy response to international environmental pressures emanating from the EC was usually defensive, its aim being less to frustrate harmonization than to persuade the Continentals of the value of the rather piecemeal, informal and decentralized, but well-tried British way of pollution control. But Britain did not make its case well and entered the Community rather too late to influence the foundations of a considerably more legalistic European policy approach to environmental protection. A phase of more active resistance followed and was aimed primarily at vetoing or at least delaying Community decisions considered to be against British interests. This phase may have come to an end in 1988.

The Conservative Government, in power since 1979, showed little interest in environmental protection and disapproved of stricter or more wide ranging regulatory measures on both economic and ideological grounds, justifying this with reference to free market philosophy, individual responsibility and the desirability of reduced state involvement in the management of both economic and social life. None of these justifications could be readily used at the international level. Economic short-termism and insufficient attention to investments into the national infrastructure are among the main criticisms levelled at this government. Taken together, neither the objectives nor the shortcomings of Tory rule have encouraged environmental protection as an active realm of public policy.

When confronted with foreign demands for costly policy changes, a defence based on the philosophy that scientific evidence of harm should proceed regulation was adopted.[32] This response most probably reflects both the important role played by scientific civil service and environmental monitoring in the control regime developed in Britain since the nineteenth century,[33] and the British legal principle that the man before a court must be assumed to be innocent until proven guilty.

Yet the demand for scientific certainty prior to the adoption of abatement measures is not, historically speaking, a part of the domestic British pollution control regime, which since the mid-nineteenth century had responded fairly well to public outcries and persuaded industry to abate pollution on the basis that specific emissions were noxious or simply a nuisance, provided that technological change made this possible. Official direction of such change did not, however, form part of this tradition. Rather different regulatory regimes evolved for air, water and land pollution, each granting considerable discretionary powers to local or regional public bodies, as well as to a number of government ministries. The courts did not play a significant role in the interpretation of legislation and its enforcement; these powers remained very much an administrative responsibility. These powers were being undermined by international developments.

During the 1980s the British pollution control regime came under growing and unsettling attack not only from international treaty law and New Right ideology, but also from the legal requirements of the EC.[34] In 1988 a rhetorical commitment to environmental values took place at the highest level of government, but it is as yet too early to judge how effective this will be in actually producing more official investment and regulation.

The recent reorganization of the institutions charged with implementing and enforcing government policy for industrial pollution control and the funding of pollution research would appear to have been motivated primarily by the desire to cut public expenditure and centralize decision-making powers, both to enable the ready implementation of European directives and to weaken local government. The expected privatization of water authorities and electric utilities may pay the way for increasing investments into this industry. Privatization would allow environmental regulations to come into effect at little cost to government, but possibly with (further) considerable regressive effects on the distribution income.

While many British scientists have long argued for a less relaxed attitude to pollution problems, as public servants or recipients of government funding handed out by poorly endowed Research Councils, they alone could not affect the political agenda. The scientific input into intergovernmental bodies has therefore tended to represent not the conclusions of 'independent' scientists, but rather an assessment of the facts produced during a first and highly informal internal negotiating process in which an overworked scientific civil service probably played an important role.

The adjustment to external demands which have been made, such as promises relating to the reduction of pollutant inputs into the North Sea and fluegas desulphurization, have followed domestic political battles which were lost by the forces supporting such demands. Instead, the degree of adjustment which did, in the end, take place, was pressed upon Ministers by external pressures related to intergovernmental negotiations. This meant that the victorious Treasury would take its preferences and arguments to Brussels where they usually came in conflict with those of several (but rarely all) other member countries. These conflicts were resolved by bargaining, after much delay and many concessions, in some cases because of the prospect of legal action by the EC.

Because the UK had adopted the strategy of defending its own preferences at the international level with reference to scientific uncertainty, international progress became linked to this factor. However, the primary causes for intergovernmental disputes over North Sea pollution and acid rain had far less to do with science than with the defence of other national priorities and regulatory traditions under challenge and also the wish to reduce compliance costs. These were invariably perceived by government as a burden on industry rather than an investment in technological change.

Several environmental issues have recently attracted the attention, imagination even, of the British Government and produced several surprising if very general policy statements in support of environmental policy objectives.[35] The motives for this apparent conversion are still being debated several months after Margaret Thatcher's famous 'green' speech to the Royal Society on 26 September 1988. Environmentalists rather cynically attributed this change in attitude to the wish of the current political leadership both to adjust to the 'greening' conservative voter and to fend off the challenge of other parties who have began to attack several Conservative policies on environmental grounds. Alliance building between the green lobby and sections of government and industry is now beginning in the United Kingdom, and environmental policy is indeed becoming less predictable and more fluid.

In particular, the British government is now taking a considerable interest in the ozone problem. From reading British official reports, one gains the impression that British scientists discovered the ozone problem and thus did a service to Britain and the world. Two British scientists, James Lockwood and Joe Farman, were indeed closely involved in the discovery of the 'hole'. Lockwood started the ball rolling in 1971/2 when he discovered ozone depletion, because he used CFCs as tracer gases, but asserted that there was no need to worry about depletion. This sparked off American investigations challenging this claim, and matters progressed from there as described. The House of Lords in early 1988 called for the tightening of the Montreal Protocol and the Foreign Office agreed.

Britain was never 'blamed' for the ozone hole, but found itself in the same boat as other nations: that of innocent polluter and likely victim. It thus did not face the issue from a 'defensive' position as happened for North Sea pollution and acid rain. Other non-scientific factors also encouraged a positive response. Only one British Company is involved (ICI), and as a large multinational concern is not likely to be bankrupted by the phasing out of a small part of its production. (The British car industry's reaction to the most stringent proposed emission values was very different.) In fact, ICI is deeply involved in the commercial competition for substitutes. The well known and now widely respected pressure group Friends of the Earth, not government institutions, have already persuaded most major retail chains to abandon products and uses involving CFCs. A greener image for government and regulation by 'market forces' is being created without any drain on the public purse and without the threat of legal compulsion, as is the British preference. Without these 'non-scientific' factors, objective knowledge is not likely to have succeeded in eliciting the mentioned positive response from the British Government at the international level.

Marine pollution presents a less optimistic picture and has only very recently appeared on the present Government's horizon of awareness — thanks to dead seals and the *Karin B*. In the last decade or so, marine pollution control in particular had conflicted with other official commitments and the study of North Sea pollution remains the task of underfunded scientists employed less to protect the sea than to defend existing government policy. It is too early to say whether real change is under way, although the promises made at the North Sea Conference in 1987 would suggest this to be the case, but largely because of pressure arising from EC legislation which expresses itself directly along established channels between Whitehall and Brussels, and via meetings of the parties to the Paris Conventions, of which the European Commission is an increasingly active member.

Conclusions

The dominance of politics over science in the regulation of pollution arises from the nature of pollution as a side-effect of technology and economic growth which is no longer unacceptable, and the nature of the policy-making process itself. Acceptability can only be defined on the basis of societal values and perceptions, and this is a profoundly political task. The assessment and evaluation of pollution must be based on a wide range of evidence not all of which needs or is subject to scientific confirmation. Evaluation includes an explicit or implicit analysis of both the economic and political control costs.

The role of science in pollution control, as distinct from the study of pollution, is best considered to be neutral. It cannot be assumed that science is on the side of environmentalists or even internationalists. Its findings are available to all interests, and this is part of its problem and strength. However, government should ensure that this availability is ensured and encouraged, and national differences in this realm are most probably at the very centre of some major international conflicts about environmental policy. The responsibility of the media is also very important and there is a widespread need for institutions and individuals which can mediate between the public and the scientists, between scientists and between scientists and the policy-makers. The area also requires further investigation.

The demand is sometimes heard that scientists should present their results in a more 'certain' and decisive manner, that they should participate fully in political battles. In my view, this would be unwise because such a strategy would harm the credibility of science, and thus its intrinsic power to encourage cooperation even among political opponents. Rather, the range of factors upon which demands for more pollution control can legitimately be based should be broadened and scientists be asked for clear statements about what is not known and might be never known. In this way, economic and social considerations, as well as morality and even intuition, could make a more explicit contribution to policy.

Notes

1. Carroll, John E. (ed.), 1988, *International Environmental Diplomacy*, Cambridge University Press, Cambridge.

2. For a somewhat different view, see Wettestad, Jørgen, 1989, 'Uncertain Science and Matching Policies', in this volume.

3. Young, Oran, 1989, 'Science and Social Institutions: Lessons for International Resource Regimes', in this volume.

4. GESAMP, the scientific experts advising UN bodies on marine pollution, set up a study group on the economic aspects of marine pollution (one group among 29) only in 1988.

5. Boehmer-Christiansen, Sonja A., 'Black Mist and Acid Rain: Science as Fig Leaf of Policy' in *The Political Quarterly*, vol. 59, no. 2, April-June 1988, pp. 145-60. See also note 23 below.

6. Sagoff, Mark, 1988, *The Economy of the Earth: Cambridge Studies in Philosophy and Public Policy*, Cambridge University Press, Cambridge. This book analyses the fundamental problems associated with a purely economic approach to resource management and is recommended for its

powerful insights into environmental policy issues.

7. See also Miles, Edward, 1989, 'Scientific and Technological Knowledge and International Cooperation in Resource Management', in this volume, pp. 000.

8. Gough, Michael, 1987, 'Environmental Epidemology: Separating Politics and Science' in *Issues in Science and Technology*, Summer, pp. 21-31. See also Schmandt, Jurgen, 1984, 'Regulation and Science' in *Science, Technology and Human Values*, vol. 9, issue 1, Winter. These authors stress the need for 'experimental rule-making' in policies strongly related to science and technology. This raises the question as to what extent international regulation can be based on such advice.

9. Nicholson, Max, 1970, *The Environmental Revolution*, Houghton and Stoughton, London.

10. For a discussion of the effects of the increased public attention towards environmental issues see Andresen, Steinar, 1989, 'Increased Public Attention: Communication and Polarization', in this volume.

11. Pepper, David, 1984, *The Roots of Modern Environmentalism*, Croom Helm, London.

12. Roberts, Marc J. et al., 'Mapping Scientific Disputes that Affect Public Policymaking' in *Science, Technology and Human Values*, vol. 9, issue 1, Winter 1984, pp. 112-21. See also Young, Oran, 1989, in this volume, pp. 000.

13. For a discussion of these issues as regards the polar regions, see Østreng, Willy, 1989, 'Polar Science and Politics: Close Twins or Opposite Poles in International Cooperation?', in this volume.

14. See also Andresen, Steinar, 1989, in this volume.

15. One example here is the scientific dispute about the validity which can be attached to national percentage contributions to sulphur depositions in Northern and Central Europe. These contributions are based on atmospheric and chemical models with high degrees of uncertainty. As M. Benaris stated at a discussion of a paper by A. Eliassen at the Conference on Air Pollution in Europe, Stockholm, 26-30 September 1988, ' . . . by cutting down all UK emissions to zero, dry and wet deposition in Norway would decrease by 10 per cent, perhaps, if that is a measurable quantity'. Such model predictions would have to be empirically confirmed before they could provide a firm scientific basis for the calculation of national reduction targets.

16. For a somewhat different view see Fløistad, Brit, 1989, 'Scientific Knowledge in the Management of Fish and Whales', in this volume.

17. Beck, Ulrich, 1986, *Risikogesellschaft auf dem Weg in eine andere Moderne*, SuhrKamp, Frankfurt am Main.

18. Collingridge, David, 1984, *Critical Decision Making*, Frances Pinter,

London.

19. Miles, Edward, 1989, in this volume.

20. For a discussion on this see also Fløistad, Brit, 1989, in this volume.

21. Bakken, Per, 1989, 'Science and Politics in the Protection of the Ozone Layer', in this volume.

22. Wettestad, Jørgen, 1989, in this volume, pp. 000.

23. Douglas, Mary, 1986, *Risk Acceptability According to the Social Sciences*, Routledge and Kegan Paul, London.

24. Luhmann, Niklas, 1986, *Oekologische Kommunikation: Kann die moderne Gesellschaft sich auf okologische Gefaehrdung einstellen?*, Westdeutscher Verlag, Opladen.

25. Boehmer-Christiansen, Sonja A., 1981, 'Limits to the International Control of Marine Pollution', unpublished D. Phil. thesis, University of Sussex.

26. Boehmer-Christiansen Sonja A., 1986, 'An End to Radioactive Waste Disposal at Sea?' in *Marine Policy*, vol. 10, no. 2, pp.119-31.

27. Boehmer-Christiansen, Sonja A. and Skea, Jim F., 1989, *Acid Politics: An Anglo-German Comparison*, to be published in 1989/90. For the German case only see note 28 below.

28. UK Terrestrial Review Group, 1988, *The Effects of Acid Deposition on the Terrestrial Environment in the United Kingdom,* first report, HMSO, London.

29. Boehmer-Christiansen, Sonia A., 1989, *The Politics of Environment and Energy in FR Germany: Forests versus Fossil Fuels*, SPRU occasional paper no. 28, University of Sussex.

30. Sætevik, Sunneva, 1988, *Environmental Cooperation Between the North Sea States*, Belhaven Press (Pinter Publishers), London.

31. Prittwitz, Volker, 1984, *Umweltaussenpolitik, Frankfurt am Main*, Campus. The only exception I know of concerns pollution control agreements between the two German states.

32. Macrory, Richard, 1986, *Environmental Policy in Britain: Reaffirmation or Reform,* IIUG discussion paper 84-6, Wissenschaftzentrum Berlin, Berlin.

33. Vogel, David, 1986, *National Styles of Regulation: Environmental Policy in Great Britain and the United States*, Cornell University Press, London.

34. Haigh, Nigel, 1984, *EEC Environmental Policy and Britain*, Environmental Data Services, London.

35. *Environmental Data Services,* Report 164, pp. 27-8, September 1988.

9

Uncertain science and matching policies: Science, politics and the organization of North Sea environmental cooperation[1]

Jørgen Wettestad

Unlike many other areas of public policy, scientific research is an integral part, a prerequisite even, of environmental policy. Without science, environmental policy would be dependent on the intuitively obvious.[2]

Introduction

In a sense, it is sufficient to whisper *chrysochromulina polylepsis* to justify the relevance of studying the role of scientific knowledge in the North Sea environmental cooperation — and 'scientific knowledge' (or simply 'science') is for the purpose of this paper somewhat narrowly defined as 'knowledge on inputs, concentrations and effects of contaminating substances in the marine environment'.[3] There are also other more general empirical and theoretical reasons for trying to understand what is really going on in this field. As indicated in the quotation above, science is obviously an important factor in environmental political decision-making. On the other hand, it is just as obvious that the relationship between these factors is not uncomplicated: 'Between the scientific study of pollution and its control lies . . . the difficult societal process of defining unacceptable or intolerable pollution levels and risks'.[4]

Thus the relationship between scientific results and related political measures will seldom be straightforward and direct; more or less wide 'gaps' between these factors may arise, especially at the international level. Hence, in an article bearing the expressive title 'Bridging the Gap Between Environmental Science and Policy-Making', Viktor Sebek maintains that 'a wide gap currently exists between scientific assessment of environmental problems . . . and their legal and administrative regulation and enforcement'.[5] However, more empirically it is not only the chrysochromulina incident that indicates that 'there is something rotten in the state of the North Sea' (at least as to the knowledge of the state of affairs). The final declaration from the 'successful' Second International Conference on the North Sea (arranged in London in November 1987) contains a call for 'the enhancement of scientific knowledge and understanding'; and in this connection, a new scientific 'North Sea Task Force' is proposed. Apparently the existing scientific-political complex is not functioning well enough; but what is wrong — and why? To what extent is there actually a gap between science and political decision-making, as indicated by Sebek? These are some of the main questions I set out to discuss in this article.

By 'scientific-political complex' here I mean more specifically the scientific and political bodies connected to the Paris Convention work (on the regulation of pollution from land-based sources) and to its more all encompassing 'offspring', the North Sea Conferences.

The relationship between science and political decision-making is complex and not particularly transparent. In the next section I discuss this relationship more thoroughly and suggest an analytical framework and some more specific questions as points of departure for the ensuing discussion.

Science and international environmental politics: a framework for analysis

As it is primarily the political fate of the scientific message that is in focus in this article, I find it appropriate to use some basic elements from general communication theory as a framework for structuring the discussion. Thus, I propose to distinguish between characteristics connected to the sender of the scientific message, i.e. the scientific community; characteristics connected to the scientific message itself; and characteristics connected to the receiver of the scientific message, i.e. the decision-makers.

Characteristics connected to the 'scientific community'

First : what kind of scientific knowledge is most relevant in connection with marine pollution issues? Following the Quality Status Report produced in connection with the Second North Sea Conference, we may distinguish broadly between (a) physical oceanography, which is basically information on sea circulation and ocean currents; (b) knowledge on concentrations of inorganic and organic contaminants, which is the main domain of chemists; and (c) knowledge on ecological effects of substances (on benthos, fish stocks etc.), which is the main domain of biologists.

When considering characteristics connected to this community, it has generally been maintained that lack of scientific credibility may weaken the persuasiveness of a given message. Studies on the International Whaling Commission have indicated that the impact of the advice of the 'official' Scientific Committee may have been weakened due to legitimacy problems: 'Some of the non-whaling nations, i.e. those with no whaling interests in Antarctic waters, had expressed dissatisfaction with the Scientific Committee; it was claimed that other considerations than purely scientific ones were taken into account . . . The point to be made is that the conflict of roles of some scientists were probably difficult, and it may have contributed to reducing the general legitimacy of the Scientific Committee.'[6] Likewise, according to Sebek's article on the international regulation of marine pollution, ' . . . problems may arise in that scientists consulted are generally civil servants, who inevitably need to take economic and political considerations into account'.[7] Thus, as Sebek indicates, it is not uncomplicated to distinguish the 'pure scientific' component in connection with these issues. However, the degree of seeking to integrate more traditionally independent scientific advice (for instance from university researchers) probably varies from country to country, partly due to basic administrative differences.

Another possible role confusion, which may weaken the legitimacy of science, has also been indicated; although both 'scientific counselling' (emphasizing proven relationships) and 'whistle-blowing' (emphasizing possible relationships and effects) are legitimate scientific roles, it has been maintained that it is important to distinguish clearly between them.[8]

Characteristics connected to the scientific message

I think it is fruitful here to distinguish analytically between 'form' and 'content' of the message, although these aspects are obviously interrelated. With regard to form, we may reasonably assume that a quantified recommendation will leave more imprint on policy than will a more qualitative assessment. However, there are obviously differences between types of policy measures with regard to the possibility of formulating quantitative recommendations. For instance, it is probably easier for marine scientists to come up with a quantitative recommendation on mesh size or TAC in fishery management than it is for scientists to recommend specific emission limits concerning toxic substances (except perhaps if the question is whether to allow emissions or not). This is mainly due to differences in types of issue, with the pollution issue in a sense being the more 'complex' one.[9] This in turn points to probable differences between the role of science in different international resource management settings.

With regard to content, we may reasonably assume that an 'alarmist' description of the state of the ecosystem is more likely to give rise to new and stricter policy measures than is a rather moderate description, although this relationship is not uncomplicated and direct.[10] The degree of uncertainty connected to an alarmist message is probably also important. It has been maintained that uncertainty may be the most apt characteristic of science where the management of marine resources is concerned.[11] However, we should note that gaining knowledge in this field *is a* complex task : 'Where the critical thresholds lie cannot be said, because of the complexity of the marine ecosystem. Tests can only reflect a very small, and not necessarily representative part of the occurrences in the marine ecosystem. Observations in the field, on the other hand, provide clear results only in the event of very drastic phenomena. For these reasons, forecasts of risk are extremely uncertain.'[12] Nevertheless, it must also be emphasized that uncertainty *can* be reduced — through national priority given to ocean research, international standardization of research methods, etc. As noted by Moltke: 'Surprisingly, there are even distinct national characteristics to research in the natural sciences, requiring elaborate structures to ensure comparability.'[13] However, no matter what the cause is, such uncertainty may have detrimental political effects: ' . . . if uncertainty is significant, it cannot be proven who is right or wrong; each player can pick and choose from the (often existing) diverging economic analyses'.[14] We may assume that scientific disagreement has similar negative effects on the influence of science.

However, we should also note that research for policy-making is a peculiar form: 'In addition to traditional research criteria, there is the need to present results in a manner that is comprehensible to the layman and to accept the fact that the ultimate judgment on the research and its uses lies not with the academic community but with policy makers.'[15] In other words, reducing uncertainty and disagreement is of little use if the (improved) message is not conveyed to policy-makers in a comprehensive and 'understandable' manner.

Characteristics connected to the political decision-makers

It has been maintained that relationships among decision-makers and the 'mood' of the decision-making process may influence the use of scientific information. Miles (1987) stresses the negative influence of political polarization (' . . . polarization is to be avoided like the plague').[16] Moreover, we should note that no matter how legitimate, certain or understandable the scientific message is, decision-makers may none the less choose to ignore it. They may, for instance, find its economic implications unacceptable, or fear implications for negotiations in other issue areas. Thus, it has been maintained that

' . . . it is rare indeed for research to lead directly to policy conclusions. Even when research results are clear and unambiguous, the policies that evolve must reflect a weighting of many conflicting priorities, and this weighting can turn out very differently in different societies.'[17] And the reverse: policy-makers may seemingly 'accept' the message, but for reasons quite unconnected to science.[18] This further underlines the proposition that the relationship between science and politics is complex, and also indicates the importance of examining other factors in the process than the scientific ones.

The organizational context

However, the importance of the organization of this communication process has to be acknowledged: 'A major general interest of political science is the study of how structures and procedures affect actor behaviour, interaction processes and decision outputs'.[19] Science and politics are formed and interact in organizational contexts which are both changing and changeable. Thus, Underdal further maintains: 'To the extent that we understand how institutional variables affect process and outcome, we have what might be called a piece of "political technology" that can, in principle, be applied to prevent negotiation failure . . . '[20]

In the case of international whaling, the legitimacy of science was seemingly enhanced when a small group of scientists from countries (and the FAO) not involved in whaling. In international fisheries management, the purpose of the creation of so-called 'dialogue meetings' between the scientific ICES organization and the nation-states seems to have been to enhance and nuance decision-makers' understanding of the scientific advice given.[21]

Several authors have pointed to the possible fruitfulness of an institutional setting which separates scientific and distributional aspects.[22] In his study on the politics of international fisheries management, Underdal finds that conflict over allocations has tended to produce 'collective inefficiency', expressed in catch quotas above the levels initially agreed upon. He proposes an alternative institutional set-up — with separate 'Scientific' and 'Management' Committees — which he argues will have several advantages: 'First, and most important, it substantially reduces the risk that distributive conflict will block effective conservation measures. It does so not by making distributive decisions on efficiency premises, but by separating as far as possible decisions on conservation from decisions on allocation.'[23]

To cite Miles: 'The organizational design criterion to be derived from this is that, when looked at from the scientific perspective, the preferred situation is when the research being conducted is of sufficient concern for governments to warrant continued support but where decision processes are deliberately designed to provide a buffer between the production of research results and their utilization for regulation and, especially, the distribution of benefits and/or apportionment of costs.'[24]

Thus, in sum, we have indicated several factors likely to influence the extent to which scientific results leave an imprint on international regulatory measures. These include scientific credibility or legitimacy; the form and content of the scientific message; the mood of the policy-making process; the organization of the communication process. However, we have not as yet explicitly discussed the basic theoretical 'rationale' for the influence of science on regulatory measures.

The 'ideal' relationship between science and politics: integrated marine policy

What is the ideal relationship between science and politics that we are really seeking in this connection? As indicated earlier, it is not scientific environmental policy. Such policy must obviously consider and contain other elements as well. However, if it is not scientific environmental policy that we are seeking, then I feel it must be something like 'integrated "rational" marine policy'. Arild Underdal has indicated three basic requirements of an 'integrated marine policy': comprehensiveness, aggregation and consistency.[25] Especially interesting in this connection is the comprehensiveness/scope dimension where Underdal defines ideal scope as one where ' . . . all significant consequences and implications of policy decisions are recognized as premises in making of those decisions. In other words, the scope of policy premises should equal the scope of policy consequences', (Underdal 1980 p.162). My interpretation of Underdal is that an integrated policy presupposes fairly distinct and unambiguous components, where the ecological component identifies the main possible ecological relationships and consequences rather clearly, the economic component identifies possible economic consequences — and so on. If such possible consequences are not distinctly identified, then — to use Sebek's formulation — policy-makers will not be in a position to establish rational priorities for legislative action. In other words, what is especially important to assess in this connection is the 'adequacy' and 'usability' of science — the extent to which the state of knowledge on inputs, concentrations and effects of contaminating inputs makes possible a rational, integrated marine policy in the North Sea with regard to ecological considerations.

Some main questions

Let us now briefly recapitulate and restate the questions we seek to answer in this article. First, it is possible to maintain that 'science is an integral part of environmental policy'. As explicitly stated in the Paris Convention text: 'In implementing this undertaking, the Contracting Parties shall take account of — the nature and quantities of the pollutants consideration; — the level of existing pollution; — the quality and absorptive capacity of the receiving waters of the maritime area . . . ' (from Article 6). Thus, the first question to answer must be: what role has changing scientific evidence played in the evolution of North Sea environmental cooperation? Is it possible to trace 'gaps' between the dominant scientific messages of the time and the corresponding political responses to these messages (cf. Sebek) — somewhat parallel to the witnessed gaps between scientific recommendations and political regulations in international fishery management?

However, science is not seen as the only important factor in environmental policy-making. Thus, in a social scientific context, identifying such gaps is only moderately interesting in itself. The next question must therefore be: has science provided an 'optimal' contribution to policy-making? This has something to do with the legitimacy, adequacy and usability of science, but it also clearly has an organizational aspect to it. Moreover, if science has not been making an optimal contribution, why not?

Finally, organizational insights have been characterized as pieces of 'political technology'. As mentioned in the introduction, a scientific North Sea Task Force has been proposed and is currently in the process of being established. Thus, organizational changes in the relationship between science and politics within the North Sea context are under discussion. To what extent are initiatives like the Task Force an adequate response to the problems identified in this report? Are other organizational changes necessary also?

The next sections

In order to be able to assess the functioning of a system/'complex', we have to know more specifically the main features and development of this system. Thus, in the next section, the main scientific and political bodies connected to the Paris Convention work and the North Sea Conferences will be identified and described. Section four will focus on the evolution of this system, 'from Parcom to the London Conference'. These sections will form the background for the analysis and discussion of five 'theses' on 'science, politics and the organization of North Sea environmental cooperation'. A brief concluding section will finish the article.

The scientific-political complex in the North Sea: an Introductory Description

Starting at the scientific end of the institutional continuum, the basic ingredient in marine scientific research in the North Sea is of course the various national laboratories and research institutes. However, since fish migrate and ocean currents disperse pollutants over wide areas, international scientific collaboration is an absolute necessity. Such collaboration takes place within several, partly interconnected, institutional settings.

The International Council for the Exploration of the Sea (ICES) is in many ways a natural point of departure in this connection, as it is the oldest intergovernmental organization concerned with marine and fishery sciences (established in 1902). The Council has 18 member countries on both sides of the Atlantic. It is involved with various aspects of oceanographic and marine biological research. Research concerning marine pollution began in the mid-1960s and is thus a comparatively new aspect of ICES' activity. Efforts have been made to determine the geographical distribution of various contaminants of the marine environment in living organisms, sea water and sediments. Contaminants investigated include various trace metals such as mercury, cadmium, lead, copper and zinc, and synthetic organic chemicals such as PCBs and DDT and other pesticides, and petroleum hydrocarbons.[26]

With regard to the external advisory function, the main body within the ICES structure is the Advisory Committee on Marine Pollution (ACMP), established at an ICES Statutory Meeting in 1972. ACMP has the task of formulating scientific advice on marine pollution and its effects on living resources to the Member Governments and to Regulatory Commissions. The Committee considers, among other things, the results of work carried out in relevant ICES working groups (these groups also report to their respective Standing Committees during the annual Statutory Meetings). At its 1988 meeting, the ACMP reviewed the most recent reports of 17 such working groups.[27] The ACMP is composed of ' . . . a number of scientists acting — when they work as Committee members — in their personal capacity as scientists, responsible only to the Council . . . The members do not act as national representatives.'[28] The composition of the Committee is split between ex-officio members (sub-committee chairmen) and co-opted members (specific scientists chosen in order for the ACMP to be able to cover different aspects of pollution problems).[29] In recent years, there have been three to four ex-officio members and nine to twelve co-opted members.

The corresponding fishery advice committee (ACFM) is differently composed, consisting solely of nationally nominated members. A proposition to constitute the ACMP along the same lines as the ACFM is currently being discussed within the ICES organization.

When the Oslo Commission, which deals with regulation of dumping, and the Paris Commission were established in the early 1970s, they set up their own scientific/technical programmes and institutional structures. First, a Joint Monitoring Group/Program (JMG/JMP) was established as the main body which should provide a basis for the assessment of ' . . . the existing level of marine pollution' and ' . . . the effectiveness of measures for the reduction of marine pollution taken under the terms of the present Convention' (from Article 11 in the Paris

Convention). Several principles for the programme were formulated: it was to be based on the national programmes of the Contracting Parties; in order to ensure that the results obtained were comparable, the various laboratories responsible for analysis should calibrate their methods, usually under the auspices of an ICES intercalibration exercise; methods to achieve these aims were to be established.[30] The programme covers 60 areas, chosen by the participating states themselves. Two main marine compartments are focused on in the programme: marine organisms and sea-water.

In some of the participating countries, JMG meetings are attended by both civil servants and representatives of ocean research institutes, while other countries have a more strictly scientific representation.[31] However, it should be noted that JMG participants are explicitly national representatives whereas ICES claims to be composed of independent scientists. To some extent, this indicates the main differences between ICES and the JMG — with ICES being the more scientific, 'internationalist' and 'methodological tool-developing' organization, and the JMG more a forum for 'national practitioners' in the field of monitoring. The reports of the work carried out in the JMG are presented at meetings of the TWG (see below) and also to the annual Joint Meeting of the Commissions.

As their name indicates, the *Technical Working Groups* (Technical Working Group (TWG) connected to the Paris Commission work; Standing Advisory Committee for Scientific Advice (SACSA) connected to the Oslo Commission work) were created as foras for discussion of questions concerning possible practical and technical solutions to pollution problems identified by marine scientific research. Thus, reports from ICES and the JMG are always reviewed as part of the agenda of TWG meetings. The groups give recommendations to the Oslo and Paris Commissions on questions of a technical nature. The groups also deal with questions concerning practical implementation of measures decided upon by the Commissions. They are intended to represent a politically neutral forum for discussions. National representatives to the groups are mostly civil servants with a background in the natural sciences. The groups now meet annually.

In connection with the North Sea Conferences, specific *Scientific and Technical Working Groups* have been established. The work of these groups has been largely based on reports and information gained through bodies like JMP and ICES. However, compared to the work of the TWG, the reports of the STWGs seem far more scientifically than technically oriented. Within this structure, the main political bodies are the *Oslo and Paris Commission Meetings* and the *North Sea Conferences*. The Oslo Convention for the Prevention of Marine Pollution by Dumping from Ships and Aircraft was signed in 1972 and entered into force in 1974. The Paris Convention for the Prevention of Marine Pollution from Landbased Sources was signed in 1974 and came into force in 1978.

Specific articles of the Conventions establish Commissions composed of representatives of each of the contracting parties to the Convention. The main duties of the Commissions are to review the condition of the seas within the area to which the Convention applies, to draw up programmes and measures for eliminating or reducing pollution from land-based sources, and to evaluate the effectiveness of the control measures adopted and the need for any additional measures. The Commissions are also to receive and assess information from the member states according to a standard procedure concerning the substances listed in the annexes to the Conventions. Programmes and regulation measures adopted by the Commissions are legally binding in the member states. The Commissions meet once a year. Continuity in work is guaranteed by a permanent joint Secretariat which organizes and prepares the meetings of the Commissions and other bodies, and distributes documentation.[32]

Supplementing the work of the Commission, two ministerial-level *North Sea Conferences* have been held: in Bremen (1984) and in London (1987). The agendas of these Conferences include major issues covered by both the Oslo and Paris Conventions. The national delegations are headed by the respective environment ministers.

Having presented the main actors in the scientific-political complex in the North Sea, let us now turn to the more intriguing task of tracing the evolution of the 'complex'.

Science and North Sea politics : from Parcom to the London Conference

The 'list approach', JMG and the evolution of Parcom: the first years

As first introduced in the Oslo Convention work, the scientific foundation for the Paris Commission work was formulated in 'black' and 'grey' lists which identified and assessed the toxicity of a large number of substances. The black list singled out those substances not readily degradable, which could give rise to dangerous accumulations of harmful material in the food chain and endanger the welfare of living organisms and thus necessitated rather urgent action. Substances included in the black list are organohalogen compounds; mercury and mercury compounds; cadmium and cadmium compounds; persistent synthetic floating materials; and persistent oils and hydrocarbons. The grey list identified substances which required 'strict control', but seemed less noxious and more readily rendered harmless by natural processes — for instance substances like the organic compounds of phosphorus, silicon and tin; non-persistent oils and hydrocarbons; arsenic, chromium, copper, etc. However, we should note that the emissions of black-list substances were not prohibited *per se*; the Convention requires elimination of 'pollution' by black-listed substances.[33]

As indicated earlier, the work of the JMG was to provide the main continuous scientific input into the work of the Oslo and Paris Commissions. In the first three years of its existence, the JMG focused on the distribution and effects of a selected group of black-list substances: mercury, cadmium and PCBs in organisms, and to mercury and cadmium in sea-water.

The results of this work were presented to the Technical Working Group at a meeting in 1983. According to the (then) Chairman of the JMG, Dr J.E. Portmann, the three years of monitoring had been characterized by a steadily improving situation with regard to the quality of data reported and the supporting information provided with it. On the whole, coverage was described as 'adequate', although some gaps could be identified for certain substances in certain areas. The main conclusion was that ' . . . although some areas could be identified as being above the normal levels for estuarine and coastal areas in terms of concentrations of one or other of the three priority substances, in no area could the concentrations be regarded as excessively high'.[34] Nor was any consistent correlation found between the concentrations of either cadmium or mercury in water and the concentrations found in biota from the same area.

Thus the JMG concluded that, as far as could be ascertained, most of the areas subject to known inputs of mercury, cadmium and PCBs were being 'adequately' monitored. This impression of 'adequacy' is strengthened in the JMP report from 1984, which stated that with regard to the findings on cadmium, mercury and PCBs, 'In each case there remain gaps in the areas for which data were provided but statements had been made on which areas appear to be most contaminated. Generally, however, it was apparent that there are few areas which are seriously contaminated by any of the three substances monitored.' However, the report also noted 'very little data availability' and 'difficulties involved in obtaining meaningful and reliable comparisons between the data from different sources'.

On the political side, the first years of the Paris Commission work did not produce very much in the form of binding, specific measures. Describing the period from 1978 to 1985, a recent analyst comments: 'Outcomes of the cooperation in the Paris Commission are characterized by few binding decisions and rather more recommendations often couched in terms inferring little in the way of obligations. One category of outcomes has been so-called "non-decisions", that is those proposals which have been postponed or have not been up for discussion.'[35] More specifically, binding measures were agreed upon with regard to the regulation of mercury and oil-based muds. Recommendations were adopted concerning the emission of mercury, oil, waste from the titanium dioxide industry, radioactive substances, aldrin/dieldrin/ endrin, PCBs, synthetic materials. Most notably, however, discussions on the black-listed cadmium emissions ended in a 'non-decision'.

Although scientific uncertainty was probably a hampering factor in these first years of the Paris Commission, Sætevik's study on the work of the Commission draws attention to the participation of the EC in this work and the constraints due to the EC Commission's 'negative' behaviour on the decision-making ability of the cooperation. Thus she notes: 'In the Paris Commission the paradox is that it has been impossible to attain binding decisions in spite of a broad majority or apparent consensus between the member states. The reason for this is that reservations from the EC Commission have blocked decisions.'

However, there was no consensus on the more important question of regulatory approach. Most of the Continental and Scandinavian countries preferred the Uniform Emission Standards (UES) approach, implying the use of the best available technical methods and equal standards for all countries. In contrast Great Britain preferred the Environmental Quality Objective approach, arguing that the essence is the quality of the marine environment. This unresolved question (although its practical implications were diffuse) probably did contribute to a somewhat polarized atmosphere within the cooperation.[36]

Nevertheless, this rather 'meagre' outcome of the cooperation — at least in terms of binding, specific decisions — may have helped to fuel the idea of the need for a new and more comprehensive forum for the discussion and regulation of North Sea pollution.

The First North Sea Conference, Bremen 1984

At the initiative of Federal Republic of Germany (partly as a response to a North Sea report produced by German scientists), a ministerial North Sea Conference was held in Bremen in 1984.[37] 'West Germany believed that such an initiative was necessary to safeguard the health of the sea. It argued that the existing plethora of conventional protocols and agencies involved in the control of pollution was too fragmented to achieve that end.'[38] As an important part of the preparatory work for this conference, a *Quality Status of the North Sea* report was produced. This report was based on national reports of perceived water quality in the national coastal areas, discussed at several preparatory meetings prior to the Conference. The synthesis work was headed by the FRG.

What, then, was the main scientific message in this report? With regard to the input of substances into the sea, it notes that some of the substances of concern (e.g. nutrients, heavy metals) may derive from natural as well as anthropogenic sources, while others (e.g. various synthetic substances) derive wholly from anthropogenic sources. More specifically, the report emphasized that rivers are still considered a major source of contamination, especially affecting the southern North Sea and the German Bight. Atmospheric deposition 'may well' constitute the main source of contamination, especially of heavy metals. Coastal discharges were considered less of a problem in general, ' . . . though they are known to give rise to local problems'.

With regard to concentrations of substances, the report noted that organic and inorganic contaminants of anthropogenic origin have been recorded in low concentrations over much of the North Sea. Elevated levels of organic and inorganic pollutants in water, sediments and biota were generally found in estuaries and coastal waters and particularly in the Southern Bight and the German Bight. Concerning synthetic substances, the report stated: 'Although newer techniques have revealed an increasing number of compounds there is clear evidence that a reduction has taken place of some of the better known organohalogen compounds, e.g. DDT and PCP.'

With regard to nutrients, no increase in nutrient levels had been recorded in the northern and central North Sea, except in limited coastal areas. An increase in nutrient concentrations could be identified in the Southern Bight, the inner German Bight and especially the Wadden Sea. The influence of this increase in nutrient concentration on primary production was not clear, ' . . . as physical factors also play a significant role in primary production'. Concerning evidence of ecological and other effects, the report concludes that: ' . . . all the numerous observations and investigations known up to now, from which only small parts were extracted for this compilation, do not in general allow clear cause-effect relationships between contaminant inputs and effects on marine organisms to be identified'. Causal relations between the occurrence of fish diseases and pollution loads has 'not yet' been established. Compared with the effects on fish stocks by fishing itself, other anthropogenic activities are said to play an insignificant role. With regard to the effects of nutrients, ' . . . so far there appears to be no evidence that anthropogenic nutrients have caused any significant change in productivity in the North Sea, or even in the Southern Bight'. In sum, the report did not give any indications of a developing 'ecodisaster' in the North Sea. Local problems were acknowledged, but the overall situation was not seen as alarming.

The Conference itself produced a Declaration which has been characterized as ' . . . long on principle but short on specific new policies, leaving ample scope for inaction by the participants until a follow-up conference is held . . . '[39] More specifically, the Declaration called for a 'reduction in pollution of coastal waters by land based sources'. The EC and the Paris Commission were called upon to introduce uniform emission standards and environmental quality standards for black-list substances, in particular organohalogens and heavy metals, as well as for 'problematic' heavy metals and metalloids on the grey list. New compounds needed to be 'examined more intensively', with a view to adding them to the two lists.

Concerning 'waste disposal at sea', it was said that 'wastes including sewage sludges, containing such amounts of substances which are or could be harmful to the marine environment will not be dumped into the North Sea'. Moreover, attention was given to 'pollution of the North Sea from the atmosphere'. Here, the Paris Commission was called upon to adopt a new protocol on the 'prevention, reduction or elimination of marine pollution through the atmosphere'. Concerning 'reduction of radioactive discharges', account should be taken of the 'best available technology' in setting discharge limits for all nuclear plants. With regard to the 'pollution by shipping', a decision whether to declare the North Sea a 'special area' was deferred until the next Conference.

The Declaration ended with a call for further development of the Joint Monitoring Programme: Efforts should be made to intensify research in the North Sea and monitoring . . . Further measures for the protection of the North Sea should above all be taken on the basis of data and information to be collected and of their evaluation and assessment.' In sum, the Conference did not introduce any major new initiatives but mostly tried to 'beef up' and vitalize existing organizations and policies.

To what extent did the scientific report, then, contribute to the outcome? To me, it seems to have been quite influential. For instance, it is maintained in ENDS-Report just after the Conference: 'Demands by German environmentalists in 1984 for sweeping clean-up measures, including a ban on waste dumping at sea and curbs on the manufacture and discharge of "black list" substances, were rejected by Ministers, not least because of a major scientific effort by the UK which showed that serious pollution is mostly confined to the major estuaries and is not a threat to the North Sea as a whole.'[40]

However, as the report was finished just in time for the Conference itself and not discussed by the delegations in advance, parts of the report were disputed at the Conference.[41] In such a more or less confrontational atmosphere, it is understandable that the numerous 'moderate' parts of the report would prevail in discussions. Other organizational and political factors also probably contributed to the outcome. Some have called attention to the fact that it was the first step in a continuing process: 'It was the first of its kind and although there had been some preparations, differences of opinion could hardly be expected to evaporate simply because the responsible ministers met in an international conference for two days.'[42] With the benefit of hindsight, we may also point to the comparatively low international attention given to environmental matters in the early 1980s. Despite scattered alarming reports, other issues dominated the agenda.

The Second North Sea Conference in London 1987: background and outcome

Preparations for the Second North Sea Conference started in January 1986. Also here a scientific report was to be produced before the Conference. Unlike Bremen, this report was to form the basis for a separate Policy Working Group prior to the Conference itself. The scientific work was this time headed by the host for the Conference, Great Britain.

Now, the interesting question is whether the 'moderate' perception of the pollution situation expressed in the scientific Bremen report was changed during the preparatory work for the London Conference. Compared to the Bremen report, certain differences and changes in emphasis can be noticed. Generally, the London report contains expanded indications and discussions of scientific uncertainty and methodological questions. Moreover, in addition to sections on 'physical oceanography', 'inputs', 'concentrations' and 'ecological effects' found in the Bremen report, this report also has specific sections on 'trends' (in the development of inputs, concentrations and effects) and a concluding 'assessment of the status of the North Sea'. The sections on 'inputs and concentrations' are mainly expanded and updated versions of the corresponding sections in the Bremen report; but the new section on 'ecological effects' seems more interesting. Here, nutrients are discussed at some length and a somewhat more worried tone is indicated, for instance with regard to plankton: 'There is a general acknowledgement that nutrient inputs, particularly of nitrate and in some cases also of phosphate, have increased, and that in some shallow coastal areas there has been an increase in phytoplankton production and in the frequency or scale of undesirable plankton blooms . . . Thus in some areas a link between nutrient inputs and plankton blooms, and nutrient inputs and plankton population structure appears possible. There is evidence also that the consequent effects are detrimental, e.g. in the German Bight and in certain Danish coastal waters.' However, problems seem to have a rather local character: 'There is clear evidence of benthic changes close to points of discharge, largely as a result of man's activity . . . The significance of these changes is often difficult to assess but the severest effects are usually local, and most studies suggest that anthropogenically-induced changes are reversible.'

The London report also seems more open to the possibility that pollution may cause fish diseases: 'Concern has arisen because many external abnormalities have been found in a significant proportion of the bottom-living fish in parts of the German Bight, Danish coastal waters, British coastal waters and in the vicinity of the Dogger Bank.'

However, the overall threat perception has not changed very much: 'There is no evidence that man's activities other than fishing are having any significant deleterious effects on the fish stocks of the North Sea as a whole although there are various limited effects . . . ' To quote from the summary report: 'In general deleterious effects, at present, can only be seen in certain regions, in the coastal margins, or near identifiable pollution sources. There is as yet no evidence of pollution away from these areas.'

In sum, the general perception of the situation in the London report seems more nuanced and multifarious, but warning is sounded first and foremost with regard to local and more limited areas and problems. The nutrient issue seems to receive somewhat more attention than in the Bremen report. However, in my opinion, it is difficult to see this new report as a significant change in the overall North Sea threat perception with regard to pollution.

Despite several similarities concerning scientific point of departure, the outcome of this Conference was definitely different from that of the Bremen Conference. With regard to inputs via rivers and estuaries of 'substances that are persistent, toxic and liable to bioaccumulate' (which include mercury, cadmium and PCBs), the 'principle of precautionary action' was endorsed: the marine ecosystem should be safeguarded by the use of the best available technology. Furthermore, ' . . . this applies especially when there is reason to assume that certain damage or harmful effects on the living resources of the sea are likely to be caused by such substances, even when there is no scientific evidence to prove a causal link between emissions and effects'. More specifically, 'urgent' and 'drastic' measures to reduce the total quantity of such substances reaching the North Sea were called for, 'with the aim of achieving a substantial reduction (of the order of 50%) in total inputs from these sources between 1985 and 1995'.

Likewise, concerning euthrophication and inputs of nutrients, the Conference called for 'effective' national steps to reduce inputs into areas which are likely, directly or indirectly, to cause pollution. Here too, the aim is to achieve a 'substantial reduction (of the order of 50%)' in inputs of phosphorus and nitrogen to these areas between 1985 and 1995. 'Urgent' preparation of plans of action to achieve these goals was also called for.

With regard to other issues, the Ministers agreed in principle to end the dumping of material into the North Sea by the end of 1988 'unless there are no practical alternatives on land and it can be shown to the competent international organisations that the materials pose no risk to the marine environment'. With respect to the dumping of industrial waste it was decided that this must end in 1989 'except for inert materials of natural origin or other materials which can be shown in the competent international organisations to cause no harm to the marine environment'. Countries that dump sewage sludge into the North Sea will take 'urgent action to reduce the contamination of such materials, so that they pose no hazard to the marine environment'. It was decided to phase out incineration at sea of dangerous liquid waste by the end of 1994 following a reduction by 65 per cent in 1991. With regard to radioactive discharges from nuclear industries like reprocessing plants, 'the best available technology' shall be applied. Other topics included 'inputs of pollutants via the atmosphere', 'pollution from ships', 'pollution from offshore installations' and 'airborne surveillance'.

Like the first North Sea Conference, the London Declaration ended with a call for 'the enhancement of scientific knowledge and understanding'. Further development of harmonized methods for monitoring, modelling and assessment of environmental conditions at national and international levels was needed. New in this connection was a request to ICES and the Oslo and Paris Commissions to set up a specific scientific *Task Force* to achieve these ends.

How then did such a 'successful' outcome come about?[43] Despite the still rather moderate overall pollution threat perception, my impression is that the STWG report none the less did contribute to the outcome of the London Conference. This was achieved by the report being both more strictly 'scientific' and more usable than earlier comprehensive efforts like the Bremen Report. By more clearly and extensively underlining and discussing the uncertainty connected to the scientific information, the report probably helped to raise the policy-makers' awareness of a 'worst-case' scenario. The concluding and synthetisizing part on 'assessment of the status of the North Sea' probably contributed to the overall usability of the report. However, the 'action-releasing' effect of the report clearly depended on several other organizational and political factors.

In my opinion, the main organizational factor was the existence of a *Policy Working Group* which discussed the possible political implications of the scientific results in a specific and institutionalized organizational setting before the Conference. This eliminated unnecessary scientific and political misunderstandings and disagreements in advance — and we may thus say that science played a more constructive and clear-cut role at the London Conference than on earlier regulatory occasions.

In explaining the change in governments' interpretation of the report and the apparent added weight given to the worst case possibility, it is also important to acknowledge the influence of a more general green upsurge in several of the participating countries in the period leading up to the Conference.[44] Environmentalist pressure groups played an important role in this process, for instance by forming specific international coalitions to campaign for stricter anti-pollution measures.[45] Nor should we underestimate the influence of quite 'conference-specific' factors like Prince Charles' 'green' opening speech. Some of the Prince's formulations undoubtedly served to increase media attention and to heighten general expectations with regard to the outcome of the Conference, as for instance: ' . . . while we wait for the doctor's diagnosis, the patient may die . . . We are right, I believe, to take the precautionary line . . . We are right to cut the input of dangerous substances, like heavy metals and organic chemicals, into the North Sea and to develop a system of measuring pollution levels which is common to all . . . '

Science, politics and the organization of North Sea environmental cooperation

In this main analytical section we shall more explicitly and fully discuss and try to answer the main questions posed at the outset. Let us briefly recapitulate these questions: (1) What role has changing scientific evidence played in the evolution of North Sea environmental cooperation — both compared to other types of resource management and assessed on its own merits? (2) Has science been making an 'optimal' contribution to North Sea policy-making? (3) To what extent are initiatives like the North Sea Task Force an adequate response to the problems identified? Are other organizational changes necessary also?

Our discussion will be structured around five main theses on science, politics and the organization of North Sea environmental organization.

The role of science in pollution control is different from the role of science in other types of resource management

In the previous section an attempt was made to trace the evolution of the relationship between science and North Sea politics at the international level. One outcome of this attempt has been to strengthen the assumption (hinted at in the theoretical introductory section) that the role of science in international pollution control is somewhat different from the role of science in other types of international resource management.

A cursory examination and comparison of the role of the ICES in international fishery management and international pollution control is quite illustrative. Through its Advisory Committee on Fisheries Management, the ICES furnishes the coastal states and the North-East Atlantic Fisheries Commission with data on stocks and advice on catch quotas. This makes it possible to compare the advice given by the Committee on total allowable catch with the quotas actually agreed on by the coastal states. With regard to international pollution control, the Advisory Committee on Marine Pollution is the comparable ICES body. However, the Cooperative Research reports of this Committee contain no parallel advice on international marine pollution regulatory action. The reports present plenty of evaluations and assessments, but advise only on methodological questions.

Likewise, as shown in the previous section, the Quality Status Reports produced in the connection with the North Sea Conferences contain, at their most 'advanced', assessments of the status of the North Sea. True, the TWG gives recommendations to the Paris Commission, but my impression is that these recommendations are based more on 'technical' than on 'scientific' considerations. Thus, Sonia Boehmer-Christiansen is probably right in maintaining that the role of science in pollution control is much more clear-cut with regard to the identification of pollution than it is in the regulation process itself.[46]

Why, then, this difference between fishery management and pollution control? As indicated earlier, I feel some issue-specific characteristics are important explanatory factors. Firstly, scientific studies of fish and fishery resources have a longer scientific tradition than do pollution studies, and the methodological tools are probably more developed. Secondly, the pollution issue is a far more complex one, with the level of pollution being determined by a multitude of factors, only some of them identifiably anthropogenic. Hence, the relationship between regulatory measures and environmental effects is indirect and uncertain, making only very broad types of scientific advice possible ('inputs should be reduced . . . ').

Nevertheless, I would maintain that although precise and more quantitative analyses of gaps between scientific recommendations and political measures are difficult (if not impossible), it is still possible more qualitatively to assess the extent to which the main scientific message has been heeded in policy-making.

The main 'message' of science has not been neglected in North Sea policy-making

Drawing upon the evolutionary account in the previous section, I do not think it is possible to uphold at least a somewhat crude version of the 'gap' thesis put forward by Viktor Sebek — which sees an alarmist scientific community being ignored by shortsighted, narrow-minded decision-makers. Rather, at a very general and abstract level, my impression is that we have a case of 'moderate overall scientific threat perception and moderate international political response'. In the period leading up to the London North Sea Conference, the main scientific message has been as summarized in the latest Quality Status Report: 'In general deleterious effects, at present, can only be seen in certain regions, in the coastal margins, or near identifiable pollution sources. There is as yet no evidence of pollution away from these areas.' Moreover, this message has clearly been taken note of and used in the political discussions — perhaps most notably at the Bremen Conference. However, 'politics' seems to have been the dominating factor in the shaping of regulatory measures.[47] This is not surprising, considering the complexity of the pollution issue.

However, another aspect of this relationship seems yet more pertinent: has science in this period developed in a way which makes it capable of making a 'satisfactory' and 'optimal' contribution to North Sea policy-making? And here I feel the answer is 'No'.

Science is not in a position where it is able to make an optimal contribution to North Sea policy-making

The theoretical point of departure and rationale for the reasoning on this point is the earlier discussed concept of 'integrated marine policy'. As I interpret this concept, an integrated policy (where significant consequences are recognized as premisses) presupposes distinct and unambiguous components, where the 'ecological' component identifies the main ecological data and relationships in a fairly distinct manner. Here we should of course note that in practice the question of reduction of uncertainty and scientific optimality must also include cost-benefit considerations. In some instances a further reduction of uncertainty will be very costly while mattering only marginally for the policy choices in question. We will, however, return to this discussion at the end of this section.

My main impression in this connection is, then, that the state of knowledge on both inputs, concentrations and effects of contaminating inputs has not developed in such a way that an international integrated marine policy in the North Sea is possible. It is important to acknowledge that we simply do not know the exact relationship between what may be termed 'ecosystemic needs' — admittedly a vague and controversial concept — and the political measures adopted. By 'ecosystemic needs' I am thinking of something in the direction of 'critical thresholds within which the contamination of a given area must be restrained in order to retain the sustainability of the marine resources in the area'. Let us look into these matters more systematically.

Research and exchange of information is often seen as the traditional (and easiest) area of international cooperation.[48] After some 15 years of international cooperation in the North Sea, which has been characterized as 'the most studied sea in the world',[49] it seems somewhat surprising to still find plenty of references to problems of intercomparability of data from different countries in the 1987 Quality Status of the North Sea-report. For instance, concerning 'inputs of inorganic and organic contaminants' it is said: ' . . . all figures for inputs, with the possible exception of dumping, are subject to considerable uncertainty, the extent of which is variable and difficult to quantify, owing to analytical variation and problems of representative sampling, among others'. Moreover, with regard to 'concentrations of inorganic and organic contaminants': ' . . . although improvements have been made in the accuracy and precision of analysis for metals in sea water over the past few years, caution must be exercised in comparing results produced by different laboratories'.

Thus when it comes to the final 'assessment of the status of the North Sea' section the report notes that: ' . . . problems arise because of the variable quality of scientific evidence. In some cases, although considerable evidence is available about the distribution of a contaminant, there is no evidence of it causing undesirable effects. In others, there is insufficient scientific information on which to base a judgement.'

Hence, according to the British newspaper the *Daily Telegraph*, ' . . . the real message of the Quality Status Report, if one examines it carefully, is that there are considerable gaps in our knowledge of what goes into the North Sea, and how these discharges affect the marine environment . . . ' Further, ' . . . the gaps show that the authors of the Quality Status Report, by which the Government sets much store, simply did not have some of the most important figures on inputs of pollutants'.[50]

How, then, should we view this uncertainty? On the one hand, and as indicated earlier, gaining knowledge in this field is a complex task. Hydrographic factors make the association between inputs, distribution of contaminants and their effects difficult to establish. As noted in the Quality Status Report, there is no exact relationship between inputs from one source and effects in coastal waters. On the other hand, my impression is that the scientific collaboration potential in the North Sea has not yet been fully tapped.

Thus as stated by a senior official and long-time participant in both the scientific and political North Sea cooperation (who understandably prefers to be left unnamed): 'The Joint Monitoring Group is a complete failure . . . ' Indeed, this has recently been more or less acknowledged also by the Parcom Secretariat. Compared to the ideal picture of what might be achieved by implementing the Commissions' monitoring programmes, ' . . . for the time being, however, it must be admitted that there is still a long way to go'. The Secretariat identifies several disadvantages of the current JMP: first, it covers only the major estuaries and coastal zones of the participating states and no open sea sites. Second, it is based on the already existing monitoring programmes of the states and little mutual 'adaption' seems to have taken place. This has made the programme 'heterogenous' and comparative assessments difficult.[51] Considering the 'crucial' and 'action-initiating' task originally assigned to JMG within the scientific-political complex — where ideally the work of both TWG and the Paris Commission was to be guided and inspired by new scientific evidence from JMG — *the malfunctioning of this group means in reality a malfunctioning of the whole scientific-political complex in this period.*

Now as has been indicated earlier, both the JMG report from 1982-83 and the Quality Status Report produced in connection with the 1984 Bremen Conference explicitly pointed to lacking and incomparable data. However, as far as I can see, this did not lead to any major political/ strategic initiatives — neither from the OsParCom Secretariat nor from any of the nation-states — to identify impeding factors in the scientific work and ways to overcome them. Why, then, this seeming inaction?

Admittedly based on rather impressionistic evidence, I think it is none the less possible to indicate some explanatory factors. One such factor could of course be that it is not until quite recently (cf. the algae and seal 'incidents') that the health of the North Sea has been alarmingly focused on, giving rise to 'serious' and widespread political concern, despite Commission meetings and North Sea Conferences. The urgency and drive to know what is *really* going on have been lacking. To some extent, this may of course be attributed to the initial stage of the cooperation. As emission limits and the classification of substances ('grey list' or 'black list') have a clear political component, it may be argued that in the first phase of cooperation a substantial proportion of the available time and energy should be devoted to the political sphere — explaining own preferences to the other participants and trying to understand their preferences; striving towards at least some consensual points, to get them transformed into decisions. At this stage, a certain degree of uncertainty may even function positively. As has been pointed out by negotiation theorists, new or more specific information may 'empty' an existing 'zone of agreement'.[52]

Second, as the Oslo and Paris Conventions cover far wider areas than the North Sea only, scientific activity connected to the Commissions has correspondingly been more widespread and diffuse, lacking any clear 'North Sea assessment mandate'.

A third (admittedly more speculative) factor — which may shed some light on the inaction of seemingly 'impatient' and 'result-seeking' nations like the Nordic countries, The Netherlands and Federal Republic of Germany — may be that the strictly scientific way of arguing in these matters has been closely linked to an actor that many have regarded as a political 'stumbling-block' within this cooperation, namely Great Britain.[53] Let me briefly sketch the background for this.

Within the field of North Sea environmental cooperation, Britain has preferred the Uniform Environmental Quality approach to international pollution control while most other countries have preferred Uniform Emission Standards, as noted in the previous section. Linked to the British preference for Uniform Environmental Quality standards has also been an insistence on 'perfect' scientific evidence before agreeing to international political measures. Most of the other countries have more or less embraced the so-called 'anticipatory' or *vorsorg* principle, which implies that measures have to be taken even if ecological damages cannot be proved. Now in a somewhat polarized political situation (especially within the Paris Commission), my impression is that the British call for convincing scientific 'evidence' before agreeing to political measures has been interpreted by the other nations as a 'play-for-time' strategy — an interpretation with probably some substance to it. But this means that the real need for scientific improvement may have been neglected. Thus, in a way, such an explanation may give support to the Miles thesis mentioned earlier, that political polarization narrows the room for science in the decision-making process.

However, no matter how this state of science may be explained, the present defects in North Sea science mean that we still lack a properly functioning feedback system with regard to the management of the North Sea environment. Due to the present gaps in knowledge, difficulties will arise when the effects of the current political measures are to be assessed in a few years time. Moreover, in my opinion the magnitude of these knowledge gaps — and the possible political consequences of reducing them — means that a reduction strategy will be clearly justified in a cost-benefit perspective. It is in this connection interesting to note some statements by Dr Brian Bayne, director of the Natural Environment Research Council's Plymouth Marine Laboratories in the UK: 'Before we can make accurate judgements about the cumulative effect human pollution has had on the North Sea, huge areas remain to be studied . . . Above all, we have very little idea how a whole host of chemicals, which are not on the Government's Red List of chemicals to be banned, behave in the marine environment . . . The question of how various compounds behave in the environment isn't ivory tower research. It's basic science. If we'd spent some money on these things four years ago we'd have some answers by now. It's all very frustrating.'[54]

In sum, this points at least to an adequacy problem. *There is 'too much' uncertainty connected to the knowledge on inputs, concentrations and effects of contaminating substances.* Moreover, I think it is also possible to identify a 'usability' problem. If it is accepted that 'research for policy-making is a peculiar form', then a continuing communication process between researchers and policy-makers is necessary.

This process does not seem to have been functioning well at all, either at the international or national level. At the international level, the scientific-political complex in the North Sea must be characterized as 'fragmented'. Scientists meet in ICES and partly JMG, policy-makers (and Ministers) in Commission meetings and North Sea Conferences. On those occasions when the two groups meet, the agenda tends to be dominated by issues of a more short-term and practical nature. This could of course be somewhat remedied by a well functioning national coordination process, but signs indicate that this is not so. [55] Thus *despite several formal meeting-points, the international dialogue between scientists and policy-makers on issues of a more basic and long-term character has been largely missing.* Now, this is where the new North Sea Task Force comes in.

The North Sea Task Force may solve some of the existing problems, but may also raise some new ones

As indicated earlier, the idea of a new scientific North Sea Task Force was launched in the final Declaration of the second North Sea Conference, probably partly as a response to problems experienced during the scientific preparatory work for the Conference. The first formal meeting of the Task Force has recently been held (December 1988). As I understand it, the purpose of the Task Force and the ensuing international programme is to reduce current uncertainty, with regard to inputs, concentrations and effects. Moreover, by developing new methodological tools and models, the relationship between these factors is to be better understood, e.g., 'The priority should therefore be to develop relatively simple methods which would provide quantitative indications of biological effects attributable to specific forms of pollution'.[56]

More specifically, the purpose is partly to produce a new and improved Quality Status Report in 1992/93. This is to be achieved partly by a more truly international scientific effort: ' . . . the work for the next QSR should be based on joint multinational collaborative studies and should use data collected on a purely national basis only when needed or appropriate, with the Task Force acting as a filter'.[57] The Task Force will comprise delegates from the eight North Sea states, the Commission of the European Communities, and representatives of ICES and OsParCom. Moreover, as stated in the summary record of the first meeting, . . . the meeting agreed that the objectives of the Task Force should include . . . to provide an organizational framework for discussion and exchange of views between policy-makers and scientists, with the aim of attaining the respective aims of the two groups'.[58] Thus to some extent it adresses also the 'usability' dimension of the science policy-making issue.

How, then should we assess the Task Force initiative? On the one hand, the potential for better and more integrated policies — both nationally and internationally — inherent in this initiative should be acknowledged and emphasized. Provided that the necessary economic and administrative resources are allotted, an important step towards a properly functioning, scientifically based feedback system for managing the North Sea environment will have been taken.

On the other hand — but not overshadowing the potential identified above — some loose ends and problematic aspects may still be suggested. For instance, the relationship between the new Task Force and the already existing bodies seems as yet unclarified. Obviously there is a difference in geographical focus between bodies like ICES and JMG and the new group, with the latter having a more specific and limited North Sea assessment focus. However, there is obviously also a geographical overlap, with the inherent possibility of duplication of efforts. Indeed this problem was pinpointed by the FRG delegation at the Inaugural Meeting of the Task Force in March 1988: 'The delegation of FRG expressed concern that the Task Force might spawn additional sub-groups, and embark upon new and large-scale data gathering exercises, rather than relying on better coordination of existing national programmes'. Moreover, in one sense, 'linking science and policy' and thus addressing the usability problem is both necessary and functional. However, the national delegation approach might raise problems concerning the scientific legitimacy of the scientists participating in the delegations. Will they be 'national scientists' or just 'scientists chosen by the nations'?[59]

Although this legitimacy problem does not seem to have fuelled much controversy or been much in focus in the past, the possibility that such conflicts may arise should not be excluded. An explicit discussion of the demarcation of the different roles and the dangers of a blurring of these roles could probably be useful.

Finally, and somewhat paradoxically, reducing uncertainty might create problems of a political and distributional kind. More generally, it has been suggested that 'the veil of uncertainty' — concerning gains and losses connected to regulatory measures — may save negotiations over such measures from failure.[60] In terms of the North Sea context, it is for instance imaginable that states agreed to the 50 per cent reduction measures at the London Conference partly because they felt they might be 'importers' of contaminating substances and would thus at least gain somewhat from a broad international reduction effort. Now, if improved research efforts lead to clearer identification of pollution sources and of the winners and losers in this game, then this in fact might reduce the willingness of specific states to agree to international measures which would first and foremost benefit other states. And this might in turn raise intriguing distributional questions.

Such objections and loose ends aside, if the Task Force is success-ful, it may mean that the scientific input to the cooperation will become more comprehensive and usable. However, this does not automatically mean that policy-makers are capable of using it (or willing to use it, but will is harder to influence than capability). And this indicates the necessity of considering also other types of institutional reforms.

Supplementary organizational changes in the scientific- political complex are necessary also

One reason why the London Conference was 'successful' may lie in the institutionalized discussions within the Policy Working Group which 'interpreted' and 'politically developed' the scientific background material *before* the Conference itself. Such an intermediary function between science and politics seems to have been weakly developed in connection with the Commission work so far. Some preparatory meetings are held within the Group of Chairmen and Vice-chairmen (CVC), but not, to my knowledge, as a part of a systematic procedure.

As the agenda of especially the Paris Commission meetings has increased considerably over the years, there is a growing danger of neglecting the more basic and time-consuming discussions of the adequacy of existing institutions and political measures in the light of available scientific and technical evidence. Expanding the CVC-mechanism or even establishing a new Policy Group could either relieve Commission meetings of some of the more routine matters and allow more time for strategic discussions, or conversely, allow these meetings to function as a more evaluative 'think-tank'. In other words, the additional information which it is hoped the new Task Force programme will provide may prove of little use if the policy-making bodies are not capable of turning this information into 'better' policies.

Now such a 'political' extension of the cooperation would necessarily involve a need for additional administrative capacity to be channelled to this work. On the other hand, in the light of the recent seal and algae 'catastrophes', such a political and administrative upgrading of this field of activity seems easily justifiable. The days where 'to demand of a politician that he accords large weight to the welfare of later generations is rather like asking him to commit suicide' seem to be over — at least temporarily.[61]

Conclusion

To sum up, then, we have identified the following characteristics of the relationship between science and politics within North Sea cooperation: first, the relationship is probably impossible to characterize and measure in quantitative terms. Speaking in more qualitative and general terms, we may say the main scientific message concerning the state of the North Sea has not been ignored in the evolving policy-making. However, this scientific message has been characterized by considerable uncertainty connected to knowledge on contaminating inputs, their concentrations and their ecological effects — nor has this uncertainty lessened much over time. Thus, the existing Joint Monitoring Group has not been a success; and due to the key organizational position of this group, the whole scientific-political complex in the North Sea has been malfunctioning and stagnant in this period. If provided with the necessary ecconomic and administrative resources, the new scientific Task Force has clearly the potential of both coming up with better knowledge and of stimulating communication between scientists and policy-makers both nationally and internationally. However, the organization of the whole scientific-political complex is in need of rethinking.

Why has this situation developed? In my opinion, the main reponsibility rests with the policy-makers. It is their job to make sure that the necessary information for 'rational' policy-making is — or will be — available. With the new Task Force initiative they now have the opportunity to improve this unfortunate state of affairs. However, we should also note that 'more priority given to North Sea issues' in this connection means both financial and administrative resources *and* more attention to the organizational aspect. More money and people might be a necessary condition for more rational policies, but they are definitely not sufficient conditions in themselves.

Notes

1. This report is partly based on interviews with civil servants and scientists in Norway, Denmark, The Netherlands, Belgium, West Germany and Great Britain — with a clear bias towards the civil servant side. Among the many who contributed to the process of writing this article, five deserve special mention: Steinar Andresen (the Fridtjof Nansen Institute), Arild Underdal (University of Oslo), Jens H. Kofoed (the Norwegian State Pollution Control Authority), Per W. Schive (the Norwegian Ministry of Environment) and Erik Lykke (former Director of the OECD Environment Directorate).

2. Moltke/Haigh, 'Environmental Protection in the North Sea', E.E.R., vol. 1, no. 3, June 1987, p. 13.

3. *Chrysochromulina polylepsis* is the Latin name of the algae that caused damage to marine life in Norwegian waters in the spring of 1988.

4. Boehmer-Christiansen, Sonja, 1981, *Limits to the International Control of Marine Pollution*, unpublished Ph.D. thesis, University of Sussex, p. 255.

5. Sebek, Viktor, 1983, 'Bridging the Gap Between Environmental Science and Policy-making: Why Public Policy Often Fails to Reflect Current Scientific Knowledge', *Ambio*, vol. 12, no. 2, p. 118. Sebek is Secretary for the Advisory Committee on Pollution of the Sea (ACOPS) in London.

6. Andresen, Steinar, 1988, 'Outcome, Science and Interests: The International Management of Whales', The Fridtjof Nansen Institute, p.14. (In revised version, 'Science and Politics in the International Management of Whales', *Marine Policy*, no 2 (1989).

7. Sebek, 1983, p. 118.

8. Roll-Hansen, Nils, 1986, *Sur nedbør — et storprosjekt i norsk miljforskning*,

NAVF, Oslo, especially pp. 11-16.

9. This question is discussed more extensively in Steinar Andresen's article in this book. For more general discussions on issue contexts and politics, see for instance Wildavsky, A., 1962, 'The Analysis of Issue Contexts in the Study of Decision-Making', *Journal of Politics*, **24** Underdal, Arild, 1979, 'Issues Determine Politics', *Cooperation and Conflict*, **14**, no. 2.

10. For instance, in Wildavsky and Tenenbaum 1981, *The Politics of Mistrust: Estimating American Oil and Gas Resources*, London, it is said that in this issue area, 'Except for the limiting case — extreme physical limits to recoverable resources — neither high nor low estimates appear to produce different policy implications' (p. 267).

11. Andresen, 1988, p. 7.

12. Sperling, K.R., 1986, 'Protection of the North Sea: Balance and Prospects', *Marine Pollution Bulletin*, vol. 17, no. 6, p.243.

13. Moltke, Konrad von, 1984, 'Needs and Action: Obstacles to International Policies', *World Resources Institute Journal* **84**, Washington, p. 11.

14. Andresen, 1988, p. 8.

15. Moltke, 1987, p. 10. This point is also emphasized by Jordijk (1988): ' . . . augmenting scientific information will not necessarily lead to the identification of suitable policies for controlling acidification of the environment. This information must be structured in a form that can be used for decision making to create a policy based on available scientific evidence and on credible judgements about the probability of future events'; 'Linking Policy and Science: A Model Approach to Acid Rain', *Environment*, vol. 30, no. 2, p. 17.

16. Miles, Edward, 1987, 'Science, Politics and International Ocean Management', *International Affairs*, University of California, Berkeley.

17. Moltke, 1983, p. 9.

18. Such an explanation is more or less hinted at in Andresen, Steinar, 1988: ' . . . why did the recommendations finally get in line with the scientific recommendations? Does this indicate that the strength of the scientific argument finally convinced the whaling nations to reduce their catches? Although this cannot be disregarded, the fact is that catch was not reduced in accordance with scientific advice until the whaling nations were unable to catch their quotas'. (pp.12-13).

19. Underdal, Arild, 1983, 'Causes of Negotiation "Failure"', *European Journal of Political Research*, **11**, p. 193. For a more general discussion of international organizations and environmental issues, see Majone, G., 'International Institutions and the Environment', in Clark/Munn, 1985, *Sustainable Development of the Biosphere*, Cambridge.

20. Underdal, Arild, 1983, p. 193.

21. See Fløistad, Brit, 1989, 'Scientific Knowledge in the Management of Fish and Whale', in this volume.

22. Miles, Edward, 1987, and Underdal, Arild, 1980, *The Politics of International Fisheries Management*, Universitesforlaget, Oslo.

23. Underdal, Arild, 1980, p. 223.

24. Miles, 1987, p. 97.

25. Underdal, Arild, 1980, 'Integrated Marine Policy: What? Why? How?', *Marine Policy*, no 3, pp. 159-69.

26. ICES Information Brochure, 1988, 'International Council for the Exploration of the Sea'.

27. These working groups are on Marine Chemistry; Baltic Marine Environment; Marine Sediments in Relation to Pollution; Statistical Aspects of Trend Monitoring; Biological Effects of Contaminants; Pathology and Diseases of Marine Organisms; Environmental Assessments and Monitoring Strategies; Benthos; Shelf Seas Oceanography; Effects of Extraction on Marine Sediments; Environmental Impacts of Mariculture; Harmful Effects of Algal Blooms on Mariculture and Marine Fisheries; Primary Production; Ecology of Algal Blooms; Acid Rain; Patchiness Investigations; Report of Seagoing Workshop on the Methodology of Fish Disease Surveys.

28. ICES Cooperative Research Report, 1987.

29. ICES Information Brochure, 1988, 'Composition of the Advisory Committee on Marine Pollution'.

30. The Oslo and Paris Commissions, 1984, *The First Decade*, p. 34.

31. Coordination problems have been indicated in connection with this 'split' in Norwegian representation in ICES and JMG. See Andresen/Fløistad, 1984, 'Overvøking av forurensnings-situasjonen i norske havområder: vektlegging, organisasjon, samordning', The Fridtjof Nansen Institute, especially pp. 89-91.

32. For more information on the Oslo and Paris Conventions and Commissions, see for instance Boehmer-Christiansen, Sonja, 1984, 'Marine Pollution Control in Europe — Regional Approaches, 1972-80', *Marine Policy*, vol. 8, no. 1, 1984; Hayward, Peter, 1984, 'Environmental Protection — Regional Approaches', *Marine Policy* , vol. 8, no. 2, 1984; Sætevik, Sunneva 1988, *Environmental Cooperation between the North Sea States*, Belhaven Press (Pinter Publishers), London.

33. See for instance Bjerre/Hayward, 1984, 'The Role and Activities of the Oslo and Paris Commissions', paper presented to the Water Research Centre Conference; *Environmental Protection: Standards, Compliance and Costs*, 1984, pp. 11-12.

34. Summary Record, Tenth Meeting of the Technical Working Group, March 1983, p. 20.

35. Sætevik, 1988, p. 134.

36. At the Parcom meeting in Berlin in 1983, it became clear that according to TWG's conclusions, it was impossible to assess which of the two approaches was the most appropriate, on the basis of the existing data.

37. For further information on the background of the Conference, see Wells/ Side, 1985, 'The Bremen Conference: Retrospect and Prospect', paper, p. 19.

38. 'Pollution and Politics in the North Sea', *New Scientist*, 19 November 1987.

39. 'UK's Defensive Efforts Pay Off at North Sea Conference', *ENDS-Report*, **118**, November 1984.

40. 'Opening Skirmishes on Health of the North Sea', *ENDS-Report*, **141**, October 1986.

41. Interview with Norwegian civil servant.

42. Andresen, Steinar, 1988, 'The Environmental North Sea Regime: A Successful Regional Approach?', The Fridtjof Nansen Institute, p. 16. (Forthcoming *Ocean Yearbook*, **8**, 1989/90.)

43. The degree of 'success' may of course be disputed. For a critical discussion of the outcome of the London Conference, see de Jong, Folkert, 'The Second Ministerial Conference on the Protection of the North Sea: An Historical Event?', *North Sea Monitor*, January 1988.

44. This is for instance illustrated by the rise of the Greens in West Germany. This upsurge was reinforced by a couple of other official factors, such as the declaration of 1987 as the 'European Year of the Environment' and the presentation of the report of the *World Commission on Environment and Development* in April 1987, with an ensuing debate (at least in the Nordic countries).

45. In 1986 environmentalist groups from all eight countries bordering the North Sea formed a coalition to campaign for stricter anti-pollution measures, with internationally organized groups like *Friends of the Earth* and *Greenpeace* playing an active role.

46. See Boehmer-Christiansen, Sonja, 1989, in this volume.

47. This 'dominance of politics' perspective is more forcefully expressed and discussed in other parts of this book; see for instance Miles' and Boehmer-Christiansen's contributions.

48. Such a point of view is discussed by Underdal, Arild, 1987, in his article 'International Cooperation: Transforming "needs" into "deeds"', *Journal of Peace Research*, vol. 24, no.2, June 1987. He notes that although pieces of

impressionistic evidence seem to support such a thesis, they can 'frequently be countered by rival interpretations'.

49. Lee, A.J., 1987, 'The North Sea - Setting the Scene', opening paper at the International Conference on Environmental Protection of the North Sea, March 1987.

50. 'North Sea or Dead Sea? The rising tide of pollution', *Daily Telegraph* Weekend Magazine special feature, 8 October 1988.

51. 'Measurement Campaigns of the Oslo and Paris Commissions', paper produced by the OsParCom Secretariat to the first meeting of the Task Force, The Hague, 7-9 December 1988.

52. This has been called the 'veil of uncertainty' (Buchanan/Tullock, 1962, *The Calculus of Consent*, Ann Arbor). The line of reasoning is discussed by Young, Oran, 1988, in his paper 'The Politics Of International Regime Formation: Governing the Global Commons', pp. 22-4.

53. For a discussion of the role of the UK within the North Sea Cooperation, see Sætevik, 1988.

54. Dr Bayne is quoted in the Daily Telegraph North Sea feature, p. 26.

55. See the report referred to in note 31.

56. Policy paper released in connection with the second North Sea Conference in London.

57. North Sea Scientific Task Force Inaugural Meeting, London, 16-17 March 1988, Report of the Meeting of the Scientific Working Group, p. 3.

58. Summary of the first meeting of the Task Force, The Hague, 7-9 December 1988, p. 4.

59. A similar problem was discussed with reference to the composition of the ACMP at the ICES meeting in Bergen, October 1988.

60. See the article referred to in note 52.

61. Elster, Jon, 1983, Explaining Technical Change, Cambridge University Press, Cambridge, p. 206.

10

Science and politics in the protection of the ozone layer

Per M. Bakken

Introduction

International agreements within the field of the environment do not have a long history. Nor are international air pollution agreements among the earliest. The first regional convention was the EEC Convention on Long Range Transboundary Air Pollution, of 1979. Still, this field of international agreements has had a rapid development over the past ten years. A significant portion of this is due to increased knowledge of our atmosphere, partly triggered by international activities in the field.

As a basis for any international environmental treaty there has to be a scientific cause-effect relationship. This might be empirical, as in the case of acid rain, or may be based on model predictions using the best available scientific knowledge, as in the case of the protection of the ozone layer. But without agreement at least in influential parts of the scientific community, the chances of reaching international agreement are small.

Since this section is devoted to empirical information, I will, through a case, indicate the role of science in the past. At the end I would also like to offer my personal views on what role science and scientists should play in the future.

The protection of the ozone layer

I would like to use the protection of the ozone layer as my prime example. There are several reasons for this. Firstly, it is an unprecedented kind of international environmental protection treaty. Secondly, in my view this is one of the best examples of how international negotiation activity varies over the years, along with varying scientific results.

As is often the case, the whole issue started recently — only fourteen years ago — as a result of research on quite another topic. In this case it was the possible influence of supersonic aircraft or SSTs on the stratosphere. Two US scientists suggested that the releases of certain man-made chemicals, the chlorofluorocarbons (CFCs), could significantly decrease the earth's protective ozone layer. This layer, found in the stratosphere 15-40 km above the earth's surface, protects us from harmful ultraviolet radiation from the sun. Their report made a significant impact: the US National Academy of Sciences as well as National Air and Space Administration (NASA) established scientific panels which published several reports about the issue during the next few years.

We have here the scientific cause-effect relationship I mentioned earlier. There was only one problem: the cause-effect relationship could not be proven. It was based on simple one-dimensional mathematical models which indicated that the depletion of the ozone layer could not be verified through actual observation before the middle of the next century. This was related to the very long atmospheric lifetime of these chemicals. From the time they were released until they reached the ozone layer would take several years. Then they would remain active in ozone destruction through a catalytic process for the next 75-100 years. To save the ozone layer we would have to stop emissions now, based on these theoretical model predictions. If we waited until the theory was proven, it would be too late.

Governments in Northern America and Western Europe reacted variously to this problem. Some accepted the threat as real, introducing a ban or severe restrictions on the use of these substances as propellant in aerosol cans, a measure which in most cases halved national consumption. Others reacted more cautiously, but still introduced what they called 'precautionary measures'. International organizations like the Organization for Economic Cooperation and Development (OECD) and some UN agencies like the UN Environmental Program (UNEP) took an interest in the problem. UNEP had already back in 1977 established a scientific panel, the Coordination Committee on the Ozone Layer (CCOL), composed of independent scientists from countries which had expressed an interest in participation. It also contained representatives from the producing industries, partly because producers had already spent significant amounts on the scientific aspects of the problem, and partly to raise the credibility of the assessment made by the CCOL, since all major interests and all those doing active research in the field would have an equal opportunity to contribute. In the years to follow this panel was to play a dominant role in the international negotiations which started under UNEP auspices in 1982.

The scientific aspects of the problems saw a rapid expansion in the years after 1974. Still in 1978-79, the use of simple one-dimensional models which covered only the height distribution of ozone in the atmosphere were used to study the simple relationship between CFCs and ozone amounts. The results seemed dramatic: at one time estimates indicated up to 18 per cent ozone depletion. However, as more knowledge was gained, scientists realized that the CFCs were not the only chemical affecting atmospheric ozone. As a result of some of the others, ozone in other parts of the atmosphere might be increasing. This was a problem in itself and one we today are familiar with when we are talking of forest death and climate change. Still, such an increase could compensate for some of the ozone depletion farther up in the atmosphere. The change in the total ozone column became the important criterion. As a result of this, as well as new reaction constants for some of the key chemical reactions, figures on ozone depletion dropped to 3-5 per cent. These figures were taken by most people as comparable with the 18 per cent mentioned earlier, and the problem seemed to have faded away.

This new information, on top of a massive and well directed campaign from the producers of these chemicals, including some of the world's leading multinational chemical companies, reduced national concern about the whole issue.[1] The industry, spending considerable amounts of money each year on science, carefully picked fields of uncertainties and processes that might reduce the negative impacts of CFCs on stratospheric ozone. The more or less annual reports from the CCOL became more diffuse and uncertainty became the dominant impression. Policy-makers were waiting for scientists to come up with a clear answer before further action was taken.[2] The result was that the framework convention, the Vienna Convention for the Protection of the Ozone Layer signed in 1985, did not contain any reduction obligations for the parties.

During the first half of the 1980s a new kind of model was presented. This was two-dimensional, covering not only vertical distribution but also latitudinal distribution of ozone. Such models all indicated that ozone depletion would not be the same at all latitudes. Near the poles, depletion would be four times greater than near the equator.

When the Vienna Convention was signed it was agreed that further negotiations would follow on specific measures for CFC reductions. After a couple of workshops organized in Europe and the US and a major scientific meeting in the US in June 1986, negotiations for a protocol began in December 1986. Leading scientists felt at this time that several of the possible uncertainties presented by industry had been dealt with, and the credibility of the newer models had increased. Even the models developed by industry gave results similar to those of independent scientists. They concluded that the problem was real and something had to be done.

However, for hard negotiations for specific measures among countries, the discovery of the *ozone hole* over Antarctica probably had an even greater impact on their attitude towards the problem. This significant depletion in the total ozone column over Antarctica during early spring should have been observed several years earlier, but NASA had programmed its satellites to ignore unusually low or high values of ozone. When the hole was found by a British scientific expedition, the discovery led to major concern among the scientists as well as policy people. NASA searched through its raw data and was able to confirm the observations. Although consistent with the 2-D models, the reduction was far more drastic than expected. Even worse, this reduction, if caused by CFCs, was appearing several decades too early, according to the models. No explanation could be given, and no one actually used that hole as an argument for strict reduction measures for CFCs. Still, in most delegations this was the 'proof' they had been waiting for. As often is the case, unexpected 'catastrophes' helped in finding rapid and significant measures to deal with the problem.[3]

During the final phase of negotiations scientists did not play an important role. Negotiations became hard and were conducted in an unorthodox way. Only a handful of countries, led by the Executive Director of UNEP, Dr Tolba, actually carried out the negotiations on this global agreement. These were the major producing countries like the European Community nations and the US, major political units like the Soviet Union, and a few 'neutral' countries like Norway, New Zealand and Canada. In addition, a few developing countries like Egypt were part of the small core negotiating group.[4]

The final negotiating session during the Montreal diplomatic conference went on until 24 hours before the Montreal Protocol was signed. At this time the problem became less important compared to the issue of securing a fair economic and trade agreement among the different parts of the world. The 'battle' was particularly hard between the US and the EC. As a result, an unfortunate new concept was accepted in the treaty: it was not to enter into force until a certain number of countries had ratified it; these countries could account for at least two-thirds of anticipated global consumption. A similar provision was accepted concerning requirements for changing the protocol: any change had to have a certain number of votes which also represented at least 50 per cent of global consumption.

All the same, the Montreal Protocol became one of the first agreements in the environmental field with the potential of being scientifically driven. At least every fourth year, starting in 1990, measures were to be evaluated in the light of new scientific, technological and economic information. One year before the evaluation, special task forces were to be established to collect information and prepare a report on the latest findings. A similar provision had never before been adopted in any international environmental agreement.

The Protocol was probably signed a few weeks too early. Two weeks after Montreal the first results from Antarctica came in showing that the hole was worse than ever: more than 50 per cent of the ozone had gone. This state lasted more than two months, and areas as far off as 60° S lat. showed significant ozone depletion. Firm proofs were presented that the CFCs were responsible for the hole. In spring 1988 NASA presented proof based on ground-based measurements from more than 30 stations in the northern hemisphere, indicating a reduction in the total ozone column over this area larger than can be explained by natural variation.

The science campaign from NASA starting in Janury 1989 might be able to tell us more about the atmospheric situation over northern areas and whether we are here facing a real threat to the ozone layer created by CFC emissions. Even if there is found to be a larger depletion caused by CFCs, this would probably not be as great as in Antarctica. The effects, however, will be far more severe, since this would take place over densely populated areas. Based on today's knowledge, scientists in several countries have made calculations showing that if we are to get rid of the ozone hole over Antarctica we will have to reduce CFC emissions by at least 85 per cent. Several multinational companies have already proclaimed that they will stop all production of these substances from the year 2000. Progress within the field of substitutes and alternatives is very rapid, and a global phase-out should therefore be possible.

This example seems like a science fairy-tale where science is given the role as the discoverer of the problem, the driving force in the development of facts and necessary for political decisions. And like all good fairy-tales, it will end happily for mankind — or so we hope.

There are, however, examples where science has been lagging behind the political will. One such example concerns the elaboration of the regional regulatory protocol on reductions of nitrogen oxides. Here the politicians decided to go ahead with actual negotiations several years before the necessary scientific basis had been established. As a result, research funds have had to be allocated to solve questions vital to the continuation of the negotiations. This is, of course, not desirable, but necessary.

The protocol signed in Sofia in November 1988 has a condition similar to the Montreal Protocol, in that the measures shall be reviewed at regular intervals in the light of new scientific findings. The protocol contains, however, another obligation to start renegotiation of measures even before six months after the protocol has entered into force, probably in 1990/91. These renegotiations are to be based, among other things, on the critical load concept. Again, this will limit the funds for research on other aspects of the problem.

Lessons to be learned

Now what can be learned concerning the role of science from these and other similar cases?

Firstly, that science is the basis for action and that it is necessary to have an understanding of the cause-effect relationship. This requires, however, that scientists recognize their responsibilities. A word of warning must be given to policy-makers at an early stage, even before a firm connection is established with 95 per cent degree of confidence. One reason for this is that if the possible effects are so severe, there is a need to locate the sources for emissions, to start work on finding possible measures to reduce these and to establish the costs involved. In addition it might be necessary to initiate research in fields which so far have not been involved. If we are aiming at a system where we can avoid jumping from one crisis to another, introducing emergency measures all the time, scientists will have to take this 'early warning signal system' seriously.

Secondly, scientists must do better in communicating with policy-makers and the public in general. The message must be presented in a clear language. I am not thinking of the more traditional problem connected with science jargon as such, but more that the message must be readable, not presented in such a way that everything is highly uncertain and nothing really can be said at the present time. This does, of course, not mean that existing uncertainty should be depressed. What is important is to try to present the results in a wider context. What aspects of society, human health, ecosystems, etc. do the results affect? In order to do this properly, it might be a good idea to integrate work with other research disciplines. Scientists should therefore consider a more comprehensive risk evaluation of their research as a natural and integral part of their reports, and scientific training should also put more emphasis on this.

Thirdly, as science has become more and more international and scientists appear in expert panels set up by international organizations, they have, whether they like it or not, become part of an international negotiating team. If scientists really believe we are faced with a problem that needs to be dealt with on an international level, their assessment should also reflect this view in a clear way. This takes, however, some training to achieve, especially since countries and industries with an economic interest in the problem might work hard to blur the picture presented in the assessment.

The job is facilitated if scientists are better trained in carrying out comprehensive risk evaluations. However, the message in international scientific assessments will be carefully worded; it takes negotiations to find the right wording which combines the concern of the problem and the different scientists' interpretations of the available data while also differentiating clearly between the real scientific uncertainty and the more political uncertainty which is based on factors other than scientific data. This is a new and challenging role for scientists.

Notes

1. For a discussion of the role of industry in the regulation of pollution, see Boehmer-Christiansen, Sonja, 1989, 'The Role of Science in the International Regulation of Pollution', in this volume.

2. For a discussion of the ability of scientists to come up with clear answers, see Andresen, Steinar, 1989, 'Increased Public Attention: Communication and Polarization', in this volume.

3. For a discussion of the effect of 'catastrophes', see for example Miles, Edward,

1989, 'Scientific and Technological Knowledge and International Cooperation in Resource Management', in this volume.

4. Miles, Edward, 1989, elaborates further on the significance of the size of the negotiating group in this volume.

SECTION 4:
Science and Living Resources

11

The role of science in international management of fish resources

Dietrich Sahrhage

International management of living resources is an important and challenging task. There is growing awareness that man must be more concerned with the protection of nature and the rational utilization of the renewable resources. Implementation of effective schemes for the management of fisheries resources has proved rather difficult, and many fish stocks are still over-exploited or even depleted. However, some progress has been made during recent years. Scientific investigations and advice have played a major role in this development.

The need for fisheries management

Experience with the development of fisheries in the world over the past 50 years has shown that the living resources of the oceans are by no means inexhaustible. The rapid increase in the number of fishing vessels and their catching efficiency, due to the introduction of more powerful fishing gear and methods such as purse-seines, pelagic trawls and acoustic fish detection, has led to an increase in total marine fish landings from about 35 million tons in 1960 to more than 75 million tons per year today. This development has contributed substantially to meet the needs of people for animal protein. However, this production has also created heavy over-exploitation of fish resources in many parts of the world, with depletion of stocks resulting in serious economic and social problems.

Prominent examples are the anchoveta fishery off Peru and the herring and mackerel fisheries in the North Atlantic. The anchoveta catches for the production of fish meal reached 12 million tons in 1970 before the fishery collapsed to comparatively low levels.[1] This was largely the result of over-exploitation, although environmental factors (El Nino events which changed temporarily the hydrographic conditions along the Peruvian coast) also played a substantial role. From the Northwest Atlantic the landings of herring were increased to almost 1 million tons in 1968 but due to overfishing of the Georges Bank, herring stock dropped thereafter to the present level of less than 200,000 tons per year. Similarly the catches of mackerel from the Northwest Atlantic decreased from 420,000 tons (1972) to less than 40,000 tons annually (1978 to the present). Even more pronounced was the rapid decline in catches of Norwegian spring-spawning herring in the Northeast Atlantic, from a peak of nearly 2 million tons in 1966 to only 44,000 tons in 1969 and 3000 tons in 1975.[2] At the same time and as a direct consequence of the collapse of the fishery of Atlanto-Scandian herring with subsequent diversion of fishing effort, landings of herring from the North Sea dropped from a maximum of 1.2 million tons in 1965 to only 79,000 tons in 1977.[3]

It can also be shown that gross over-exploitation of several other fish stocks has led to their depletion or serious reduction one after the other, but it is extremely difficult if not impossible to quantify the influence of such changes in relation to the effects of fishing. Quite often these developments have been reinforced by environmental changes.[4] Obviously pelagic species, due to their shoaling behaviour, are highly vulnerable to extensive fishing with modern detecting and catching methods. Over-exploitation is, however, observed not only in pelagic fish stocks but also in demersal resources in many waters of the world oceans,[5] so there is a great need for proper management.[6]

This need has long been recognized. Also it was realized early on that the development and management of fisheries must be based on the results of scientific investigation. This idea was instrumental in the foundation of the International Council for the Exploration of the Sea (ICES) as early as 1902, and later (1950) the International Commission for the Northwest Atlantic Fisheries (ICNAF), converted in 1979 into the Northwest Atlantic Fisheries Organization (NAFO). While this latter organization is concerned with both fisheries research and management, there is in the Northeast Atlantic a separation between ICES, which coordinates research activities and provides scientific advice for management purposes,[7] and other organizations responsible for fisheries management, namely the Northeast Atlantic Fisheries Commission (NEAFC), the International Baltic Sea Fishery Commission (IBSFC), and the North Atlantic Salmon Conservation Organization (NASCO), and more recently the European Communities (EC). Moreover, various organizations exist in other parts of the world.[8] Most of these are regional fisheries bodies of the Food and Agriculture Organization of the UN (FAO) or have been created on initiatives taken by FAO, like the International Commission for the Conservation of Atlantic Tunas

(ICCAT) and the International Commission for the Southeast Atlantic Fisheries (ICSEAF). The latest management organization is the Commission for the Conservation of Antarctic Marine Living Resources (CCAMLR), established in 1980 under a convention which for the first time has as its objective not only the protection of living resources but also the prevention of longer term changes in the marine ecosystem.

Endeavours for the conservation of fish resources

The legal provisions, instruments and mechanisms of the various management bodies differ considerably due to historical developments, political conditions and special requirements. In the beginning, management considerations were limited to a few heavily exploited commercial species. Management measures concentrated on the introduction of minimum mesh sizes in the cod-end of trawls so as to allow small fish to escape. Furthermore minimum sizes of fish in the landings were introduced to discourage the capture of young fish, and protected areas and closed seasons were established to improve recruitment in fish stocks.

Although these regulatory measures have been useful, they have proved insufficient to manage the resources properly. Experience in NEAFC and ICNAF showed that it was difficult to apply minimum mesh sizes in trawl fisheries which were simultaneously catching a number of different species ('mixed fishery'). Large catches, particularly of pelagic fish, resulted in good profits and provided incentives to the fishing industries to invest in an increasing number of new and powerful vessels and fish processing installations. The result of these unrestricted actions was a large increase in fishing effort and a level of catches much higher than the natural production of these resources. As a consequence, yields declined steeply, fisheries came to rely more and more on young fish in the absence of larger ones (growth overfishing), and recruitment was endangered due to reduction of spawning stocks (recruitment overfishing).

These detrimental effects were clearly identified by biologists, and scientists warned against this over-exploitation at an early stage. However, it was unfortunately only under hard economic and political pressure that governments finally were prepared to agree to the introduction of more efficient management regulations.[9]

Many fisheries had become less and less profitable and governments were increasingly forced to subsidize the industries to avoid negative social repercussions. Thus political pressure developed and governments had to react to this. There was also an increase in conflicts between countries on fisheries matters.

Since effort limitations, like reducing the number of fishing vessels, were rather difficult to achieve, endeavours concentrated on limitation of catches. With major national economic and political interests involved, it took a long time until total allowable catches (TACs), and in particular national catch quotas, were accepted. The first quotas in the Northwest Atlantic were agreed on in 1973 and in the Northeast Atlantic in 1975. The number of fish stocks covered increased in both areas rather quickly during the following years. However under pressure from the fishing industries, most catch quotas were set far higher than recommended by scientists on the basis of stock assessments.[10]As a result, yields of several highly important commercial fish species declined further; fisheries became unprofitable; and finally in 1977 a total ban of fisheries on certain stocks had to be accepted. (See the example of North Sea herring, figure 11.1.)

Extended fisheries' jurisdiction of coastal states

The introduction of 200-mile Exclusive Economic Zones (EEZ) mainly around 1977, which brought 35 per cent of the world's oceans and 95 per cent of the marine living resources under national jurisdiction, was certainly speeded up by the inability of existing international management bodies to implement adequate management of the fish resources. After the establishment of the EEZs many of the old problems of management under the open-access regime remained and new ones developed.[11] Instead of competition between fishing fleets of various nations there was now competition between different branches of their own national fishery which governments of coastal states had to regulate in their EEZ. Furthermore, various disputes arose between two or more states concerning the utilization of joint resources within EEZs. However, there is no doubt that progress has been made in schemes of resources management. The enforcement of rigid surveillance of fishing zones and inspection of fishing vessels has greatly contributed to this development.[12]

Management of resources under the jurisdiction of one nation is less complex than multinational management. Examples of the former are Canada (see 'Cod off Labrador', figure 11.2), Iceland and Norway; an example of the latter is the management scheme established under the EC.

According to the Rome Treaties, the member countries of the EC entrusted the EC Commission with responsibility for fishery policy, including the management of the joint living resources and relations with third parties (e.g. Canada, Faeroes, Greenland, Iceland, Norway) in this respect. Like other coastal states, the members of the EC in 1977 claimed a joint fisheries zone of 200 miles. This was followed by long, rather difficult negotiations on fisheries policies which in 1983 resulted in a 'fisheries regime' agreed for a ten-year period, for the present. Part of this regime is a percentage distribution of catch quotas for fish stocks in EC waters to member nations based on requirements of national fisheries and their fishing efforts during earlier reference periods. It was agreed to fix TACs and national quotas annually on the basis of scientific advice on the status of stocks. This procedure has since been implemented successfully following regular meetings of the Council of Ministers. Agreements have also been reached with a number of non-EC countries concerning the exploitation of joint resources, exchanges of fishing opportunities and fishing rights in exchange for trade facilities or other means. Scientists from the countries concerned have made considerable contributions during these developments in advising national delegations.

Scientific advice for management purposes

The management of fisheries and resources is the responsibility of policy-makers and administrators, but it is generally agreed that sound management measures must be based on proper scientific advice. This puts considerable responsibilities on the shoulders of scientists as well, not least in view of the great economic and political implications.

Scientific advice is mainly expected from fisheries biologists who are specialized in the assessment of stocks and conversant with the structure, activities and problems of commercial fisheries. These must be suitable persons with mathematical skill and the right 'feeling' for problems of diplomatic negotiations. In their assessments and advice they rely heavily on the work of other fisheries scientists who investigate the various fish species and obtain the various types of data needed.[13] Regular collection of adequate data and statistics over long time periods is a basic requirement for the critical examination of trends in the status of living resources under the influence of fisheries utilization and natural events. It is the responsibility of governments to ensure this work without interruptions by providing the necessary specialized personnel, ships, travel funds, etc. Scientific advice and subsequent resources management can only be as good as the underlying data base. Proper management must take into account not only biological aspects but also economic factors. Input on the latter is provided by representatives of the fishing industries; but scientific advice in the field of economics to the management bodies has been rather limited so far, and more activity in this sector should be encouraged.

Scientific advice from fisheries research started with the provision of suitable and detailed statistics on fish catches, landings and fishing effort. Investigations on mesh selection and fish behaviour formed the basis for the introduction of, and later adjustments in, minimum mesh sizes of fishing gear. The creation of closed areas and seasons relied on knowledge of the biology of the species concerned.

Driven by the need for scientific advice and by experience obtained over the years, substantial progress has been achieved in methods of fish stock assessment.[14] Following general production models using catch and fishing effort statistics to calculate the optimum sustainable yield, age-specific methods (cohort analysis and virtual population analysis) have been developed which allow estimation of annual stock size and fishing mortality by age groups starting with the current year. On this basis the presumable catch in subsequent years under certain assumptions can be calculated and more up-to-date management advice can be provided.

As a consequence of the introduction of TACs and national catch quotas (sometimes a total ban on fisheries), the quality of fishery statistics deteriorated because of misreporting of quantity, area and species. Therefore it became essential to shift progressively to fishery-independent estimations of stock size made from research vessel surveys of the commercially most important species, using standardized fishing gear, hydro-acoustic surveys with echo integration, and egg and larval surveys. Internationally coordinated young fish surveys were introduced to estimate recruitment of various stocks. Whenever possible, different methods were applied to the same stocks in order to verify results obtained.

The techniques of fish stock assessment and manner of scientific advice have gradually been improved over many years, but during the early period there were often considerable uncertainties. Through close collaboration between scientists from various countries, considerable standardization of the assessment methods has been achieved in recent years. Today's stock estimates are now fairly reliable and can form a sound basis for management actions.[15]

While it is important for the credibility of scientific advice to apply agreed assessment methods over longer periods, this should of course not prevent the further development of more refined or new approaches. So far assessments have concentrated on single species. There is, however, increasing awareness that each species is closely linked with other parts of the marine ecosystem through simultaneous exploitation as well as predator-prey interaction. Therefore any management measure for one species could also be of consequence for one or more other species, either also used commercially or important as food source for other animals.[16] A good example is the regulation of fishing for Northeast Atlantic capelin, a species which is an important food source for cod and haddock and also seals. Extensive fishing can alter the natural balance within marine ecosystems and even lead to damage, sometimes irreversible. It is therefore an important task for resources management to prevent such developments. CCAMLR has taken this into account in its legal provisions. Several multi-species assessment models have been developed, and it is now necessary to verify them on the basis of actual biological data. Such models may then play an increasing role as a tool for fisheries management.

Results of environmental research can also be of great importance for the resource management. An example is the regular West German and Greenlandic oceanographic investigations off West Greenland which, closely coordinated with biological studies, have shown that fluctuations in cod recruitment are in those waters obviously related to long-term fluctuations in the physical environment.[17] Thus for certain areas it may be possible to predict the likelihood of increasing or decreasing recruitment from trends in the oceanographic conditions.

Mechanisms for providing scientific advice

Since most of the stocks of living resources interest more than one nation, mechanisms exist for providing international scientific advice. In the Northeast Atlantic ICES has established a number of working groups (at present 25) in which fisheries biologists from the various countries concerned pool data and information for regular reports on the status of one or more stock(s), with assessments of stock sizes, level of exploitation and expected recruitment. These reports also contain catch projections for different levels of exploitation in future years, mostly in the form of various options for corresponding management measures. The reports by the working groups are reviewed and if necessary amended by the Advisory Committee on Fishery Management (ACFM). This Committee is composed of one assessment specialist from each of the ICES member countries and the chairmen of some standing fish committees of the Council. ACFM executes a certain control function, and only the final reports by ACFM are considered official advice of ICES to the various management bodies and member governments. If necessary, the reports contain recommendations for total allowable catches (TACs) and other management measures, such as changes in minimum mesh sizes or closed areas and seasons, for further consideration and decision by the management bodies.

A further 'filtering' mechanism exists in the EC. The Commission of the European Communities obtains special advice from its Scientific and Technical Committee for Fisheries (STCF) when developing proposals for management actions to be adopted by the EC Council of Ministers before they become binding for EC waters. Also in STCF there is substantial input from ACFM and the fisheries biologists of the member countries.

Other management bodies, like NAFO or CCAMLR, do not usually rely on scientific advice from separate organizations but possess their own scientific councils or committees in which fisheries biologists from many nations collaborate extensively. This collaboration also helps to neutralize scientific arguments in cases where these seem biased to promote national interests.

The results of international cooperation and scientific advice are of great importance also to the programmes of national fisheries management and development, since they provide a common ground for the proper protection and utilization of the resources in question.

Interaction between scientific advice and management decisions

The role of science in international management of living resources has grown considerably in recent years. Not long ago warnings issued by biologists against over-exploitation of stocks were disregarded by policy- makers and managers who had to negotiate under hard economic and political pressure and difficulties. It was less on the strength of the arguments presented by scientists and rather by the obvious collapse of fisheries that action to protect these resources was finally taken. After this painful experience it is now widely accepted that scientific investigations and advice in this field are indispensable. Adequate structures and mechanisms for the necessary on-going dialogue between managers and scientists have been established for the North Atlantic and some other areas of the world.

There is no doubt that the total annual landings of fisheries in the world can be increased substantially through better resource management. According to the international law of the sea, responsibility for these resources and their management lies with the coastal states. Not all of these states, particularly developing countries, are yet in a position to handle this important task due to lack of experienced personnel and of adequate administrative and scientific instruments. Better resources management should therefore be promoted through assistance and training in this field. Scientific institutions with specialized experience can play a most useful role in this regard if governments provide them with the necessary facilities.

Scientists can also be of great help to policy-makers by explaining to fishermen, to representatives of the fishing industries and to the public the aims and needs of management actions. Proper management can best be achieved if those most directly involved can be convinced that measures are being taken in their own long-term interest. Much educational work still remains to be done. Of course, this requires scientists able to present these problems in a language and style which can easily be understood.[18]

At this stage, however, what is most important for successful resources management is the political will by governments to introduce and to act with determination upon management regulations once the need has been identified, even if this may mean short-term losses in catches. Too often policy-makers tend to hide behind such arguments as 'scientists do not yet have sufficient data' or 'more scientific studies are needed before we can take any action.'[19] Also, policy-makers often fail to provide sufficient guidance to the scientific advisory bodies on special tasks which they want to be investigated. More longer-term management strategies need to be developed in close collaboration between managers and scientists. Through their work and publications, scientists can exert substantial influence on the decision-making processes.

Achievements in management through scientific advice

The question arises whether the considerable efforts and financial and other means required for proper management are justified in fact by positive results. I think the answer is 'yes'. The following two examples may demonstrate what achievements can be expected.

Herring in the North Sea

After an increase during the post-war years, the landings of herring from the North Sea fluctuated from 1953 until 1963 around 700,000 tons annually (see figure 11.1). In 1964 and subsequent years fishing effort and landings rose dramatically. In 1965 and 1966 more than 1 million tons of herring were caught, but after this peak there followed a steep decline in catches which continued until a total ban of herring had to be implemented in 1977. A considerable quantity of the landings, on average 100,000 tons per annum, consisted of young, immature herring caught for industrial purposes.

Scientific investigations have shown (figure 11.1b) that, due to excessive fishing with increasing fishing mortality, the size of the adult herring stock decreased after 1965 to an extremely low level of only about 200,000 tons in 1977. The catch of immature herring was particularly detrimental to the stock.

As early as 1970 scientists recommended a reduction of fishing mortality by 50 per cent, and their proposals for protective measures became more pressing every year until in 1975 they recommended a total ban on all directed herring fisheries. It was not, however, until the beginning of 1977 that all countries involved were prepared to agree to such a serious step. In the absence of fishing, further development of the stock was then observed by biologists through scientific catches, egg and larvae studies, and hydro-acoustic surveys.

When there were indications of an increase in stock size, the herring fishery was re-opened at the end of 1980 with rather limited TACs. In accordance with scientific advice these TACs were raised in subsequent years, and by 1987 a total catch of more than 600,000 tons could be permitted, with different allocations to various sub-areas of the North Sea and Skagerak.[20] As a result of such careful management, the adult herring stock had increased again almost to levels observed in the 1960s, and with the appearance of a number of good new year-classes (1982-5) there are now good prospects for continuous adequate catches of North Sea herring. However, the delay in appropriate management action, with the consequence of a complete ban on North Sea herring fishing, resulted in serious disruptions in the herring market which could have been avoided if less dramatic action had been taken some years earlier.

Cod off Labrador

Landings of cod from the waters off Labrador amounted during the 1950s to around 300,000 tons annually. When European fishing fleets started to utilize this stock, catches increased steadily to a maximum of 800,000 tons in 1968 (see figure 11.2). Despite higher fishing effort which led to

Figure 11.1 Landings of herring from the North Sea, 1946-86 (above 11.1a), and spawning stock biomass and fishing mortality (below 11.1b), from Anonymous, 1988.

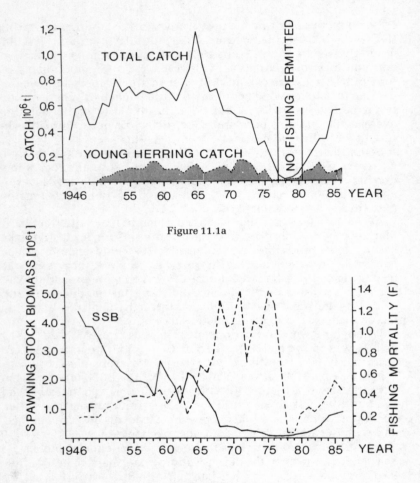

Figure 11.1a

Figure 11.1b

Figure 11.2 Landings of cod from the waters off Labrador, 1953–85 and fishing mortality (above 11.2a). Cod stock size and abundance indices from Canadian and German (FRG) investigations (below 11.2b).

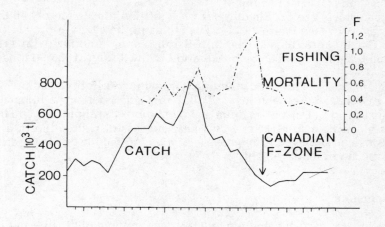

Figure 11.2a

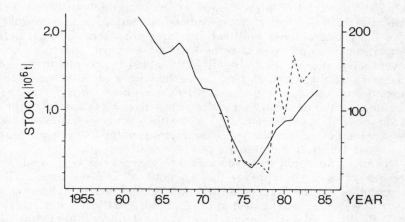

Figure 11.2b

drastic increases in fishing mortality, also of young cod, catches
declined during the following years to a minimum of 150,000 tons by
1978. This decline, together with warnings from scientists, resulted in
1973 in an agreement within ICNAF to establish a total allowable catch
for this cod stock. Unfortunately this TAC was set at 600,000 tons, far too
high, so stock size declined from over 2 million tons to merely 300,000
tons by 1975 (see figure 11.2b). The status of the stock improved only
after Canada introduced a 200-mile fishing zone, combined with a rigid
scheme of surveillance and a reduction of the TAC to 160,000 tons per
year.

The recovery of this stock is evident from the results of Canadian[21] and
West German investigations.[22]. Today this cod stock has a biomass of
about 1 million tons, and annual catches amount to about 230,000 tons.
This example also clearly shows how successful restoration of a fish
stock can be achieved through a productive interaction between science
and resources management.

Conclusion

In summary, we can conclude that the development of the international
management of fish resources has been a painstaking process over a
rather long period of time. Biologists had already warned at a rather early
stage against the overexploitation of resources. However, under strong
pressures from national fishing industries for economic reasons,
governments were not prepared to agree on regulatory measures
effective enough to protect the resources. Thus one valuable fish stock
after the other was fished down. Only when fishing became unprofitable
did the economic and political pressures grow large enough to force
governments into negotiations on more rigid measures which
eventually, after considerable difficulties, led to acceptable regimes of
fisheries management. During the earlier times of open access to fish
resources, international management bodies proved unable to
implement the necessary regulatory measures. The situation improved
after coastal states established 200-mile exclusive economic zones
under the new law of the sea. This put most of the fish resources under
national jurisdiction, but many problems still remain.

There is no doubt that considerable progress has been achieved in
recent years in the proper management of fish resources. This is
exemplified by the successful regulation of the fisheries on herring in the
North Sea and cod in the waters off Labrador and the restoration of these
fish stocks. However much needs still to be done for other fish stocks in
the North Atlantic and elsewhere.

Science has played an increasing role in providing the necessary
advice for fisheries management. In earlier times this advice was often
disregarded in favour of rather short-term profits. Scientists had little if
any means of exerting political pressure. Under the sobering influence of
firsthand practical experience with the reduction or even collapse of fish

stocks, however, a major change has taken place; today regular advice from assessment biologists forms an important part in schemes of fisheries regulation. After a period of trial and error, methods of stock assessment have been improved and are now internationally more or less standardized. They are also being further developed, particularly in the direction of multi-species models.

At least for the North Atlantic and Antarctic waters, suitable administrative and scientific instruments and schemes exist to improve or implement adequate management measures. Most important at this stage is the political will by governments to participate actively and positively in management schemes — even in cases where this may imply some losses in catches until the situation in over-exploited or depleted fish stocks is restored to healthy and productive conditions.

Notes

1. Valdivia, J.E., 1978, 'The Anchoveta and El Nino', Rapp.P.V.Reun Cons.Int.Explor. Mer. 173, pp. 196-202.

2. See Dragesund, O., 1980, 'A Review of Management Practices and Research Activities on Norwegian Spring Spawning Herring' in B. R. Melteff and V. G. Wespestad (eds.), *Proceedings of the Alaska Herring Symposium*, Anchorage, Alaska, 19-21 February 1980, Alaska Sea Grant Report 80-4, pp. 207-38; and Jakobsson, J., 1985, 'Monitoring and Management of the Northeast Atlantic Herring Stocks', *Can.J.Fish.Aquat.Sci.*, **42** (suppl. 1), pp. 207-21.

3. Schumacher, A., 1980, 'Management of the North Sea Herring Fisheries', in B. R. Melteff and V. G. Wespestad (eds.), pp. 239-49.

4. See also Andresen, Steinar, 1989, 'Increased Public Attention: Communication and Polarization', in this volume.

5. FAO, 1987, 'Review of the State of World Fishery Resources', FAO Fish.Circ. 710, rev. 5.

6. FAO, 1980, 'ACMRR Working Party on the Scientific Basis of Determining Management Measures', FAO Fish. Report 236.

7. For a discussion on the role of ICES in this respect, see Fløistad, Brit, 1989, 'Scientific Knowledge in the Management of Fish and Whale', in this volume.

8. Koers, A.W., 1973, *International Regulation of Marine Fisheries*, Fishing News (Books) Ltd., West Byfleet, London.

9. A parallel development is pointed out as regards the management of whales by Argrimsson, Haldor, 1989, 'Developments Leading to the 1982 Decision of the International Whaling Commission for a Zero Catch Quota 1986-90', in this volume.

10. For a discussion of the significance of industry pressure in environmental matters, see Boehmer-Christiansen, Sonja, 1989, 'The Role of Science in the International Regulation of Pollution', in this volume.

11. Rothschild, B.J. (ed.), 1983, *Global Fisheries: Perspectives for the 1980s*, Springer-Verlag Inc., New York.

12. For a general discussion on the role of science concerning compliance, see Young, Oran, 1989, 'Science and Social Institutions: Lessons for International Resource Regimes', in this volume.

13. For a discussion of different implications of a more interdisciplinary approach, see Andresen, Steinar, 1989, in this volume.

14. Gulland, J.A. (ed.), 1977, *Fish Population Dynamics*, John Wiley, New York; and Cushing, D.H., 1983, 'The Outlook for Fisheries Research in the Next Ten Years' in B. J. Rothschild (ed.), *Global Fisheries: Perspectives for the 1980s*, Springer, New York, pp. 263-77.

15. For a discussion on reliability of scientific recommendations, see Fløistad, Brit, 1989, in this volume.

16. For further discussion on the multi-species approach, see Asgrimsson, Haldor, 1989, and Fløistad, Brit, 1989, in this volume.

17. Stein, M. and Messtorff, J., 1988, 'Are Fluctuations in Cod Recruitment Off West Greenland Related to Long-Term Variations of the Physical Environment?', NAFO SCR Doc. 88/36.

18. This question is addressed by several authors in this volume. See, for instance, Timberlake, Lloyd, 1989, and Young, Oran, 1989, in this volume.

19. This question is also discussed by, for instance, Boehmer-Christiansen, Sonja, 1989, in this volume.

20. Anonymous, 1988., 'Reports of the ICES Advisory Committee on Fishery Management, 1987', ICES Cooperative Research Report 153.

21. Baird, J.W. and Bishop, C.A., 1986, 'Assessment of the Cod Stock in NAFO Divisions 2J+3KL', NAFO SCR Doc. 86/47.

22. Messtorff, J., 1985, 'Cod Biomass and Abundance Estimates for NAFO Division 2J from Stratified Random Bottom Trawl Survey Results over a Time Series of 12 Years, 1972-1983', NAFO SCR Doc. 85/95.

12

Developments leading to the 1982 decision of the International Whaling Commission for a zero catch quota 1986-90

Halldór Agrímsson

Introduction

The history of whaling is a prime example of international resource management. Although the history of modern-type whaling spans only about a century it clearly reveals some of the worst extremes of any international resource utilization. In brief it could be said that in the twentieth century the attitude towards whaling has changed from lack of knowledge and over-exploitation (1900-46) to increasing awareness and regulatory measures (1946-75) and finally to emotional and moral campaigns against whaling (since 1972). Scientists certainly played a fundamental role earlier this century in pointing out the imminent depletion of whale stocks and in formulating the rules for regulation. Those against whaling on emotional grounds also claim to base their arguments on scientific advice. In this sense, recent developments in the international regulation of whaling has politicized science and divided scientists.[1] This certainly raises challenging questions on the role of science in initiating a new policy versus supporting a predetermined policy.

Developments leading to the establishment of the International Whaling Commission

In 1925 the steamship *Lancing* was fitted with a slipway in the stern so that whales could be hauled up on deck for processing. This was the beginning of the floating whale factories, and five years later Norwegian and British ships in the Antarctic caught so many whales that the world market for whale oil collapsed. Subsequently, the whaling companies agreed to limit whale oil production, but this only succeeded partially because of large-scale German and Japanese whaling expeditions in that area in the late 1930s.

Because of this development, the International Council for the Exploration of the Sea (ICES) expressed its concern about the state of the whale stocks in the Antarctic and the necessity for international cooperation in whale management. The first systematic research on the stocks of whales in the Antarctic was initiated by the British Government which set up the Discovery Committee in 1924 to investigate the whales in that region. Norway also took an active part in this research effort.

In 1929, as a result of the Norwegian Whaling Act, the International Bureau of Whaling Statistics was set up in Norway to collect and publish catch statistics from all over the world which gradually became essential for estimating the state of the stocks and the industry. Following a further ICES recommendation, the first Convention for the regulation of whaling was established under the auspices of the League of Nations in 1931. This convention became effective in 1935 and gave total protection to right whales and further prohibited the catching of females with calves. However, no quotas or seasonal limitations were set, and no catch areas were closed. Furthermore there was no office established to operate and administer the Convention, which was signed by 26 nations. The absence of important whaling nations like Japan, the Soviet Union, Germany and Chile, represented a further weakness of the Convention.

By this time it was evident that the blue whales and the humpbacks in the Antarctic were over-exploited and whale oil production was only maintained by catching more and more fin whales. In 1937 a second international agreement was signed in London, establishing a detailed system of species regulation such as protection of the grey whale and minimum lengths for blue, fin, humpback and sperm whales. The Antarctic whaling season was limited to three months and pelagic whaling was forbidden in all areas north of 40^0s except in the Pacific.

During World War II little whaling was carried out and a large part of the pre-war whaling fleet was destroyed through war operations. In 1944 a conference was held in London to reorganize the whaling industry after the war. At this meeting a quota of 16,000 blue whale units was set for the first post-war season in the Antarctic as compared to 30,000 units in the 1938/39 season. This quota was an educated guess but the Blue Whale Unit, which was introduced by the Bureau of International Whaling Statistics in 1939 to measure the catches of various species in terms of oil production, became the standard yardstick for whaling regulations for the next quarter of a century. This unit, which was introduced by the industry to aid in self-regulation, consisted of one blue whale, 2 fin whales, 2,5 humpback whales, or 6 sei whales.

After the Washington Conference in 1946 these regulatory measures were soon replaced by the International Convention for the Regulation of Whaling (ICRW). This Convention was signed by 14 nations including all major whaling nations and it became effective two years later. It established the International Whaling Commission (IWC), a permanent body created through the treaty where each party has one vote. The preamble to the Convention recognizes the interest of the member nations to safeguard the great natural resources of the whale stocks for future generations. It also emphasizes that proper regulations will secure that the number of whales caught will not endanger the future of the stocks and that it is of common interest to achieve the optimum level of the whale stocks as rapidly as possible without causing widespread economic and nutritional distress. The aim of the Convention was thus to provide for a proper conservation of whale stocks as a resource and the orderly development of the whaling industry.

An important part of the Convention is the Schedule which is an annex to the treaty but forms an integral part of the Convention. The Schedule is quite flexible and is constantly being reviewed according to changing management needs. The Schedule makes specific provisions for the classification of whale stocks and protection, such as catch limits by species, areas and sex, minimum size limits, duration of whaling seasons, limitations of areas where factory ships can be used, inspection of whaling operations and, finally, collection of data. Amendments to the Schedule have to be adopted by a three-quarters majority of the voting members. However, they are not binding on any member government which lodges an objection to the decision within a period of ninety days. This means that most decisions of the Commission have to be unanimous in order to be successfully implemented, but without this provision it is considered unlikely that the Convention would have been concluded at all.[2]

Scientific foundations for the regulation of whaling

In the early years of the IWC a great deal of effort was devoted to biological research and related studies necessary for conservation and management of the whale stocks. Because of the lack of quantitative stock assessment scientists had great difficulties in convincing the whaling industry about the progressive depletion of the stocks. These years were actually the 'black period' in the history of the IWC and it was not until the stocks had reached a critical point in 1960 that the Commission set up an independant group of scientists, the Committee of Three (later Four) Scientists, to assess stock levels and give advice on allowable catches. This committee worked from 1961 to 1964 in cooperation with the Scientific Committee of the Commission and analysed the biological and catch data according to the techniques which were then used for fisheries assessments. This work provided the basis for present methods of whale stock analysis. As early as in 1964 the

Committee point out the unsuitability of the Blue Whale Unit as a basis for management and proposed regulations on a species-by-species basis. This advice was supported by the Commission's Scientific Committee. In spite of that, species quotas were not introduced until 1969 when catch limits were set for fin and sei whales in the North Pacific. In the Southern Hemisphere the Blue Whale Unit was not abandoned until the 1972/1973 season.

In 1975 the Commission adopted the so-called New Management Procedure (NMP) which was based on the principle that all whale stocks should be stabilized at a level of the maximum sustainable yield (MSY). For stocks of baleen whales the Scientific Committee used as the maximum sustainable yield level 60 per cent of the initial stock level, and as the maximum sustainable yield 4 per cent of the maximum sustainable yield stock level. According to the new rules the stocks were divided into three categories:

1. An initial management stock (IMS) is a stock more than 20 per cent above the MSY stock level. [Commercial whaling should be allowed on these stocks on the advice of the Scientific Committee without the risk of bringing them below the MSY level. The permitted catch should not be more than 90 per cent of the MSY as far as this was known.]

2. A sustained management stock (SMS) is a stock not more than 10 per cent below the MSY level, and not more than 20 per cent above that level. [When a stock had remained stable for a considerable period of time giving rather constant catches it should be classified as an SMS stock. Whaling should be permitted on sustained management stocks in accordance with the advice of the Scientific Committee. For stocks at or above the MSY stock level the permitted catch should not exceed 90 per cent of the MSY. For stocks between the MSY level and 10 per cent below that level the permitted catch should not exceed the number of whales obtained by taking 90 per cent of the MSY and reducing that number by 10 per cent for every 1 per cent by which the stock falls short of the MSY stock level.]

3. A protection stock (PS) is a stock that is 10 per cent or more below the MSY stock level. These stocks should be protected.

During the next decade it became increasingly evident that the Scientific Committee was not in a position to give the Commission solid advice on stock classification and quotas, despite the new management procedure. The main reason for this was the lack of reliable data for stock size calculation and the uncertainty of the models used. Eventually, it became clear that a number of stocks were over-exploited even under the NMP.[3]

Developments leading to the 1982 zero quota decision.

Until 1970, the IWC was more or less a whalers' association, which tried to allocate catches and regulate the competition between its members.

The Commission was evidently showing more concern for whale products than the state of the stocks, and it had a bad name with regard to conservation of marine resources. During the years 1972-84, the number of contracting parties to the Convention nearly tripled, i.e. from 14 to 40 member nations. This was possible since admittance to the Commission is open to any nation. Most of the newcomers were non-whaling nations with no tradition or interest in commercial whaling. On the other hand, many of the new members were deeply concerned about the ethics of whaling, advocating a general moratorium on all commercial whaling.[4]

A few weeks before the 1972 annual meeting of the IWC, the United Nations Conference on the Human Environment in Stockholm recommended a ten-year moratorium in commercial whaling. This proposal was forwarded to the IWC Annual Meeting, but since eight of the 14 members of the Commission in that year conducted commercial whaling, the moratorium proposal was not adopted. However, at the next year's meeting the Scientific Committee of the IWC proposed an International Decade of Cetacean Research and, furthermore, the NMP was adopted in 1974 and implemented from 1975. Thus, the Stockholm resolution was undoubtedly a great impetus to the whale protectionist movements.

The 1972 moratorium proposal was thoroughly discussed in the Scientific Committee which concluded that 'a blanket moratorium can not be justified scientifically. Prudent management requires regulation of the stocks individually'. The Committee further noted that a moratorium would probably also bring about a reduction in the amount of research whereas there was a prime need for a substantial increase in research activity.

In 1973 the US proposed a ten year moratorium on commercial whaling, but the Scientific Committee again stated that there was no biological necessity for such a measure. It was, however, decided to protect fin whales in the Antarctic as from the 1976 season. In 1974, the US again proposed a moratorium but instead the NMP was adopted on the basis of an Australian amendment to the proposal and thus came about as a kind of compromise to the moratorium issue. These new regulations, however, did not substantially affect the fishery since the overall quota was only reduced by 3.5 per cent in the years 1972 to 1974, and no catch quota was set for the stocks of whales in the North Atlantic.

In 1977 the Scientific Committee suggested that the NMP should be revised as it was not considered adequate to protect the whale stocks. Although no changes were adopted by the Commission, the NMP led to the end of sei whaling in the Antarctic in 1975, and catch limits were introduced in the mid 1970s in the North Atlantic with respect to sperm, fin, sei and minke whales. In the years 1975 to 1978 the total quota was reduced by 37 per cent, from 33,000 whales to 21,000 whales, a clear sign of stricter regulations and with the consent of the whaling nations.

In 1979 Australia proposed a ban on all whaling but this did not get enough support. At the same meeting the Seychelles proposed a whale sanctuary in the Indian Ocean and this was adopted by the Commission. A new US proposal for a moratorium on all commercial whaling of baleen whales was adopted in a much modified form. It would only apply to pelagic whaling, and minkes were exempted from the moratorium. In this way fin and sei whales were protected, except in the North Atlantic where no pelagic whaling was carried out. However, the impact of these measures on the whaling nations was rather small, since minke and sperm whales could be hunted pelagically and coastal stations could continue their operations. In 1980 a sperm whale moratorium was proposed and adopted.

The membership of the IWC not only changed drastically during the period mentioned above, but also its character and the balance between the two main interest groups; i.e. whaling nations and non-whaling nations. Of the 14 members of the IWC in 1972, eight conducted whaling for commercial purposes. By 1980 the number of whaling nations in the Commission had increased to ten, but two nations had stopped whaling. During the same period the number of non-whaling members in the Commission had increased from six to 30 which gave them decisive control in the Commission. In 1972 the whaling nations constituted 57 per cent of the Commission members. In 1976 they were down to 47 per cent and in 1982 their percentage had shrunk to 23 per cent, bringing them into a definite minority in a Commission where the three quarters decision rule governs. The majority has been called the group of 'like-minded' anti-whaling nations.

The big victory of the whale protectionist movement came in 1982, when the IWC adopted a three-year phase-out of commercial whaling. At the thirty-fourth annual meeting of the Commission in 1982 five proposals seeking an end to commercial whaling were introduced. The proponents were the representatives of the so-called like minded group, i.e. Seychelles, UK, US, France and Australia. In support of the Seychelles' proposal the other moratorium proposals before the meeting were withdrawn.

The Seychelles' proposal provided for an additional clause to paragraph 10 of the Schedule and introduced a three-year phase-out period for the whaling-industry to accommodate to zero catch limits. Extensive discussion on this proposal focused on the following topics:

1. The need for rational management and sustained utilization.
2. The scientific uncertainty and lack of data in assessments.
3. Past over-exploitation and decline in whale stocks.
4. The present size of some whale stocks.
5. The humaneness of whaling.
6. The distinction drawn between commercial and aboriginal/subsistence whaling.
7. Compatibility of the proposal with the intents and purposes of the International Convention for the Regulation of Whaling.
8. Coastal state sovereignty within the 200 mile Exclusive Economic Zones.
9. United Nations Convention of the Law of the Sea.

After some amendments the final proposal was as follows:

Notwithstanding the other provisions of paragraph 10, catch limits for the killing for commercial purposes of whales from all stocks for the 1986 coastal and the 1985/86 pelagic seasons and thereafter shall be zero. This provision will be kept under review, based upon the best scientific advice, and by 1990 at the latest the Commission will undertake a comprehensive assessment of the effects of this decision on whale stocks and consider modification of this provision and the establishment of other catch limits.

All the whaling nations present at the meeting opposed the proposed amendment of the Schedule. They argued that there was no scientific justification for a moratorium and that the proposal lacked a necessary scientific basis as required under the Convention. In fact, the Scientific Committee was not able to support the proposal. Furthermore, the whaling nations also questioned the distinction created between aboriginal/subsistence whaling operations and commercial whaling operations. Some of them maintained that the proposal infringed upon sovereign rights of nations in coastal waters and that it did not conform to the ICRW of 1946. Some of the non-whaling nations expressed their concern over the lack of humane killing methods in the whaling industry and the strength of world-wide public opinion on the issue and ecological uncertainties. Other non-whaling nations believed that the proposal was a good solution for the conservation of whales and the various interests of the whaling industry.

The amendment to the Schedule was adopted by 25 votes in favour, with 7 against and 5 abstentions. The majority — 'like-minded nations' — had achieved the necessary three-quarter majority vote required for an operative Schedule Amendment.[5] Subsequently four whaling nations used their right under the Convention to object to the Zero Catch Quota. The Icelandic Parliament recommended that Iceland not object to the decision.

Comprehensive assessment of whale stocks 1986-90: divergent intentions and definitions

As already pointed out, the proposal for a zero quota as from 1986 included a provision for a comprehensive assessment of the effects of this decision on whale stocks. Since 1982, the definition, timing, and implementation of a 'comprehensive assessment' has been a constant bone of contention. At its annual meeting in 1984, the Scientific Committee of the IWC stated that it did not believe that it was in a position to define what comprises a comprehensive assessment. In 1985 the Scientific Committee pointed out that the IWC had come to use the term 'comprehensive assessment' to mean two rather different things:

1. An ex-post evaluation of the effects of setting catch limits to zero for the 1986 season and thereafter.

2. An ex-ante in depth evaluation of the current status of whale stocks in
    the light of management objectives and procedures.

The Scientific Committee concluded that the latter definition of
comprehensive assessment would better enable the Committee to carry
out the IWC's terms of reference. Not only the timing but also the
methodology of a comprehensive assessment has been a matter of
disagreement. The Scientific Committee, for example, pointed out at its
1985 meeting that for many important stocks essentially no new data had
been obtained since exploitation had ceased many years previously. To
obtain current information on the status of these stocks, the Scientific
Committee concluded that direct observations would have to be made.

In order to clarify the intent and procedures of the Comprehensive
Assessment, the Scientific Committee convened a special meeting on the
subject in April 1986. At this meeting the Scientific Committee agreed
that a comprehensive assessment can be considered an in-depth
evaluation of the status of whale stocks in light of management objectives
and procedures. In order to achieve this objective the Committee agreed
that it would need to:

1. review and revise stock assessment methods;
2. collect new information to facilitate and improve assessments;
3. examine alternative management regimes.

The shortcomings in assessment methods is not a new issue at the
IWC. Since the late 1970s, the Scientific Committee encountered
problems in implementing the NMP mainly due to difficulties in
estimating initial stock sizes and MSY and the Maximum Sustainable
Yield Level (MSYL). The call for a Comprehensive Assessment of whale
stocks placed a new emphasis on management procedures and a new
focus on the weaknesses in methodology and uncertainties in estimated
quantities.

Therefore, if current trends in whale populations were to be studied
seriously, the Scientific Committee concluded that IWC member nations
should place a high priority on continuing monitoring studies. The
Scientific Committee assumed that all national research programmes
would at least continue at their present levels and that new resources
would be provided by the Commission and member nations in order to
fulfil the intentions of the Comprehensive Assessment.

Japan, Norway and Iceland decided to commit substantial amounts of
new resources and manpower to fulfil the research requirements of the
comprehensive assessment. However whale research by other members
of the IWC has been negligible and limited special effort has been noted
in connection with the comprehensive assessment.

Conclusions

Following the Stockholm Conference in 1972, many large
environmental activist groups intensified their campaign against

whaling. These groups have claimed that our knowledge of whale stocks is not sufficient to determine sustainable yield or to set catch quotas. Therefore, it would be necessary to protect whales and emphasize benign research in the near future. The real drive behind these groups is often the feeling that any kind of whaling, regardless of stock size, is morally wrong and barbaric. To further their cause these groups have, therefore, used repulsive images of whaling in their campaigns, although the taking of whales with modern methods is probably no more inhumane than slaughtering of livestock. They claim that civilized people must stop such inhumane activities. But in recent years, whale protectionists have sought to apply pressure mainly on two fronts:

1. by boycott actions against whaling nations by encouraging the public to avoid their products; and
2. by pressure on the United States government to apply coercive provisions of the 1971 Amendment to the Fishermen's Protective Act of 1967 and the 1979 Amendment to the Magnusson Fishery Conservation and Management Act of 1976.

In some cases emotional protectionist campaigns have been bolstered by outspoken support from respected scientists. In this sense, science has been misused. These scientists have not shown the same enthusiasm for research on the status of the world whale stocks, including multi-species interactions, in order to carry out the Comprehensive Assessment.[6] The lack of resources committed to this important task of the Commission by the majority of IWC member nations is a reverse example of the ignorance during the years of over-exploitation earlier this century.

It has been pointed out that the so called 'like-minded' group within the IWC does in fact base much of its strength on the provisions of United States' laws, as a main enforcement instrument of IWC resolutions. This in turn gives a temptation to misinterpret and misuse IWC resolutions and proceedings. Thus, if the IWC would state its concern about an issue, it could very well be interpreted by some pressure groups as a legal ordinance. For example, these groups claim that the taking of any whale for scientific purposes should not be permitted and is illegal, although such a take is in fact allowed under Article VIII of the 1946 ICRW.

From 1982 it became apparent that most of the 'like-minded' nations seemed to have limited intentions to carry out serious whale research and, thus contribute to the completion of the Comprehensive Assessment. It gradually became clear that the protectionist movement had come to a moral conclusion which would not necessarily be based on better scientific knowledge. It is of concern that the existing majority block of nations within the IWC does not need to base a three-quarter majority vote on scientific knowledge. In fact the most significant development that has taken place in the past two decades is that the IWC has gradually moved from an organization of whale management towards protectionism. This has eroded the role of science in the regulation of whaling, while there has been an increasing tendency to refer to IWC resolutions for a political purpose with regard to United States' laws.

The heated moral campaigns against whaling of any kind are in principle against the utilization of whales as a resource.[7] The boycott actions of the pressure groups can in fact be considered economic and cultural terrorism against local populations. A prime example is the socio-economic and ecological disaster brought about by Greenpeace's systematic destruction of the seal fur industry. In addition to the economic collapse of many eskimo communities, a further consequence of that action is an explosion in the seal population and an ecological disaster in northern waters.

In addition to the inherent weakness of the IWC as regulatory body, because of the open rules of admittance, the single-species orientation of the Commission is inadequate to deal comprehensively with marine resource management in line with current scientific knowledge.[8] For example, it is believed that the Antarctic minke whale stock is in direct competition with blue whales in the area. Not only does the size of one whale stock affect other whales, but also other parts of the ecosystem which implies that a broader multi-species management approach is needed. This is the most apparent shortcoming of the IWC as a regulatory body if we can, indeed, look upon whales as a resource that can be rationally utilized, which is clearly stipulated as one of the main objectives of the Convention. It is perhaps only clearly evident to those nations that base a major part of their economy on fisheries and have experienced at first hand the strong interrelationships within the marine ecosystem. In the future we need an ecological approach to the conservation and management of marine mammals in order to restore the role of science as the basis for policy making and thus restore confidence in the regulatory functions of the IWC. Therefore, we need increased international cooperation among scientists, which in turn requires increased funding and support of applied research programmes.

Notes

1. For a more general discussion of the politicization of science, see for instance Miles, Edward, 1989, 'Scientific and Technological Knowledge and International Cooperation in Resource Management', and Young, Oran, 1989, 'Science and Social Institutions: Lessons for International Resource Regimes', both in this volume.

2. For a history of whaling and the IWC up until approximately 1970, see for example McHugh, J.L., 1974, 'The Role and History of the International Whaling Commission' in W.E. Schevill (ed.), *The Whale Problem: A Status Report*, Harvard University Press, Cambridge, pp. 305-35.

3. For a general discussion of various aspects of the regulation of whales see Allen, K.R., 1980, *Conservation and Management of Whales*, Butterworths & Co., London.

4. For an extensive discussion of the effect of the strong increase in membership in the IWC, see Hoel, A.H., 1985, *The International Whaling Commission 1972-84: New Members, New Concerns*, The Fridtjof Nansen Institute, R:003-1985 (171 pp.).

5. For a history of the IWC, see Beek, J.G. Van, 1987, 'Historical Review of the Management Measures Taken by the International Whaling Commission', *Lutra 30*, 166-192, and 'International Whaling Commission 1973-87', the Chairman's report, *Rep.int.Whal.Commn*, vols. 23-37.

6. For a discussion of this, see also Fløistad, Brit, 1989, 'Scientific Knowledge in the Management of Fish and Whale: Global or Regional Organizations, Single and Multi-species Approach', in this volume.

7. For a discussion of the effect of the increased public attention towards the management of whaling, see Andresen, Steinar, 1989, 'Increased Public Attention: Communication and Polarization', in this volume.

8. For a discussion of other organizational aspects of the IWC, see Fløistad, Brit, 1989, in this volume.

13

Scientific knowledge in the management of fish and whale: global or regional organizations, single and multi-species approach

Brit Fløistad

Introduction

The point of departure in this paper is the need for scientific knowledge in the management of fish and whale. Realizing that science is but one aspect in marine resource management does not change the point made by representatives from the scientific [1] and the political [2] world alike, namely that scientific information constitutes the necessary basis for such management. The challenge is thus to identify how science can best perform this function.

One fruitful approach may be to view the relationship between science and policy as consituting three different process levels. In the first process the collecting and appraisal of information and data on marine biology is the basis for scientists to *provide scientific advice* on resource management. In the second process this advice is *mediated* through communication between scientist and policy maker. This process has been referred to as a 'buffer between research results and their utilization for regulation'. [3] The actual weighing between the scientific advice and economic and political consequences of this advice is left to the third process: the *formulating of management policy*.

Although there are thus three processes, I will in this paper deal only with the first two. More specifically I want to look into *how scientific*

advice is provided and mediated in the management of fish and whale.
As both these resources have a 'common' characteristic, in that they are
not entirely under one state's national jurisdiction, international
cooperation is required both in providing scientific advice, in the
mediating process and in formulating management policy.

Scientific advice in fishery is provided by the International Council for
the Exploration of the Sea (ICES) while fisheries commissions and
nation states formulate management policies. In whaling, the
International Whaling Commission (IWC) provides scientific advice and
formulates regulatory measures as well.

My point of departure in discussing the provision and mediation of
scientific advice in fishery and in whaling will be certain variables
considered necessary for making such advice *credible* and *acceptable*.
Credibility in the scientific process in essential for acceptance in the
mediating process. The result of the mediating process is in its turn
crucial for the role of science in actual management policy. [4]

An important aspect of today's resource management is the increasing
need for a 'multi-species approach'. [5] As this implies taking into account
all interrelated marine living resources, it makes for a more
comprehensive and a more complicated process both in providing
scientific advice, in mediating this advice and in formulating the
management policy. Relating this to the present organizational structure
in fisheries and whaling, I want to ask if this structure is inconsistent
with a *multi-species approach*. Today this structure implies a regional
'many-species' (not multi-species) assessment in fisheries and a global
one-species assessment in whaling.

Providing scientific advice; what makes it credible?

Obviously no scientist involved in providing scientific advice on
resource management will be totally unaware of the national interests of
his or her country in the sharing of this resource. But, since 'reading the
mind' of the scientist is impossible, we can never know exactly to what
extent such non-scientific considerations affect the formulation of
scientific advice. [6] What can be done is to try to indicate some aspects
that may influence the possibility of other considerations playing a role.
While 'science' here refers to biological data and information on the
various marine living resources, 'other considerations' are the economic
and political consequences of implementing the advice. Aspects
discussed here are scientific tradition, organizational structure,
membership in the organzations, the closeness of the scientific process
and the concord between and the record of scientists.

Scientific tradition

Let me start with a rather diffuse but no less important aspect, namely
what could be designated as the scientific tradition. Reviewing the

effectiveness of past management of some pelagic stocks, it has been maintained 'that scientists needed time to deal adequately with the research problems'.[7] Whether a scientific organization came as a response to a need for managing the actual resource, or had its own tradition for scientific investigations prior to this need, may mean a difference in its ability to provide adequate scientific advice, but also in its detachment from national management interests and thus in its scientific independence. One may argue that the longer the scientific tradition, the more independent and objective the scientific investigation, and, thereby, the more credible the scientific advice.

Relating this to the two sets of organizational structures dealt with here, the ICES, established as far back as 1902, is the oldest international marine organization in the world.[8] Concern for regulatory measures to protect fish stocks played a role in the founding of the ICES, but a general wish among scientists in different countries to cooperate on marine research was stressed as well. It was not until the 1950s that the situation became alarming for many species and management measures essential. That this could happen despite the existence of a scientific body like the ICES is connected to the fact that the 'state of the art' of fishery science does not always lead to timely and adequate advice, nor are scientists always heeded. This does not, however, undermine the point made here: namely that when the need for regulatory measures became evident, a body for assessing stocks and providing scientific advice was at hand. In the case of whaling regulation, various attempts at international cooperation had been made in the 1930s. [9] An International Committee on Whaling Statistics was established in 1929 and the first Convention for the Regulation of Whaling was signed in 1931. Such measures, however, could not prevent a situation where generally 'all sizes and all species were fair game'.[10] Even though concern for the effect on whale stocks had earlier been expressed by some scientists, it is fair to say that the establishment of international scientific cooperation in whaling — namely the International Convention for the Regulation of Whaling (ICWR) in 1946 and the International Whaling Commission in 1949 — concurred with the urgent need for regulatory measures. This meant a situation where a rather immature body of scientific cooperation was set to provide scientific advice for managing the different whale stocks. If we link this to the assumption made initially about scientific tradition, we may summarize that the International Whaling Commission may have been less capable of providing proper scientific advice. The fact that conflicting interests in the managing of whale stocks developed parallel to the scientific cooperation may have weakened the possibility of independent and objective scientific advice.

Organizational structure

In elaborating further on what makes scientific advice credible, we now turn to the difference in organizational structure between fisheries and whaling to elucidate the importance of this aspect.

Since the founding of the ICES in 1902, the premiss of its activities has been that international cooperation on scientific research constitutes the basis for a rational conservation and exploration of marine resources. The purpose of the ICES is thus to promote and coordinate research undertaken by scientists within its 18 member countries, and to utilize this information in providing scientific advice on resource management. While the member countries are responsible for collecting catch statistics and conducting the actual research, the *Council* of the ICES, consisting of two delegates from each member country, coordinates this activity through the formulation of ICES research programmes. The information and data on various stocks resulting from the national research activities constitute the basis for the cooperation on stock assessment taking place in the various ICES *working groups.* Each working group specializes in one or a set of stocks; groups consist of scientists from the member countries doing research on the stocks in question. Reports from these working groups on estimates of fish stocks and fishing patterns are in turn utilized by the *Advisory Committee* on Fishery Management (ACFM) in providing scientific advice on resource management.

While the number of scientists taking part in the working groups may vary from country to country, each member state has one representative in the ACFM. This national representation differs from what had been the case until 1978, when the advisory function had been handled by a 'Liaison Committee', with representation not by country but by 'co-opted experts from ICES member states, appointed by the Council'. [11] By linking the providing of scientific advice to a representative body, the ICES introduced an element of national interests in formulating scientific advice. This must, however, be seen in the light of extended national jurisdiction and the reduced role of the North East Atlantic Fisheries Commission (NEAFC). The increased role of the nation-states did thus reflect itself in the scientific cooperation. This nationalistic impression is softened by the fact that, even though scientists meeting in the Advisory Committee on Fishery Management are nominated by the member states, they are appointed and also paid by the Council. This should indicate a balance between loyalty to the nation-state and to the ICES.

As indicated earlier, the ICES is responsible solely for the providing of scientific advice, while fisheries commissions (North East Atlantic Fisheries Commission, International Baltic Sea Fisheries Commission and North Atlantic Salmon Conservation Organisation) and nation states (either unilaterally or in cooperation with states sharing the same stock) are responsible for regulatory measures.

The International Whaling Commission differs from the ICES in that the providing of scientific advice and the formulating of regulatory measures take place under 'the same organizational roof'. The objective of the International Convention for the Regulation of Whaling (ICRW) is to provide for the 'conservation, development and optimum utlization of whale resources' but also 'to take into consideration the interests of the consumers of whale products and the whaling industry'. [12] This means in other words that economic and political aspects are to be considered within the organizational structure of the IWC responsible for implementing the ICRW. In doing so the IWC is to base its regulatory measures on scientific findings.

Handling both scientific and management aspects under the same organizational roof does not imply, however, that the two processes are one and the same. In implementing the ICRW the International Whaling Commission may establish 'such committees as it considers desirable' [13]. A *Scientific Committee* is thus responsible for considering scientific data while the formulation of regulatory measures takes place in the *Commission*. Like ACFM the Scientific Committee also bases its appraisal and assessment on information from scientists operating in different *working groups*. As in the working groups of ICES, member states may send as many scientists as they see fit. They may also send any number of scientists to the Scientific Committee. Information from this committee is passed on to the *Technical Committee* which forwards proposals on advice for managing whale stocks to the Commission. The Technical Committee may consider factors other than purely scientific; and proposals may formally be passed by simple majority, each country having one vote. Both in the Technical Committee and in the Commission, the general aim is to achieve consensus and avoid voting. [14]

In neither of the two scientific processes, that of ICES or IWC, can the providing of scientific advice completely ignore the fact that different national interests are involved. The difference here is in the way it is handled. Being a scientific organization *per se*, in the Advisory Committee on Fishery Management the element of national representation is as such 'out of place'. To what extent it impinges on the content of the advice is of course an open question. The important point here is that there does exist an element of national representation, and thereby the possibility that national interests may play a role. Here, however, the element of scientific tradition mentioned earlier may help reduce such influence.

When it comes to the provision of scientific advice on the management of whale stocks, the national element is more openly acknowledged as part of the process. This is manifested by the fact that the Technical Committee has a broader mandate than 'pure' science when formulating its proposal on management. This indicates an organizational structure with possibilites of a closer and more blurred relationship between science and national interests. The fact that the 1982 moratorium on whaling was passed by the votes of non-whaling nations, while whaling nations voted against, and while the Scientific Committee made no recommendations for such a moratorium, certainly indicates that national interests played a major role in this regulatory measure.

Membership

Another aspect that may be important for the credibility of the scientific advice, relevant for both the organizations discussed here, has to do with membership. Both organizations are open to membership by countries not directly involved in the management of the actual resource. In ICES scientists from the United States and Canada take part in the scientific work. By representing an impartial element, in the sense that these countries are not fishing in the area, this membership must be said to increase the objectivity, and thus the credibility, of the advice provided.

In the case of whaling, however, the Icelandic Minister of Fisheries, Halldor Asgrimsson, has made a very strong case for extended membership in the IWC having undermined the credibility of the organization's scientific advice. According to Asgrimsson, the increase in number of member nations from 14 to 41 has changed the IWC from 'an organization of whaling nations to a protectionist oriented body . . . '[15] What he says in fact is that membership by non-whaling nations has had an effect contrary to what can be said for ICES. Important here is no doubt that being a non-whaling nation does not imply impartiality on the management issue: rather the contrary. The whale is considered a 'common resource' and its management obviously raises common ethical and moral questions. Extended membership in the International Whaling Commission, therefore, has implied an extension in the scope of interests involved in the management of this resource. The effect has been members not impartial to the management of whales, but rather with a different view on management policy. Even though whaling nations may consider this conservationist view out of place, it is important to bear in mind that such an attitude is founded on the extensive over-exploitation of whales in the first half of this century.

It may be argued, as Asgrimsson does,[16] that science is here being used to further conservationist interests. It may, however, then be countered that science has been used to further the interests of whaling nations as well. The fact of the matter is that a situation of scientific uncertainty makes it possible for political interests rather than scientific knowledge to play a major role in management policy; 'the higher the level of conflict, the greater the constraints on utilizing scientific research'. [17] The situation today is that while the objective of some members seems to be a ban on whaling regardless of scientific information, others see increased scientific information as a means to further continued whaling. What must be done is to better our scientific knowledge on the various whale stocks and thereby help reduce the use of scientific uncertainty as a base for different managing strategies.

A closed scientific process

One other aspect that may be of importance for the credibility of scientific advice concerns scientists being able to appraise data and provide their advice in a closed scientific process. Now, openness on scientific data, allowing the public and organizations to get information on and take part in the managing of resources is considered positive. What I say here is not contrary to that. My point is that keeping media and public attention out of the *process of providing* scientific advice can help to prevent other considerations from playing a role. Scientists will be more free to express 'pure' scientific views without having to look to distributional effects.[18]

The difference in the public concern for managing fish and whale is reflected in the far greater attention given to the meetings of the International Whaling Commission than to those of the International Council for the Exploration of the Sea. One obvious reason is that IWC deals with both management and distributional aspects. This, together with the rather strong conflict of interest attached to whaling, makes public attention both appropriate and understandable. The important question is, however, whether this attention impinges on the work of the Scientific Committee.

As indicated earlier, member states can be represented by as many scientists as they see fit in the Scientific Committee. This may open the way for representation by 'science politicians',[19] representatives who in addition to their scientific work also look to the political aspects. As they are dealing here with the rather 'hot' issue of marine mammals, these representatives may see an interest in public attention at this point. Since meetings of the Scientific Committee are held immediately prior to meetings of the Commission, public attention may already have been aroused.

In fisheries the fact that only one scientist from each country can take part in the working of the ACFM makes the presence of 'science politicians' less likely. The modest public attention generally attached to fishery and the longer scientific tradition help support the assumption that providing scientifc advice in fishery matter is a 'closer process' than is the case in whaling.

The assertion that public attention should be kept at a certain distance from the scientific process is supported by the fact that meetings of the Council, the highest body of the ICES, allow only two delegates from each country. No observers from nation states and organizations or representatives from the media may be present at these meetings.

The concord between scientists and scientific record

This leads me to the final set of aspects with a bearing on the credibility of scientific advice, namely the degree of concord between scientists and their scientific record. We may assume that disagreement between scientists will represent a poor basis for providing credible scientific advice. In most cases it leads to a lesser, or at least more accidental, role for science in the policy-making process. As indicated earlier, this also paves the way for policy-makers to interpret scientific information to their liking.

Now, it is of course unlikely that all scientists will fully agree on the assessment of a particular stock or on the consequences of a certain catch volume. What seems important for credibility is, however, that there be fundamental agreement on the methods and procedures for collecting and appraising scientific data.

As for the two organizations providing scientific advice on fish stocks and marine mammals, it seems fair to say that there has been greater disagreement between scientists regarding information on whale stocks than has been the case for fishery. One reason seems to lie in the collection and processing of data.

The main data base for assessment for all marine resources is catch statistics based on landings by fishermen. Regulating a fishery may, however, lead to deterioration in fishery statistics due to misreporting in forms of quantity, areas and species. This underlines the need for independent estimates from research vessel surveys. [20] While such surveys are part of fisheries data collection under the auspices of the ICES, catch landings have been the main, if not the only, base for stock assessment of whales. In addition to uncertainties related to the catch reports themselves, this also means that assessment estimates are based on constructed models, allowing for a greater difference among scientists on aspects inherent in the model. Such aspects may be the time-span on which their estimates are based, and also whether it involves aspects such as the development of a more efficient fleet, new catching methods and so on.

Of the two management strategies — continued whaling or a zero quota — it could be argued that in a situation of uncertainty, a protectionist strategy is the safest way. This does not necessarily imply the most effective management in the sense of optimal resource exploitation. The ultimate goal must therefore be to provide management knowledge that may constitute a credible base for a proper conservation of the resource — implying either a stop or continued exploitation. The research vessel surveys on whale stocks in the Northeast Atlantic region now being conducted by Norway and Iceland stem from a need for scientific information more reliable than that provided by the methods now in operation.

The credibility of advice and recommendations coming from scientists also relates to their scientific record. In both fishery and whaling it is fair to say that awareness of the need for regulatory measures manifested itself mainly in connection with over-exploitation and depletion of stocks rather than scientific advice and warnings. As for whaling, 'it was not until the stocks had reached a critical point'[21] that the need for management was acknowledged, even though scientists had been pointing to the over-exploitation of certain whale stocks. And in fisheries it was 'less on the strength of the arguments presented by the scientists but rather by the obvious collapse of certain fisheries that actions for the protection of the resource were finally taken'. [22]

To what extent appropriate and timely advice was at hand but disregarded by policy-makers is a difficult, but still highly relevant question. Also, a record of providing advice not in accordance with what later proved the actual situation, or advice coming too late, may have influenced the role of science in managing these resources.

This touches on the relationship between the advice coming from scientists and acceptance of this by policy-makers. Accepting scientific advice as a base for formulating management policy makes for a greater role for science not only in management policy, but also in abiding by the regulatory measures in the actual fishery.

Mediating scientific advice; what makes it acceptable to the policy-maker?

The mediation of the scientific advice to the policy-maker has been referred to as an intermediate stage between providing scientific advice and formulating management policy. A policy-maker may view some scientific advice as both credible and timely, while at the same time knowing that it implies socio-economic consequences that are not — and should not be — inherent in the advice. In the event that this touches on politically difficult distributive aspects, such scientific advice may have to be rejected or drastically adjusted. The management of both fishery and whaling has many examples of this. 'For several of the main fisheries in the Northeast Atlantic the magnitude and timing of agreed measures fell considerably short of the scientifically recommended requirements to achieve these goals.' [23]

This is certainly related to the fact that 'since major national economic and political interests were involved, it took a long time before total allowable catches and in particular national catch quotas were accepted'. [24] However, marine biologists are not supposed to — nor are they in most cases able to — link socio-economic aspects to their scientific advice. Even though they may be aware of the difficulties of the fishing industry, 'they were in some respects to be considered the representatives of the fish, and this task should not be taken from them'. [25] As stressed earlier, precisely such distance from other considerations is essential for the credibility of scientific advice. What might however seem important is an *awareness* among scientists of the socio-economic consequences of their advice. This may then imply a way of mediating their scientific advice that can increase the possibility that policy-makers will accept the advice as a basis for their management policy.

Mediating scientific advice in fisheries

Within the field of fishery, the past ten years have seen increasingly closer contact between marine biologists, fisheries administrators and the fishing industry. A driving force in this has been the new ocean regime of national economic zones and the nationalization of many fish resources. While the main recipients of scientific advice formerly were the different fisheries commissions, now one or possibly several states are to consider the advice under the new regime. This could imply a challenge to the scientific advice coming from the ICES, as nation-states might be tempted to provide scientific advice more in line with national management interests. This might apply particularly to the European Community, leaving it to their own Scientific and Technical Committee on Fisheries (STCF) to provide scientific advice for the formulation of the Community management policy. EC today comprises half the member states of the ICES and is in itself an international scientific body. The STCF has however so far not constituted a challenge to the scientific work of the Advisory Committee on Fishery Management. An agreement has been reached between the ICES and the Commission of the European Community giving the Commission the right to ask the Council for scientific advice on fishery resources management. Thus the Commission can get the information directly from the ACFM rather than through their member states.

Such possible 'competition' from other scientific bodies might, however, have had a triggering effect towards increased awareness within the ICES of the economic and political implications of scientific advice. This awareness is referred to by Sahrhage in pointing to the heavy responsibility put on the shoulders of scientists 'considering the great economic and political implications' of their advice.[26]He does not go any further in indicating what implications this might have, but it seems to me that here lies the real challenge of the close linkage between scientific advice and its political and economic consequences. The relationship between science and policy means in other words to strike a balance between making scientific advice usable as a base for formulating management policy, without at the same time jeopardizing the integrity of science by opening up for other considerations in scientific appraisals.

Within the ICES there are procedures that indicate that such an awareness does influence the mediation of scientific advice to policy-makers. For one thing, the advice is given in 'the form of *various options* for corresponding management measures'.[27] This opens up for the second aspect, namely a *dialogue* around these options between scientists and managers. Before discussing these aspects, let me mention one obvious but still important aspect: as scientific information is seldom understood by non-scientists in its original form, making scientific advice the basis for management policy thus also means rendering it *comprehensible* for the policy-maker.

As for formulating advice in the form of options, this of course has to be kept within certain biological limits. It seems that giving managers the possibility 'to choose between biologically acceptable alternatives, with information about the consequences of the option they select', instead of 'being faced with a *fait accompli*'[28] has increased the applicability of the advice provided — because it relates to a range of alternative management strategies. Scientists stress, however, that there may be instances where one single recommendation is desirable; furthermore, scientists may have the right to state their preference for a certain options.

As for the other aspect — mediating advice in the form of a dialogue — Dialogue Meetings between scientists, fisheries administators and the fishing industry were initiated by the ICES in 1979. The Council had, 'following the demise of the North East Atlantic Fisheries Commission, been concerned about the lack of an effective dialogue between fishery scientists responsible for assessment of the fish stocks on the one side and national authorities responsible for the management of the stocks on the other'.[29] These meetings are organized in the form of debates with one expert representing each of the three groups involved in the fishery management process. These experts give their statements on the topics selected for consideration at the meeting, with provision for open discussion involving the audience. In 1987, more than 120 persons attended the Dialogue Meeting, where the topics were management systems and long-term objectives for resource utilization.

These Dialogue Meetings do not imply that scientists adjust their advice to fit political realities. Rather their advice is mediated in a form and a way that helps policy-makers understand the underlying data base and content. For scientists this means a better understanding of the distributional effects of implementing scientific advice. While scientists often stress the need for a more long-term perspective in resource management, policy-makers tend to concentrate on short-term gains. This intermediate stage may help to reduce the gap between short-term political interests and long-term management considerations.

Mediating the advice in a forum consisting of policy-makers who are later to negotiate on allocating the resource, may also mean a better atmosphere when actual management policy is formulated.

Mediating scientific advice in whaling

As for an intermediate stage in relation to whaling the Technical Committee, as the 'meeting-place' for scientific information and other considerations, might be said to represent such a stage. The Technical Committee is to view information coming from the Scientific Committee and to propose scientific advice to the Commission. As this involves taking into account political aspects as well, the formulation of management policy — actually the function of the Commission — starts at the 'mediating' stage. While the sole function of the Dialogue Meetings is to increase understanding between the scientific and the political aspects of managing resources, and thus create a better atmosphere for the negotiators in the management process, the Technical Committee actual weighs scientific and political aspects. This must be said to create a more 'blurred' relationship between the scientific and the political process.

It may thus be argued that an awareness of a mediation stage between provision of scientific advice and formulation of management policy is less apparent in whaling, and that a clearer distinction between the three processes is therefore needed. One possibility is to make the IWC a management organization, basing its recommendations on scientific advice from an outside scientific body, namely the ICES. An interesting parallel can be drawn with the North Atlantic Salmon Conservation Organization (NASCO), which is in charge of formulating regulatory measures on the exploitation of salmon. The scientific base for this management is advice from the ACFM.

A multi-species approach in resource assessment and management

In their articles, both Sahrhage and Asgrimsson express the need for a multi-species approach in the assessment of marine resources. One example of the shortcomings of a single-species approach can be found in the ecological changes in the Barents Sea in the 1980s. Depletion in the prey stock of capelin resulted in failure in rebuilding cod stocks. Even though the interrelationship between the various species had been known for some time, Nature itself pointed to the need for a multi-species approach.

Interrelationships in the marine ecological system are complex, involving not only various fish stocks but plankton and marine mammals as well. In addition there are oceanographic factors like water temperature and currents. Multi-species assessment therefore requires a more encompassing way of thinking and interdisiplinary cooperation. In turn this means more sophisticated and more efficient ways of organizing data and information: models able to handle many species simultaneously, and ultimately the entire marine ecological system.

The main reason for multi-species assessment is that it enables more reliable predictions on the resource situation. This is of course vital for policy-makers to be able to formulate management policy and for fishermen and the fishing industry to plan their future activity. The interrelationship between species will make providing scientific advice more complicated, but also more important, as it increases the options for management policies. In turn this will have distributional effects, not only between fishing communities within one's own country, but also between fishing states sharing stocks that interact biologically. A multi-species approach will thus be required in management policy as well. Rather than elaborate further here on the management and distributional effects of a multi-species assessment, I will now relate this approach to the present organizational structure for resource assessment and management of fish and whale.

*A multi-species approach: a challenge to the present organizational
structure?*

One important aspect of a multi-species approach is the need for more
knowledge on the relationship between marine mammals and fish
stocks. The research programmes launched by Norway and Iceland on
the Northeast Atlantic mink whale is expected to elucidate the
consequences of a stop in this whaling for fish stocks in the area.
Increased knowledge on the interrelationship between fish and whale
will add to the set of arguments in the comprehensive assessment of the
effects of the IWC moratorium, to take place in 1990.

Asgrimsson makes a point of the single-species orientation that
characterizes the IWC,[30] and he touches on a very important aspect. A
single-species approach giving insufficient ecological knowledge,
combined with the protectionist objective that today charcterizes the
IWC, can very well lead to management based on what Asgrimsson
describes as a moral conclusion rather than scientific knowledge. Thus
the comprehensive assessment called for by IWC on the 1982
moratorium must focus on the interrelationship between marine
mammals and fish stocks. Asgrimsson seems rather disillusioned as to
the 'like-minded' nations wanting to contribute to such an assessment,
not least in view of their resistance to a rather modest research quota.
Taking as a point of departure that a certain scientific catch is necessary,
resistance towards such catch will fail because of its own absurdity.
Being opposed to exploration in a situation of scientific uncertainty is
one thing: opposing attempts to diminish this uncertainty is quite
another matter.

For a multi-species approach that includes marine mammals as well
as fish stocks to emerge, a relevant question is to what extent this can be
achieved with the present organizational structure for providing
scientific advice on whaling and fishery. Today's structure is
characterized, as noted, by a global single-species approach in whaling
and a regional many-species approach in fishery. Asgrimsson maintains
that the IWC is not competent to deal comprehensively with marine
resource management, precisely because it is single-species oriented.
While a managing body may be single-species orientated, this is
incompatible with the multi-species approach needed in scientific
assessment. Alternatively, then, can the answer lie in assessing whale
stocks within an organization already dealing with assessment of fish
stocks, i.e. the ICES? In fact dealing with whale assessment would not be
new to the ICES. A concern for this species was raised as far back as in
1927 when the Whaling Committee in the ICES formulated a programme
for whaling. A marine mammals committee is still part of the committee
system of ICES. This would, however, imply a change in the scope of
whale assessment from the global to the regional level. As the whale is a
highly migratory species, the important question is to what extent a
regional assessment could comprise the whole migratory range.

It seems reasonable to argue that a multi-species approach cannot have the global level as its only point of departure. This would be too extensive. The region seems the only practical level for such an assessment; however, dealing with a highly migratory species may make this too limited. The important thing is not so much the geographical extention of the assessment area, as whether it covers a total ecological system. I will not venture here to suggest the biologically most suitable structure for a multi-species approach in assessment. The main point is the increasing awareness of the need for knowledge on the interrelationship between fish and marine mammals, and the challenges this entails for the scientific community.

When the stage of multi-species assessment has been reached — there is still some way to go — it will place added responsibility on those giving scientific advice. More specifically this means making sure that the consequences of various options — which then might constitute a rather complicated pattern — are clearly conveyed. It will also imply a more complicated pattern of economic and political consequences to the various options, calling in turn for a more multilateral approach in managing stocks that interact biologically. A multi-species approach is thus a challenge not only to the natural scientist, but to the social scientist as well.

Conclusions

Two conclusions can be drawn from my discussion above. Firstly, there are differences in the process of providing scientific advice and in mediating this advice in fisheries and in whaling. Secondly, certain aspects seem to influence the credibility and the acceptance of a scientific advice. Let me start by summarizing what seems to make scientific advice credible and how this differ between fisheries and whaling.

In fisheries, the scientific process preceeded if not the actual need for, at least the political acknowledgement of, a need for regulatory measures. This seems to have given a certain independence in scientific work. In whaling the scientific process came as a response to the management process and developed parallel with it, and this may imply less scientific independence, especially since the scientific and the management process take place under the same organizational roof.

This touches on an essential element in making scientific advice credible: namely that national managment interests be kept at some distance from the providing of scientific advice. As we cannot read the minds of scientists, an important question is to what degree the organizational structure opens for a 'blurred' relationship between science and policy. Here I have argued that having an organization solely responsible for providing scientific advice is a better point of departure for keeping such a distance, than having one organization in charge of both scientific advice and regulatory measures alike. In the latter, the opening for different management interests is of course legitimate, but the great challenge is to keep the two processes separate. This is more difficult and thus less likely when there is only one organization, as is the case in whaling.

Membership by parties with no distributional interests in the actual resource is likely to represent an impartial element in the scientific process. This is no doubt the case in fisheries. In whaling, however, not having economic interests in the resource is not the same as being impartial: on the contrary, the moral and ethical aspects related to whaling imply a broadening of the interest picture. The difference in the effect of extended membership in fisheries and in whaling is thus found primarily in the inherent difference between the actual resources.

This is very much the case when it comes to having a closed scientific process. The fact that whaling has become a 'hot' political issue implies a greater public attention. In turn, this also means greater pressure on scientists to take a political stand as well.[31] This is the main reason why 'science politicians' are more likely in whaling than in fisheries — not least when the scientific process in whaling makes it possible for any number of scientists to take part in this process.

It seems fair to say that, in both fisheries and whaling, it is the actual depletion of stocks rather than warnings from scientists that has been the driving force behind regulatory measures. However, that there is greater scientific uncertainty in whaling than in fisheries is probably because disagreement on procedures and methods is greater as well. This again has to do with the fact that assessment in whaling is based primarily on constructed models, rather than on research vessel survey.

In order to make a clearer distinction between the scientific and the political process, while at the same time making scientific knowledge the basis in management policy, having an intermediate stage or a 'buffer' seems a good starting point. The fact that the organizational structure creates a rather blurred relationship between the scientific and the political aspects of whaling is one important reason for the lack of credibility as to scientific advice on the various whale stocks.

The increasing need for a multi-species assessment has, however, added to the debate concerning the appropriateness of the IWC as a provider of scientific advice. Having a single-species orientation goes contrary to such an approach, not least when the interrelationship between fish and marine mammals is increasingly acknowledged and thus added to the set of arguments used concerning the future management of whales. In other words, the need for a more comprehensive approach both in assessing and in managing marine living resources seems likely to constitute a challenge to the organizational structure as well.

Table 13.1 Aspects related to the credibility of scientific advice.

	Fisheries	Whaling
Scientific tradition:		
Independent	x	
Response		x
Organizational structure:		
Separate	x	
'Blurred'		x
Membership:		
Impartial	x	
Partial		x
Closed scientific process:		
'Pure' scientists	x	
'Science politicians'		x
Concord between scientists:		
Research vessel survey	x	
Constructed models		x

Notes

1. Sahrhage, Dietrich, 1989, 'The Role of Science in International Management of Fish Resources', in this volume.

2. Asgrimsson, Halldor, 1989, 'Developments Leading to the 1982 Decision of the International Whaling Commission for a Zero Catch Quota, 1986-90', in this volume.

3. Miles, Edward, 1987, *Science, Politics and International Ocean Management. The Uses of Scientific Knowledge in International Negotiations*, University of California, Berkeley, p.70.

4. Gunnar Sætersdal seems to think along these lines when he expresses that 'the acceptability is again a function largely of the credibility of the scientific case produced' (Sætersdal, Gunnar, 1980, *A Review of Past Management of Some Pelagic Stocks and its Effectiveness*, ICES Report **177**).

5. Asgrimsson, Halldor, 1989, in this volume.

6. 'New scientific theory' maintains that scientists traditionally have been too naïve in believing in the objectivity of their conclusions. (Roll-Hansen, Nils, 'Ønsketenkning eller vitenskap. Subjektivismen i vitenskapsteori og forskningspolitikk', in *Nytt norsk tidsskrift*, 1987:2)

7. Sætersdal, Gunnar, 1980.

8. For the history of ICES see Went, A.E.J., 1979, *Seventy Years Agrowing. A History of the International Council for the Exploration of the Sea 1902-1972*, Andr. Fred Host al Fils., Copenhagen 1972, pp. 252.

9. For the history of whaling see Birnie, Pat,. 1985, *International Regulation of Whaling*, New York, vol.1-2 and Tønnesen, I. and Johnsen, A., 1959-70, *Den moderne hvalfangsts historie. Opprinnelse og utvikling*, Sandefjord, vol.1-5.

10. McHugh, J.L., 'The Role and History of the Whaling Commissions' in W.E. Schevill (ed.), 1974, *The Whale Problem: A Status Report*, Harvard University Press, 322 pp.

11. Parrish, Basil B., l988, *Scientific Advice for Management of Northeast Atlantic Fisheries. Fishery Science and Management: Objectives and Limitation*, Springer Verlag, New York.

12. *International Convention for the Regulation of Whaling*, 1946, Article V, 2.

13. Ibid., Article III, 4

14. 'Conference report. Whaling Negotiations and Hard-core Issues' in *Marine Policy*, January 1989, p. 69.

15. Asgrimsson, Halldor, 1989, in this volume.

16. Asgrimsson, Halldor, 1989, in this volume.

17. Miles, Edward, 1987.

18. Andresen, Steinar, 1989, 'Increased Public Attention: Communications and Polarization', in this volume.

19. Østreng, Willy, 1989, 'Polar Science and Politics: Close Twins or Opposite Poles in International Cooperation', in this volume.

20. Sahrhage, Dietrich, 1989, in this volume.

21. Asgrimsson, Halldor, 1989, in this volume.

22. Sahrhage, Dietrich, 1989, in this volume.

23. Sahrhage, Dietrich, 1989, in this volume.

24. Sahrhage, Dietrich, 1989, in this volume.

25. ICES Cooperative research report: *Reports on Dialogue Meetings*, 20-21 May and 4 October 1980, 25.

26. Sahrhage, Dietrich, 1989, in this volume.

27. ICES 1980 Cooperative research report: *Reports on Dialogue Meeting*, 20-21 May and 4 October. 1980.

28. ICES 1980 Cooperative research report: *Reports on Dialogue Meeting.*

29. ICES 1980 Cooperative research report: *Reports on Dialogue Meeting.*

30. Asgrimsson, Halldor, 1989, in this volume.

31. Young, Oran, 1989, 'Science and Social Institutions: Lessons for International Resource Regimes', in this volume.

Conclusion

14

The politics of science in international resource management: a summary

Arild Underdal

Introduction

Preceding chapters have provided a rich variety of inputs to our understanding of the complex relationship between scientific research and resource management. A concluding chapter can hardly aim at rendering full justice to all these contributions. It seems to me, however, that four general questions stand out as the major, recurring themes of this volume:

1. Does scientific research have a *legitimate claim* to a major role in resource and environmental management? If so, which role(s)?
2. Do findings from scientific research *in fact* have any significant impact on international resource management? And, if so, what kind(s) of impact?
3. Under which circumstances, if any, are inputs from scientific research *likely* to serve as important premises for management decisions?
4. How can scientific research itself survive as an independent undertaking if its findings or hypotheses are to be used as salient premises in the making of politically controversial decisions?

I propose to conclude this volume by summarizing what appears to me to be some of the main lessons that we can infer about these four questions from preceeding contributions.

Can scientific research legitimately claim a major role in resource management?

The general consensus among decision-makers as well as scientists may, in essence, be summarized in three very general propositions: (1) Knowledge, in the form of theoretical understanding of cause-effect relationship as well as descriptive information about relevant variables and parameters, is a *necessary* condition for rational resource management. Scientific research is, at least in principle, the major — but certainly not the only — supplier of such knowledge. (2) Although being a necessary input, even the best available theories and information do not constitute a *sufficient* basis for rational management. Sound management policies can not simply be derived from the findings or hypotheses of scientific research. And precautionary management may often have to proceed without any conclusive scientific evidence. (3) The case for acknowledging scientific research as a major supplier of inputs needed to develop sound resource management is substantially stronger than the case for admitting or encouraging scientists to take over the role of manager.

In this context, knowledge may be considered a tool, necessary for accurately 'diagnosing' environmental problems as well as for prescribing an effective 'therapy'. Thus, knowledge enables; it accounts for much of the difference between taking charge and passively resigning oneself to one's fate or just kneeling in prayer to some Superior power. More specifically, rational resource management requires knowledge about two *kinds of systems* — ecological systems as well as systems of human activities — and the interface between the two. The former is the domain of natural sciences, while systems of human activities (the 'superstructure') are studied by social sciences and to some extent the humanities. The interface between man and his environment constitutes an interface also between or among disciplines, with technology as a critical link. Moreover, we need two *kinds of knowledge*: information, used first of all to describe; and theory, enabling us to predict and explain. The relationship between the two is 'dialectical' in the sense that theory makes sense of data, and data is required for constructing empirical theories as well as for applying them to specific problems.

Science is not the only producer of knowledge. But the more technical the measurement required, the more complex and less transparent the cause-effect relationships, and the more stable the dynamics of the system studied, the greater seems to be the comparative advantage of systematic research over more impressionistic modes of generating knowledge. This proposition has at least two interesting implications:

First, if decision-makers turn to science mainly for answers to the more complex and difficult questions, the research community in a sense starts with a handicap, and may have a hard time 'delivering the goods', at least by the decision-maker's deadline. This is all the more so since the standards of evidence and validity applied in scientific research are more strict than those normally applied by decision-makers and the public. By his own deadline, the decision-maker may receive only highly tentative and probabilistic answers to his specific questions. Thus, in his perspective the short-term pay-off from investment in scientific research may very well be zero. The incongruence between the demands of decision-makers for definite answers and 'instant expertise' and the capacity of scientific research to deliver only tentative conclusions — and then perhaps only in the long run — makes for an uneasy partnership. Hence, it should be emphasized that the claim of research to a role in resource management is based primarily on its general capacity to advance beyond any other mode of generating knowledge, and less on its ability to provide instant expertise on each specific and acute problem facing the decision-maker. Moreover, resource management implies making decisions under uncertainty, and most often there is no way even the most generously funded and well staffed programme can relieve the decision-maker of that chore.

Second, in terms of contributing to rational management natural sciences and technology seem to have a comparative advantage over social sciences. The main reason is not that the former is more 'relevant'; arguably, knowledge about systems of human activities can be as critical to environmental management as is knowledge about the state and dynamics of ecological or technical systems. Rather, the advantage of natural sciences and technology stems, I suspect, largely from their likely ability to make a greater marginal contribution in terms of advancing further beyond the informed judgement of the decision-makers themselves or the immediate experience of the general public.[1] More specifically, this greater capacity of advancing beyond immediate experience and lay judgement seems to be due to greater and certainly more exclusive technical sophistication in measurement, and partly from the privilege of having a subject that seems, at least in some respects, less inscrutable and intractable than the human mind (implying, among other things, more favourable conditions for the accummulation of knowledge). Whether the 'rate of return' on investment in research will be higher in the natural sciences is quite a different question; also the costs of relevant programmes are likely to be substantially higher in the natural sciences and technology than in the social sciences.

The proposition that knowledge is a necessary input to rational management may be a truism, but if we ask how much knowledge we need, the answer is far from obvious. Other things being equal, we would assume that the more extensive, exact and reliable knowledge available to us, the better management decisions we would be able to make. But this statement begs the question. How much knowledge is required depends on the complexity and specification of the decision model and the purpose for which the model is used: the more complex and precise our concept of social welfare, and the finer we can tune the policy 'cure', the more extensive and exact knowledge is needed to select the optimal response. Conversely, if our criteria are very simple or highly diffuse, our policy options few and crude, and our ambitions confined to 'muddling through', the marginal utility of more exact knowledge is likely to drop sharply once the basics are known.

In the issue area of resource management one may probably find cases corresponding reasonably well to the former scenario, and others corresponding better to the latter. I strongly suspect, though, that the latter kind of situation may be more common than the former, particularly at the international level. In international negotiations decision-makers seem often to face, or at least to focus on, crude choices between or among discrete options — such as whether to declare an unconditional ban on dumping of some toxic waste at sea or merely to require a government permit. Moreover, they rarely have a precise set of agreed criteria against which available options can be evaluated. If the policy options considered are few and crude and the criteria of social welfare diffuse, the choice of 'cure' is likely to be rather insensitive to the fine print of the problem 'diagnosis'. I have yet to see a government document outlining some kind of formula prescribing that restrictions on, for example, emissions of sulphur oxides should be reduced by x per cent over the next ten years if acid rain is estimated to account for y per cent of the decline in the population of fish stocks in European lakes and rivers, and by x+n per cent if the rate of damage is believed to be y+m per cent.

Even a precise policy response, such as a convention committing governments to achieve a reduction of at least 50 per cent in certain emissions by a certain date, is rarely if ever derived from a precise 'therapeutic theory' identifying the figure 50 as the optimal response to one particular diagnosis of the problem. Most likely, the figure 50 would be more or less arbitrary; it might as well have been 44 or 62. And the governments involved probably have no policy criteria stipulating whether and how much the target should be modified in response to a different, more exact or more definite estimate of damage or abatement costs.

The answer to the 'how much is enough' question also depends on the decision rules applied to deal with uncertainty. As pointed out above, managers frequently have to make decisions under uncertainty. In the field of environmental management some of the potentially most critical decisions will have to be taken under conditions approaching *fundamental* uncertainty (i.e. where even the range of possible consequences is unknown). Under such conditions demanding 'conclusive evidence' or 'perfect knowledge' would not only be misplaced; such demands would in fact contradict the basic idea of management. The 'burden of proof' can usually not be satisfied in time for precautionary action to be taken. By the time we approach 'conclusive' evidence, the only kind of 'curative' action available to us would most likely be to 'repair'. Thus, in environmental management precautionary action shall most often have to be undertaken on the basis of more or less weak indices, or not at all. Moreover, some of the uncertainty pertaining to environmental management may be more aptly attributed to inherent characteristics of the objects themselves rather than to imperfections in our knowledge about these objects. The outcome of a lottery can be predicted only in stochastic terms, and so can in some respects the behaviour of 'nature' and 'man' as well. There is no way in which science can ever remove this hard core of uncertainty, inherent in stochastic processes in the objects themselves.

The preceding argument has at least two important implications: first, the fact that knowledge, *sui generis*, is a necessary input to rational management does not imply that extensive, exact and conclusive knowledge is generally required — nor, indeed, that such knowledge could always be utilized for policy-making purposes had it been available. Second, it should be abundantly clear that knowledge can never be a *sufficient* basis for rational management. Conclusions from scientific research do not, however exact and reliable they may be, in themselves have any clear-cut policy 'implications'.[2] Environmental management will have to be guided by some aggregate notion of social welfare and some normative decision rule(s) for dealing with uncertainty. Research can help clarify possible criteria and the dilemmas and trade-offs involved, and it can help compute the score of alternative options on whatever criteria are adopted. But the basic question of what shall be considered 'good' or 'bad' can not be answered by science. Nor can scientists as professionals claim any comparative advantage in deciding the 'utility function' of society. The claim of scientific research to a role in resource management is based entirely on its ability to provide valid, accurate and relevant knowledge — beyond what can be achieved through more impressionistic, common-sense methods. This applies also to the research community — except, perhaps, in the rare and fortunate circumstances where scientific research is the only human activity to be managed.[3]

The actual impact of scientific research

Being capable of supplying inputs needed for rational management is certainly not a sufficient, perhaps not even a necessary, condition for actually having one's findings recognized as decision premises. And if the basis for claiming a major role is circumscribed as indicated above, there is all the more reason to ask whether the findings or hypotheses produced by scientific research do in fact have any significant impact on resource and environmental management.

The general answer clearly is: sometimes, and at two different levels. First, as pointed out by Young and Miles,[4] scientific research affects resource management indirectly — notably through its impact upon the systems to be managed. Some of the major problems that resource management tries to solve or alleviate are to some extent caused by the use of technology growing out of scientific research. And the 'first-order cures' to these problems will frequently take the form of new or modified technologies for production, pollution abatement, etc. In its capacity as the principal developer of technology, scientific research thus serves in a dual role as a major supplier of management problems *and* as a major producer of technology needed to solve such problems. Arguably, it may be in this 'technological' role that scientific research leaves its most substantial impact on resource management.

Our major concern here, however, is the use of research findings as premisses in the making of management decisions. Preceding contributions have clearly shown that decision-makers sometimes respond, though perhaps slowly and inadequately, to new findings or hypotheses; sometimes they do not. This suggests that we should rephrase the question so as to focus on *the circumstances* under which conclusions from scientific research are likely to serve as premisses for management decisions. Before pursuing this latter version of the question, however, there are two methodological traps that merit attention.

First, in this volume inputs from scientific research seem most often to have been conceived of as impetus to *policy* change. Accordingly, impact has been conceived of largely in terms of the extent to which management policy changes in response to new findings or hypotheses. Although a perfectly reasonable perspective in the context of environmental management, I strongly suspect that it may lead us to underestimate the actual impact of conclusions from scientific research. Findings and theories may also be interpreted — legitimately or not — as reassuring, in the sense of confirming established policies. This reassuring effect is, of course, also a kind of impact; it may even be the more frequent one. At least the odd seem to be in favour of this 'conservative' function: other things being equal, less energy is usually needed to preserve than to change an established policy (or a stable 'non-policy').

Second, a (pluralist) society can respond to environmental stress not only through its government but also through other institutions, of which the market may be the most important. Even fairly small groups of consumers might, by shifting their demand from one product to another, provide incentives for producers to come up with new products or shift to more 'benign' production processes. Though perhaps a less likely response, 'exit' in markets may in some circumstances be as effective as 'voice' in politics.[5] Though evident that we cannot rely on the market itself to secure the optimal use of common pool resources or the optimal provision of collective goods, limiting our focus exclusively to governmental regulation may lead us to underestimate society's capacity to respond to environmental stress or resource depletion. In which circumstances are inputs from scientific research likely to have a significant impact on management decisions? Taken together, the previous chapters point explicitly at several such circumstances. And even more suggestions seem to be implicit in arguments and interpretations submitted. In trying to convert the latter into explicit statements, I have interpreted my role as summarizer quite liberally. In doing so, I have come up with nine *ceteris paribus* propositions (see Table 14.1). The list is, of course, not exhaustive, but it seems to me that it includes the essence of most of the suggestions made elsewhere in this volume. Two of the propositions listed pertain to the nature and quality of the input itself, four refer to the substantive content of the 'message' (i.e. to characteristics of the effects or developments described or predicted) and another three concern the political setting into which this message is fed. Let us take a brief look at the rationale behind each of these propositions.

Table 14.1 Conditions affecting the impact of scientific inputs

Impact likely to be	
Strong	Weak
'Definite' or at least consensual conclusion	Tentative or contested hypothesis
Feasible 'cure' available	'Cure' unclear or not feasible
Effects close in time and (social) space	Effects remote
Problem affecting 'social centre' of society	Problem affecting 'periphery' only
Problem developing rapidly and surprisingly	Problem developing slowly and according to expectations
Effects experienced by or at least visible to the public	Effects not (yet) experienced by or visible to the public
Political conflict: low	Political conflict: high
Issue linkage: none, or on substantive merits only	Tactical issue linkage; issue 'contamination'
Institutionalized setting, interative decision-making	Not institutionalized, *ad hoc* decision-making

Nature and quality of input

Although, in principle, no conclusion of scientific research is ever definite, some are clearly more tentative and contested than others. Other things being equal, the more tentative and contested a finding or hypothesis appears, the more easily it can be disregarded. Uncertainty pertaining to the direction and strength of cause-effect relationship ('theory') seems to be more paralysing than uncertainty pertaining to descriptive knowledge. At least in international negotiations, *consensual* knowledge seems to be more important than 'advanced' knowledge.[6] And the more demanding the decision rules, the less uncertainty is needed to block regulatory action. Particularly in international negotiation processes substantial uncertainty about cause-effect relationships may serve as the political equivalent of live ammunition in the hands of actors opposed to (new) regulatory measures. Here the advocates of new regulatory measures tend to find themselves in a position of asymmetrical disadvantage. This is so for at least three different reasons.

Firstly, the way international negotiations works anyone advocating new restrictions will have to 'prove' his case, while scientifically based uncertainty tends to be accepted as a legitimate reason for declining to go along. Removing or even reducing uncertainty is generally far more difficult than producing or substantiating critical questions and objections — particularly, of course, when it comes to predicting future effects for which no record of experience from earlier history is yet available. And at least some of the industrial actors concerned are indeed well equipped to foster such critical questions. Even in the industrialized world, most governments would find it hard to match the R&D capacity of, for example, the transnational chemical industry. If such an R&D establishment can be geared to demonstrating that available evidence is yet inconclusive and provides no compelling basis for demanding new restrictions, we can easily see that the fusion of uncertainty and commercial interests can make a formidable 'opponent.'[7]

Secondly, this asymmetry is reinforced by the fact that at the national level producer interests tend to be better organized than those of consumers.[8] This probably applies also to the 'producers' and 'consumers' of pollution and resource depletion. This institutional bias may be weakening, but one of the laws of political science is that building institutions takes time. At any one particular point in time, the interests of 'yesterday' therefore tend to command relatively more institutional energy than those of 'tomorrow'.

Thirdly, since effective international management usually requires agreement among all states playing a significant part in the system of activities concerned, 'vetoing' is far easier than 'engineering'. Whenever collective goods are concerned, any major actor may — by refusing to contribute — in fact be able to block the entire project.

A scientist may invest all his professional energy in validating or refining a certain problem diagnosis, but a decision-maker would almost certainly be more interested in possible solutions. Other things being equal, we may therefore assume that scientific input identifying some *feasible cure* would attract more attention than input merely describing and diagnosing a problem[9]. Thus, however convincing the evidence that the burning of fossil fuels produces CO_2 and therefore contributes to what is known as the 'greenhouse effect', decision-makers are likely to pay more attention if provided with at least the prospects of some feasible solution(s) to the problem. The word 'feasible' is ambiguous, but none the less important — particularly as a reminder to some of our fellow social scientists: whatever its validity, the proposition that the 'world capitalist system' (or, for that matter, human greed) is to blame for resource depletion or environmental stress is almost certainly a non-starter — simply because neither proposition identifies any operational policy instrument that is or can be made accessible to any decision-maker or government. And we should immediately forgive the politician or civil servant who finds no guidance in applications of the game theory concept of 'mixed strategy' to her specific negotiation problem. To the decision-maker, the most relevant contributions of research are those providing a cure that is feasible within the constraints of her decision-making authority and resources.

The substantive content of the 'message'

Decision-makers as well as the mass public tend to be myopic in more than one sense of that word: we probably tend to care more about 'us' than about 'them', more about 'here' than 'there', and 'today' is likely to be more urgent than 'tomorrow'. More generally stated, we tend, everything else the same, to put more energy into solving problems that are close rather than those that are in some sense remote. By implication, inputs from research are more likely to be taken into serious consideration if they deal with problems that are at the forefront of the decision-makers mind.

Moreover, it should be recognized that some are in a better position than others to take advantage of the benefits of scientific research. Generally stated, the more the problem affects the 'social centre' of society the more intellectual, economic and political resources are likely to be mobilized in the search for a solution. At the national as well as the global level, the centre controls a disproportionately large share of relevant resources, including R&D capacity. This distribution of capabilities is likely to affect research priorities as well as the ability to utilize the knowledge produced. Thus, the poor peasant of rural Africa is much less likely to have his specific environmental problems studied, let alone solved, than is the resident of some upper middle-class suburbia in the 'northwest'. By implication, however, if the problem facing the centre is a collective or global problem, the centre is likely to take a leading entrepreneurial role in developing an effective policy response.

The propositions linking development and visibility to impact both pertain mainly to what Young [10] has termed the agenda-setting function. The reasoning behind them may be summarized as follows: to most of us, and to high-level decision-makers in particular, time and energy are *scarce* resources. Therefore, at any point in time, only a limited number of problems can be under active consideration. If decision-makers are to pay attention to research findings, the *problem(s)* for which these findings are relevant must itself belong to this subset. What, then, characterizes those problems that succeed in catching the attention of decision-makers? Though the answer certainly is far more complex, suffice it here to concentrate on two dimensions:

Other things being equal, I would suspect that problems that are perceived to develop rapidly and surprisingly tend to get more attention than those that develop slowly and conform to expectations. Speed probably helps to inject a sense of urgency, and surprise is likely to stimulate new search for explanations as well as for policy responses. The attention threshold of the mass public will most often be higher than that of government agencies, and perhaps also different in profile. Other things being equal, we may expect the mass public to respond more readily to problems which it can actually experience itself. [11] In the absence of personal experience, the public depends heavily on mass media for guiding its attention, and mass media tend to focus their reporting on what is spectacular and dramatic. To the man or woman in the street, there are few things in life as devoid of social drama as a correlation matrix or a regression equation. The televized suffering of dying seals on the shores of Northern Europe, and the devastating effects on marine life of the algae 'invasion' into the fjords of Southern Norway last spring probably had a far greater impact on the public's attention to marine pollution than any research report. And Mr Timberlake's reminder that even the members of the World Commission on Environment and Development referred more frequently to the statements of 'common people' should come as no surprise: 'The testimony of these people was almost always more *dramatic, memorable* and *easier to comprehend* than the testimony of the technocrats'.[12]

Now, the relationship between 'surprise' and 'drama' on the one hand and attention to findings and hypotheses from scientific research on the other is likely to be curvilinear. If a problem really comes as a surprise even to the expert, there may yet be only a small amount of applied research available. Moreover, as pointed out by Galtung,[13] a mobilized mass public tend to react in an 'absolutist' manner. If the mass public should react very strongly to some environmental problem, its reaction will certainly not be tuned to the fine print of scientific knowledge. The optimal condition for findings from (applied) scientific research to get to the attention of the mass public will probably be an atmosphere characterized by serious and widespread concern for the problem, but not by real alarm or outrage. Following Downs (1972) we may add that public excitement tends to ebb and flow, and this ephemeral character makes it a shaky basis for rational management.[14]

The political and institutional setting

If I should point to one conclusion that stands out as strongly supported throughout this volume (see for example the contributions by Young, Miles, Andresen, Wettestad and Østreng), it would have to be the proposition that political conflict tends to disturb the development of consensual knowledge as well as the rational utilization of research findings.[15] First of all, political conflict tends to shift attention away from the search for solutions improving collective welfare to concern about protecting one's own interests. Second, political conflict tends to exploit and even reinforce uncertainty by infusing political energy into diverging interpretations of available evidence. Particularly where findings from research can be related directly to actor interests, political conflict may even 'contaminate' scientific research itself. Third, political conflict may give one or more of the actors incentives to go for what Haas has called tactical issue linkage.[16] Tactical issue linkage may in some circumstances facilitate international cooperation,[17] but the direct impact of scientific inputs is likely to decline since solutions to the problem will no longer be considered on their own merits alone.

Miles has aptly summarized the essence of the argument in two propositions: (1) 'The higher the level of conflict, the greater the constraints on utilizing scientific results', (2) ' . . . contamination of the issue by external political issues of high salience . . . is a wild card in the process of knowledge utilization'.[18]

As also pointed out by Miles (1987;1989), it seems that an institution-alized framework providing a firm basis for *iterative* decision-making creates the most favourable conditions for establishing a constructive dialogue between decision-makers and scientists.[19] This is so partly because such a setting gives government representatives opportunities to reconsider and improve existing solutions in the light of whatever new evidence that may be available, and hence encourages them to learn by trial and error. At the same time it enables the scientific community to respond more systematically and directly to remaining concerns of the decision-makers. Perhaps, special procedures or institutions, like, for example the former Liaison Committee of ICES and NEAFC, can be developed to foster the dialogue between managers and scientists. [20] Moreover, institutionalized cooperation in resource management is likely to encourage cooperative research efforts. To the extent that such efforts succeed in contributing to the development of consensual knowledge, they may in turn facilitate progress in negotiations on international regimes and regulations. [21 22]

Mediating 'truth' to 'power'

Even in the most favourable circumstances, the transformation of research findings into premises for management decisions is not necessarily a straightforward process easily controlled by the scientists concerned.

As emphasized above, conclusions from scientific research are in themselves devoid of clear-cut policy 'implications'. Only after being transmitted to or 'discovered' by decision-makers, reinterpreted in the context of some policy concern(s) and infused with political energy, can a finding have some impact on management policy. The end product of this 'translation' may be quite different from the finding as originally reported by the scientists. Some, including Timberlake and Bakken, have argued that scientists should involve themselves more actively in this process.[23] And, arguably, scientists do have a responsibility to make sure that their findings are easily available also beyond the confines of the research community, and — perhaps — also to seek to minimize the distortion that might occur if others take over the transformation process. Others, including Boehmer-Christiansen, take a more sceptical view regarding what can be accomplished by the scientists themselves — particularly, I suspect, when it comes to inferring policy implications and mobilizing political energy.[24] Scientists are not necessarily good at making policy nor effective in terms of mobilizing political support. Moreover, in becoming players in the game of politics they run a serious risk of compromising their credibility as scientists. In the absence of Plato's philosopher kings, the use of research findings in the making of management policy often seem to depend on some kind of mediating agent or amplifyer other than the scientists or the ultimate decision-makers themselves. If so, who might these agents be?

The answer seems to depend to some extent on the character of the political process. At the national level civil servants of specialized government agencies are supposed to serve as the main regular channel. It seems reasonable to expect the mediating role of government bureaucracies to be particularly dominant in the making of routine decisions in a consensual and specialized setting.[25] Until quite recently, however, environmental management has not been well established as a specialized policy arena; rather, institutions as well as policies have been 'in the making'. In this context, environmental protection has, at least in Western democracies, been a cause championed very much by non-governmental organizations, relying heavily on mass media to help bring environmental concerns on to the political agenda. Some of these organizations have contributed substantially to translating findings and hypotheses from scientific research into premises or even demands for new policy proposals. Complaints have been voiced about some of these translations. And, admittedly, the game of public campaigns played by several of the main non-governmental organizations is one where the fine print of scientific reports is unlikely to be preserved. None the less, some of these organizations today serve as important elements of an early-warning system, amplifying whatever causes for environmental concern that can be found in publications from scientific research as well as in other available sources.

At the international level, secretariats of intergovernmental organizations are rarely in a position to serve as functional equivalents of national governmental agencies in this respect. Several of the contributions to this volume (in particular those of Miles and Wettestad)[26] suggest that institutionalized links such as the former Liaison Committee of ICES/NEAFC and the Policy Working Group of the Second International Conference on the North Sea provide an optimal setting for utilizing inputs from scientific research. At a more general level, even *ad hoc* bodies like the World Commission on Environment and Development can contribute substantially to developing a consensual diagnosis of, and perhaps even a consensual response to, common environmental challenges. Other things being equal, however, *ad hoc* committees with no institutionalized links to specific management functions seems to be at a disadvantage, at least once we move beyond the agenda-setting stage.

The mixed blessing of being 'relevant'

How can scientific research itself survive as an independent undertaking if its findings and hypotheses are to be used as salient premisses in the making of politically controversial decisions?

Before pursuing this final question, two brief reminders may be appropriate. First, in a global perspective the Western concept of science as critical and independent inquiry may in fact be considered somewhat parochial. In most countries of the world scientific research today suffers under more or less severe political constraints even when its relevance to political conflict seems, at most, to be marginal. Second, in a liberal democratic society increased attention from decision-makers is not necessarily a bad thing for the scientific community. Most scientists never make the headlines (as scientists), nor will they ever be invited to submit their advice to cabinet level decision)makers. To the average scientist, therefore, the prospect of having the attention of the media or of men in power may be most welcome and flattering. Should fame and power prove beyond reach, he may at least take some comfort in the fact that perceived relevance to the current concerns of high-level decision-makers tend to have a positive effect on funding.

Yet, having one's findings recognized as relevant to policy decisions may be a mixed blessing, particularly if these findings can be linked directly to competing actor interests. In at least three different ways political conflict may contaminate scientific research itself.

First, whenever empirical research has to rely on information provided by the parties themselves, there is a serious risk that access to 'sensitive' data will be restricted, or that actor activities will be misreported. We all know that when catch statistics are used as a basis for allocating or enforcing scarce quotas in marine fisheries, the reliability of catch reports tends to decline.

Second, in intense conflict the parties themselves are likely to search for research reports that are 'favourable' in terms of legitimizing own positions. If scientific inputs are being valued by decision-makers mainly as a legitimizing device, 'truth' becomes a secondary or auxiliary criterion. And if scientists are being rewarded for producing 'favourable' rather than 'true' reports, a disproportionately large share of the funding may be granted to research of poor quality. If so, 'poor' science may in the long run squeeze out high quality research.

Third, scholars producing reports relevant to current policy concerns may soon find themselves in a boundary role for which they are not well prepared. Most scholars would probably find the role of scientist hard to combine with that of policy advocate; the latter tends to damage the credibility of the former. As a policy advocate a scientist may have to commit herself strongly to conclusions that are still quite open to the independent scholar. And a strong personal stake in a certain conclusion easily impair one's ability to pursue independent and critical research.[27]

The best protection known against these and other forms of 'perversion' of scientific research can probably still be found in the classical virtues of open and critical peer review, honoured and supported by a pluralist scientific community. If scientific research is to serve as a constructive partner in the development of resource and environmental management, the research community will be heavily dependent upon those members of the profession who care more about quality than about relevance.

Notes

1. This is a probabilistic statement, meaning that it most certainly does not apply to every management problem.

2. Boehmer-Christiansen, Sonja, 1989, 'The Role of Science in the International Regulation of Pollution', and Young, Oran, 1989, 'Science and Social Institutions', both in this volume.

3. As pointed out by Young (1989) and Østreng, Willy, 1989, 'Polar Science and Politics', in this volume, pp. 000, the scientific community has none the less in fact provided leadership in some cases of regime formation *outside* its own particular domain.

4. Young, Oran, 1989, and Miles, Edward L., 1989, 'Scientific and Technological Knowledge and International Cooperation in Resource Management', both in this volume.

5. Hirschman, Albert O., 1970, *Exit, Voice and Loyalty*, Harvard University Press, Cambridge, MA.

6. Miles, Edward L., 1987, *Science, Politics and International Resource Management: The Uses of Scientific Knowledge in International Negotiations*, University of California, Institute of International Studies, Berkeley, CA (Policy Papers in International Affairs, no.33, and Young, Oran, 1989, in this volume.

7. Bakken, Per M., 1989, 'Science and Politics in the Protection of the Ozone Layer', in this volume.

8. Olsen, Johan P., 1983, *Organized Democracy*, Norwegian University Press, Oslo.

9. Timberlake, Lloyd, 1989, 'The Role of Scientific Knowledge in Drawing up the Brundtland Report', in this volume.

10. Young, Oran, 1989, in this volume.

11. Sahrhage, Dietrich, 1989, 'The Role of Science in International Management of Fish Resources', in this volume.

12. Timberlake, Lloyd, 1989, in this volume. Italics are mine.

13. Galtung, Johan, 1965, 'Foreign Policy Opinion as a Function of Social Position' in *Journal of Peace Research*, **2**, 206-30.

14. Downs, Anthony, 1972, 'Up and Down with Ecology: The "Issue-Attention Cycle"' in *Public Interest*, **28**, 38-50.

15. See in particular Andresen, Steinar, 1989, 'Increased Public Attention: Communication and Polarization', in this volume.

16. Haas, Ernst B., 1980, 'Why Collaborate? Issue Linkage and International Regimes' in *World Politics*, **32**, 357-405.

17. Sebenius, James, 1983, 'Negotiation Arithmetic: Adding and Subtracting Parties and Issues', *International Organization*, **37**, 281-316.

18. Miles, Edward, 1987 and 1989, the latter in this volume.

19. Miles, Edward, 1987 and 1989, the latter in this volume.

20. Fløistad, Brit, 1989, 'Scientific Knowledge in Management of Fish and Whale', in this volume.

21. Scott, Anthony, 1976, 'Transfrontier Pollution: Are new institutions necessary?' in OECD, *Economics of Transfrontier Pollution*, Paris, pp. 178–218.

22. In extremely favourable and probably rare circumstances, successful cooperation in scientific research may even have what functionalist integration theory would label a genuine 'spill-over' effect on international resource management (see Østreng, 1989).

23. Timberlake, Lloyd, 1989, and Bakken, Per M., 1989, both in this volume.

24. Boehmer-Christiansen, Sonja, 1989, in this volume.

25. Hermann, Charles F., 1969, 'International Crisis as a Situational Variable', in James N. Rosenau (ed.), *International Politics and Foreign Policy*, The Free Press, New York, pp.409-21, and Underdal, Arild, 1979, 'Issues Determine Politics Determine Policies: The Case for a "Rationalistic" Approach to the Study of Foreign Policy Decision-Making' in *Cooperation and Conflict*, no.14, pp. 1-9.

26. Wttestad, Jørgen, 1989, 'Uncertain Science and Matching Policies: Science, Politics and the Organization of North Sea Environmental Cooperation', in this volume.

27. Of course, even with no commitment to a certain policy, a scholar will to some extent stake his *professional reputation* on the scientific findings he reports.

Appendixes

Appendix A: Overview of selected international organizations

Compiled by Øystein B. Thommessen

Advisory Committee on Pollution of the Sea (ACOPS)
Established: 1952. **Headquarters:** London, UK. **NGO. Members:** Representatives of 24 UK organizations, 11 international organizations. **Aims:** Attention focused on marine pollution; oil pollution, chemical and other hazardous substances; sewage; radioactivity in waters around British Isles.

Commission for the Conservation of Antarctic Marine Living Resources (CCAMLR)
Established: 7 Apr. 1982. **Headquarters:** Hobart, Australia. **IGO. Members:** Governments of 18 countries. **Aims:** Conserve the Antarctic marine ecosystem while allowing for rational use of resources.

Commission for the Convention on Future Multilateral Cooperation in North-East Atlantic Fisheries
Established: 18 Nov. 1980. **Headquarters:** London, UK. **IGO. Members:** Governments of 22 countries and territories. **Aims:** Ensure management of fisheries in the North Atlantic. **Activities:** Annual meeting.

Committee on Space Research (COSPAR),
see **International Council of Scientific Unions (ICSU)**

Committee on the Peaceful Uses of Outer Space (COPUOS)
Established: 12 Dec 1958, within the UN framework. **Headquarters:** UN, New York, US. **IGO. Members:** 53 States — Members of the UN. **Aims:** Review international cooperation in the peaceful uses of outer space; study the practical and feasible means of giving effect to programmes that might be undertaken under United Nations' auspices; study legal problems that might arise from the exploration and use of outer space. **Activities:** Recommendations made on exchange of information, international programmes, training and education.

Consultative Meeting of Contracting Parties to the London Dumping Convention,
see **International Maritime Organization (IMO)**

Convention on Long-Range Transboundary Air Pollutions
Established: 13 Nov. 1979. **Headquarters:** Geneva, Switzerland. **IGO. Members:** Governments, Parties to the Convention, of 31 countries. **Aims:** Limit and, as far as possible, generally reduce and prevent air pollution, including long-range transboundary air pollution.

European Company for the Financing of Railway Rolling Stock (EUROFIMA)
Established: 20 Oct. 1955. **Headquarters:** Basle, Switzerland. **IGO. Members:** National railways of 16 countries. **Aims:** Facilitate for the associated railways the acquisition of railway rolling stock of standard type or of standard performance as necessary for their traffic operations.

FAO,
    see **Food and Agriculture Organization of the United Nations (FAO)**

Food and Agriculture Organization of the United Nations (FAO)
Established: 16 Oct. 1945. **Headquarters:** Rome, Italy. **IGO. Members:** Membership is confined to nations. 158 Nations. **Aims:** Raise the levels of nutrition and standards of living of the peoples in the member countries; secure the conditions of rural populations; thus contributing towards an expanding world economy and ensuring humanity's freedom from hunger.

Friends of the Earth International (FOEI)
Established: 1971. **Headquarters:** London, UK. **NGO. Members:** Full members in 29 countries, associates in 3 countries. **Aims:** Promote conservation, restoration and rational use of the environment and the Earth's natural resources through public education and campaigning at local, national and international levels. **Activities:** Instrumental in creating networks of environmental, consumer, human rights and peace organizations worldwide.

Global Environment Monitoring System (GEMS),
    see **United Nations Environment Program (UNEP)**
Global Resources Information Data-Base (GRID),
    see **United Nations Environment Program (UNEP)**

Greenpeace International
Established: 1971. **Headquarters:** Lewes, UK. **NGO. Members:** Individuals in 123 countries. **Aims:** Halt and reverse destruction of the biosphere, end nuclear testing; carry out uncompromising but peaceful action in defence of the environment, taking the responsibility of bearing witness at the site where damage is being done. **Activities:** Projects include: stopping whaling; preventing dumping of toxic and nuclear wastes; campaigning against nuclear tests and manufacturing of bombs as a first step towards disarmaments.

Group of 77
Established: Oct. 1967. **Headquarters:** c/o Perm. Representatives UN, United Nations, New York, US. **IGO. Members:** Governments of 125 countries. **Aims:** Promote economic cooperation among developing countries; provide the means for the Third World to articulate and promote its collective economic interests and enhance its bargaining power in negotiations for the establishment of a 'New Economic Order'. **Activities:** Produces joint declarations on specific topics. Programme of cooperation in the fields of trade industry food and agriculture, energy, raw materials, financial and monetary cooperation.

ICES,
    see **International Council for the Exploration of the Sea (ICES)**

Intergovernmental Oceanographic Commission (IOC)
Established: 1960, within the UN framework (UNESCO). **Headquarters:** Paris, France.

IGO. Members: Governments of 116 states. **Aims:** Promote marine scientific investigations and related ocean services, with a view to learning more about the nature and resources of the oceans through concerted action of members. **Activities:** Coordinates international marine scientific research and services at intergovernmental level; develops ocean-observing systems; coordinates UN agency activities, training, education and mutual assistance in marine sciences. Several sub-commissions, technical and regional subsidiary bodies. Mentioned in this volume:

    IOC International Oceanographic Data and Information Exchange (IODE)

International Arctic Committee (ICA)
Established: Feb. 1979. **Headquarters:** Monte Carlo, Monaco. **NGO. Members:** Specialists in 10 countries. **Aims:** Study the present situation of the arctic regions and advise on their future.

International Association of Meteorology and Atmospheric Physics (IAMAP)
Established: 1919. **Headquarters:** Innsbruck, Austria. **NGO. Members:** National Committees in 79 countries. **Aims:** Promote meteorological research and investigation including all aspects of atmospheric physics, particularly in those fields which require international cooperation; provide a forum for discussion of results and trends in research, and of those subjects of atmospheric research and investigation which overlap the fields of other sciences. **Activities:** Commissions: 1. International Commission on Atmospheric Chemistry and Global Pollution of IAMAP (ICACGP); 2. International Commission on Atmospheric Electricity (ICAE); 3. International Commission on Climate (ICCL); 4. International Commission on Cloud Physics (ICCP); 5. International Commission on Dynamic Meteorology (ICDM); 6. International Commission on the Meteorology of the Upper Atmosphere (ICMUA); 7. International Commission on Planetary Atmospheres and their Evolution (ICPAE); 8. International Commission on Polar Meteorology (ICPM); 9. International Ozone Commission (IOC); 10. International Radiation Commission (IRC). Commission of special relevance for this volume:

    International Ozone Commission (IOC)
    Established: 1948, as Commission of International Association of Meteorology and Atmospheric Physics (IAMAP). **Headquarters:** Downsview, Canada. **NGO. Members:** Individuals (distinguished scientists in their individual capacity for 8-year terms) in 17 countries. **Aims:** Stimulate improvements in the measurements and analysis of atmospheric ozone; advise other scientific and/or intergovernmental bodies in matters relevant to atmospheric ozone including possible effects on human activities. **Activities:** Establishes working groups and appoints rapporteurs on important topics. Organizes ozone symposia (every 4 years). Prepares statements on current topics relevant to atmospheric ozone.

International Atomic Energy Agency (IAEA)
Established: 29 July 1957 within the framework of UN. **Headquarters:** Vienna, Austria. **IGO. Members:** 113 states. **Aims:** Seeks to accelerate and enlarge the contribution of atomic energy to peace, health and prosperity throughout the world; ensure, so far as it is able, that assistance provided by it, or at its request, or under its supervision or control, is not used in such a way as to further any military purpose. **Activities:** The Agency fosters, encourages and advises on the development of peaceful uses of atomic energy throughout the world; organizes meetings; publishes books; establishes safety standards for all types of nuclear activity; prepares feasibility and market studies; operates three laboratories. By the end of 1986, a total of 164 safeguards agreements were in force with 96 states to ensure that nuclear materials are used only for their intended peaceful purposes.

International Baltic Sea Fishery Commission (IBSFC)
Established: 13 Sep. 1973. **Headquarters:** Warsaw, Poland. **IGO. Members:** Governments of 5 countries. **Aims:** Establish regulation of fisheries and conservation of living resources in the Baltic Sea; promote coordination of scientific research and joint programmes. **Activities:** Prepares and submits recommendations on a year-to-year basis regarding total allowable catches, types of fishing gear used, establishment of closed seasons or areas, total

fishing effort and other measures related to conservation and national exploitation of living resources.

International Centre of Insect Physiology and Ecology (ICIPE)
Established: Apr. 1980. **Headquarters:** Nairobi, Kenya. **NGO. Members:** Representatives of scientific institutions in 12 countries. **Aims:** Promote and conduct fundamental studies on insects of world-wide economic importance; carry out high quality research in various fields of insect science in order to develop environmentally sound and effective biological pest management systems not based on the use of harmful synthetic insecticides.

International Civil Aviation Organization (ICAO)
Established: 4 Apr. 1947, within the UN framework. **Headquarters:** Montreal, Canada. **IGO. Members:** 115 contracting states. **Aims:** Develop the principles and tehniques of international air navigation and foster the planning and development of international air transport so as to ensure safe and orderly growth of international civil aviation throughout the world. **Activities:** Regularly revises Standards and Recommended Practices contained in the annexes to Chicago Convention and procedures for Air Navigation Services. Studies current problems aiming to apply new technology in different fields of civil aviation such as air navigation, air transport, legal matters. Tecnical assistance, in the form of country and inter-country projects, was provided to the developing countries through UNDP and other funding sources.

International Commission for the Conservation of Atlantic Tunas (ICCAT)
Established: 21 Mar. 1969. Headquarters: Madrid, Spain. **IGO. Members:** Governments of 23 countries. **Aims:** Maintain the populations of tuna-like fish in the Atlantic Ocean at levels which will permit maximum sustainable catch.

International Commission for the Southeast Atlantic Fisheries (ICSEAF)
Established: 23 Oct. 1969. **Headquarters:** Madrid, Spain. **IGO. Members:** 17 Governments. **Aims:** Ensure a rational exploitation of the maritime sector of the Southeast Atlantic region. **Activities:** Statistical data; information and research.

International Commission on Radiological Protection (ICRP)
Established: 1928. **Headquarters:** Didcot, UK. **NGO. Members:** Commission and its committees comprise a total of 75 individuals in 20 countries. **Aims:** Ensure progress in the whole field of radiation protection, publish recommendations on radiation safety standards, mainly dealing with basic principles of radiation protection. **Activities:** Produces recommendations which are adopted by many intergovermental organizations and are kept continually under review in order to cover the increasing number and scope of potential radiation hazards, and to take account of new knowledge concerning the effects of ionizing radiations.

International Council for the Exploration of the Sea (ICES)
Established: 22 July 1902. **Headquarters:** Copenhagen, Denmark. **IGO. Members:** Governments of 18 countries. **Aims:** Promote and encourage research and investigations for the study of the sea, particularly those related to the living resources thereof, draw up programmes required for this purpose, and organize, in agreement with the contracting parties, such research and investigations as may appear necessary; publish or otherwise disseminate the results of research and investigations carried out under its auspices or encourage the publication thereof. **Area:** Atlantic Ocean and its adjacent seas, and primarily North Atlantic.

International Council of Scientific Unions (ICSU)
Established: July 1919. **Headquarters:** Paris, France. **NGO. Members:** National Members (67): principal scientific academies, national research councils, associations of institutions, in 66 countries. **Aims:** Encourage, for the benefit of humankind international scientific activity which will serve scientific and technological development and so help to promote the cause of peace and international security throughout the world; facilitate

and coordinate the international scientific activities of national members; enter through the intermediary of the national adhering organizations, into relations with the governments of their respective countries in order to promote scientific research in these countries; maintain relations with the United Nations and its agencies, and with other international intergovernmental or non-governmental organizations. **Activities:** Established several Committees, Commissions, and Services to facilitate and coordinate planning of scientific activities on an international basis. Mentioned in this volume:

Committee on Space Research (COSPAR)
Established: 2-6 Oct. 1959. **Headquarters:** Paris, France. **NGO. Members:** National scientific institutions, adhering to ICSU, in 36 countries. **Aims:** Provide the world scientific community with the means to exploit the possibilities of satellites and space probes for scientific purposes; exchange data on a cooperative basis. Terms of reference expanded by ICSU, Sep 1975, to include space research experiments with balloons.

Scientific Committee on Antarctic Research (SCAR)
Established: May 1959. **Headquarters:** Scott Polar Research Institute, Cambridge, UK. **NGO.Members:** National delegates of 18 countries. **Aims:** Initiate, promote and coordinate scientific activities in the Antarctic.

International Frequency Registration Board (IFRB)
see **International Telecommunication Union (ITU)**

International Institute for Environment and Development (IIED)
Established: Jan. 1971. **Headquarters:** London, UK. **NGO. Members:** Associations; Individuals. Number of members not available. **Aims:** Survey and analyse international policies and activities affecting development and the environment, their interrelationships and their consequences; serve as a clearing- house for ideas on environmental problems, informing public and private sectors as well as international institutions. **Activities:** Undertakes policy studies on issues of concern to international development institutions, national governments and non-governmental organizations. Focuses on such issues as: forestry; future energy; development of basic needs which are culturally sensitive and sustainable; national management and exploitation of marine and polar resources; environmental consequences and sustainability of social and economic development, especially in the Third World. Runs an international news and information service, *Earthscan.*

International Maritime Organization (IMO)
Established: 6 Mar. 1948, within the UN system. **Headquarters:** London, UK. **IGO. Members:** Governments of 131 countries. **Aims:** Provide machinery for cooperation among governments on technical matters affecting international merchant shipping and, with special responsibility for the safety of life at sea, to ensure that the highest possible standards of safety at sea and of efficient navigation are achieved; prevent pollution of the sea caused by ships and other craft operating in the marine environment, encourage removal of hindrances to international shipping services. Responsible for convening international maritime conferences and drafting international maritime conventions. **Activities:** Adoption of conventions, codes and other instruments dealing with maritime safety and prevention of marine pollution from ships. Activities mentioned in this volume: Maintain secretariat of;

Consultative Meeting of Contracting Parties to the London Dumping Convention
Established: 13 Nov. 1972, as governing body of Convention on the prevention of marine pollution by dumping of wastes and other matters. **Headquarters:** c/o IMO. **IGO. Members:** Contracting Parties to the Convention, governments of 61 countries. **Aims:** prevent and control marine pollution caused by dumping and incineration of wastes at sea, world-wide. Works with OSCOM, see **Oslo Commission (OSCOM) and PARCOM, see Paris Commission (PARCOM)**

International Maritime Satellite Organization (INMARSAT)

Established: 16 July 1979. **Headquarters:** London, UK. **IGO. Members:** Signatory states (50). **Aims:** Make provision for the space segment necessary for improving maritime and aeronautical communications, thereby assisting in improving safety of life at sea communications, efficiency and management of ships, maritime aeronautical and mobile public correspondence services and radio determination capabilities; serve the world-wide maritime and aviations community exclusively for peaceful purposes.

International Organization of Space Communications (INTERSPUTNIK)
Established: 14 Nov 1971. **Headquarters:** Moscow, USSR. **IGO. Members:** Governments of 15 countries. **Aims:** Establish a communication system using artificial earth satellites to meet the requirements of member countries in the exchange of television and radio broadcasting programmes, as well as of telephone and telegraph traffic; ensure cooperation and coordination of effort in design, establishment, operation, and development of the system. **Activities:** Intersputnik communication satellites and related facilities are owned by Intersputnik or leased from members. The system's earth stations are owned by the states where they are located. Bilateral agreements for the use of satellite facilities are concluded between the organization and its members.

IOC International Oceanographic Data and Information Exchange (IODE),
    see **Intergovernmental Oceanographic Commission (IOC)**

International Rice Research Institute (IRRI)
Established: 8 Mar. 1960. **Headquarters:** Manila, Philippines. **Members:** Individuals; organizations; governments. Numbers of members not available. **Aims:** Conduct basic research on the rice plant and on rice production, management, distribution and utilization, with the objective of improving quantity and quality of rice available for food.

International Telecommunication Union (ITU)
Established: 17 May 1865. Since 1947 within the UN framework. **Headquarters:** Geneva, Switzerland. **IGO. Members:** Governments of 163 countries. **Aims:** Maintain and extend international cooperation between all members for the improvement and rational use of telecommunications of all kinds, as well as promote and offer technical assistance to developing countries in the field of telecommunications. **Activities:** Elects, coordinates and makes financial and administrative arrangements for the four permanent organs at ITU headquarters: 1. ITU General Secretariat; 2. International Radio Consultative Committee; 3. International Telegraph and Telephone Consultative Committee; and mentioned in this volume, 4. International Frequency Registration Board (IFRB).

   International Frequency Registration Board (IFRB)
   Established: 1947. **Headquarters:** Geneva, Switzerland. **IGO. Members:** Member countries of ITU (163). **Aims:** Effect an orderly recording and registration of frequency assignments made by different countries in accordance with procedures provided for in the Radio Regulations and with any decision which may be taken by competent conferences of the Union.

International Telecommunications Satellite Organization (INTELSAT)
Established: 20 Aug. 1964. **Headquarters:** Washington DC, US. **IGO. Members:** 114 countries. **Aims:** Carry forward on a definitive basis the design, development construction, establishment, operation and maintenance of the space segment of the global commercial telecommunications satellite system.

International Union for Conservation of Nature and Natural Resources (IUCN)
Established: 5 Oct. 1948. **Headquarters:** Gland, Switzerland. **NGO. Members:** Members in 123 countries and territories. **Aims:** Promote scientifically-based actions directed towards the sustainable use and conservation of natural resources so that natural resources are conserved and the many species and varieties of plants and animals can persist in adequate numbers; protect areas of the land, and of fresh and sea waters, which contain

representatives or exceptional communities of plants and animals; devise special measures to ensure that species of fauna and flora do not become endangered or extinct. **Activities:** 1. Monitoring what is happening in conservation and drawing conservation requirements to the attention of organizations which can undertake action; 2. planning conservation action at strategic, programme and project levels, which is scientifically sound and realistic in socio-economic terms, using the information obtained through monitoring; 3. promoting conservation action by governments, intergovernmental bodies and non-governmental organizations through the effective dissemination of information; 4. providing assistance and advice necessary for the achievement of conservation action.

International Whaling Commission (IWC)
Established: 2 Dec. 1946. **Headquarters:** Cambridge, UK. **IGO. Members:** Governments of 38 countries. **Aims:** Provide for proper conservation of whale stocks and thus make possible orderly development of the whaling industry; encourage, recommend and organize studies and investigations relating to whales and whaling. **Activities:** Regulation of whaling; enforcement of whaling controls; exploration of stocks of whales and other cetaceans. All whale stocks are classified into one of 3 categories according to the advice of Scientific Committee.

IOC Data and Information Exchange,
see **International Ozone Commission (IOC)**

North Atlantic Salmon Conservation Organization (NASCO)
Established: Feb. 1984. **Headquarters:** Edinburgh, UK. **IGO. Members:** Governments of 8 countries and EEC. **Aims:** Contribute through consultation and cooperation to the conservation, restoration, enhancement and rational management of salmon stocks subject to the Convention.

Northeast Atlantic Fisheries Commission (NEAFC),
see **Commission for the Convention on Future Multilateral Cooperation in North-East Atlantic Fisheries**

Northwest Atlantic Fisheries Organization (NAFO)
Established: 1979. **Headquarters:** Dartmouth, Canada. **IGO. Members:** 22 states. **Aims:** Carry out and promote investigation, protection, and conservation of the fishery resources of the Northwest Atlantic Ocean in order to provide the optimum utilization and rational management of these resources. **Activities:** planning and cooperation of research work; compilation and consideration of results; collection and publication of fisheries statistics and samples of commercially caught fishes; proposals for regulating fisheries.

Nuclear Energy Agency (NEA),
see **Organization for Economic Cooperation and Development (OECD)**

Organization for Economic Cooperation and Development (OECD)
Established: 30 Sep. 1961. **Headquarters:** Paris, France. **IGO. Members:** Governments of 24 countries. **Aims:** Promote economic and social welfare in member countries, as well as the sound and harmonious development of the world economy, notably by improving the lot of developing countries. **Activities:** Concerned with all aspects of economic and social policy, covering the following fields of interest: 1. Economic Policy; 2. Energy; 3. Nuclear Energy; 4. Development Cooperation; 5. International Trade; 6. Financial and Fiscal Affairs; 7. Agriculture and Fisheries; 8. Environment; 9. Science; Technology and Industry; 10. Manpower; Social Affairs and Education; 11. Road Research; 12. Publications. Bodies mentioned in this volume:

OECD Nuclear Energy Agency (NEA)
Established: 20 Apr 1972, as a semi-autonomous body. **Headquarters:** Paris, France. **IGO. Members:** Governments of 23 countries of OECD. **Aims:** Promote international

cooperation within the OECD area for the development and application of nuclear power for peaceful purposes through international research and development projects, and through the exchange of scientific and technical experience and information. The Agency also contributes to the development of uniform standards governing nuclear safety and health protection, and a uniform legislative regime for nuclear liability and insurance.

Organization of the Petroleum Exporting Countries (OPEC)

Established: 10-14 Sep. 1960. **Headquarters:** Vienna, Austria. **IGO. Members:** Membership open to countries with a substantial net export of crude petroleum, having fundamentally similar interests. Governments of 13 countries. **Aims:** Coordinate and unify petroleum policies of member countries and determine the best means for safeguarding their interests individually and collectively; devise means of ensuring stabilization of prices in international oil markets so as to eliminate harmful and unnecessary fluctuations. **Activities:** Conducts a continuous programme of research, with particular emphasis on energy and related matters; monitors, forecasts and analyses development in the energy and petrochemical industries and studies the evaluation of hydrocarbons and products and their non-energy uses; analyses economic and financial issues and maintains data services. Gives attention to training, transfer of technology to developing countries, information exchange, development and management of tanker fleets and, through OPEC Fund for International Development, financing of development projects and other financial assistance to developing countries.

Oslo Commission (OSCOM)

Established: 15 Feb. 1972. **Headquarters:** London, UK. **IGO. Members:** Government representatives of 13 countries. **Aims:** Control disposal of waste at sea by the regulation of dumping/incineration activities. **Activities:** Annual Commisssion meetings. Joint monitoring programme with Paris Commission. Regulates dumping and incineration operations in the Northeast Atlantic through test procedures, prior consultation procedure and codes of practice.

Paris Commission (PARCOM)

Established: 4 June 1974. **Headquarters:** London, UK. **IGO. Members:** Governments representatives and Observers in 14 countries. **Aims:** Prevent marine pollution in the Northeast Atlantic Region arising from land-based sources. **Activities:** Annual Commission meetings. Joint monitoring programme with Oslo Commission. Carries out programmes for reduction of land-based discharges of polluting substances.

Scientific Committee on Antarctic Research (SCAR),
    see **International Council of Scientific Unions (ICSU)**

Secretariat for the Convention on International Trade in Endangered Species of Wild Fauna and Flora (CITES Secretariat) **Established:** 3 Mar. 1973 within the UN framework.
Headquarters: Lausanne, Switzerland. **IGO. Members:** Contracting Parties to the Convention (Governments of 96 countries). **Aims:** Regulate international commerce in wild flora and fauna to conserve and manage natural resources, protect certain endangered species from over-exploitation through international trade.

UNEP,
    see **United Nations Environment Programme (UNEP)**

United Nations Economic Commission for Africa (ECA)

Established: 29 Apr. 1958. **Headquarters:** Addis Ababa, Ethiopia. **IGO. Members:** Full independent countries. Members of UN and belonging to the African continent and its associated islands. Governments of 50 countries. **Aims:** Promote and facilitate concerted action for the economic and social development of Africa; maintain and strengthen economic relations of African countries, both among themselves and with the other countries of the world.

United Nations Environment Programme (UNEP)

Established: 15 Dec. 1972, within the UN system. **Headquarters:** Nairobi, Kenya. **IGO.** **Members:** Governing Council, consisting of 58 member states. **Aims:** Promote international cooperation in all matters affecting the human environment; to ensure that environmental problems of wide international significance receive appropriate governmental consideration; and to promote the acquisition, assessment and exchange of environmental knowledge. **Activities:** In addition to distributing both technical and general information, notably through its 'state of the environment' reports, UNEP acts as a catalyst within the UN system on environmental matters. Its operations encompass a Global Environmental Monitoring System (GEMS), a Global Resource Information Data Base (GRID), a global information network on the environment (Inforterra), an International Register of Potentially Toxic Chemicals, various advisory services and a clearing-house, established in 1982, to mobilize additional resources from governments, private groups and intergovernmental and non-governmental organizations to address environmental concerns. Mentioned in this volume:

Global Environment Monitoring System (GEMS)

Established: 1974. **Headquarters:** c/o UNEP. **IGO. Members:** 58 member states. **Aims:** Coordinate and implement environmental monitoring, research and assessment; provide an environmental data management service throughout the United Nations. **Activities:** Comprises technical environment monitoring and assessment programmes and projects, providing governments with information necessary to understand, anticipate and combat adverse environmental changes. Established in 1985 the **Global Resource Information Data-Base, (GRID) Aims:** 1. Coordinate existing environmental data sets; 2. Analyse existing information to pinpoint areas of environmental concern; 3. Train personnel from developing and developed countries in use of GRID technology. The aim is to collect and channel key environmental data to scientists and planners world-wide.

World Bank/International Bank for Reconstruction and Development (IBRD)

Established: 27 Dec. 1945, from Nov. 1947 as a specialized agency of United Nations. **Headquarters:** Washington DC, US. **IGO. Members:** 150 states. **Aims:** Promote the economic development of member countries by making loans to governments, or with a government guarantee, below conventional rates of interest for high-priority productive projects in cases where capital is not obtainable from other sources on reasonable terms; provide member countries with technical assistance on matters relating to their economic development; try to increase the effectiveness of the international development effort by fostering cooperation with and among other donors of financial and technical assistance.

World Commission on Environment and Development (WCED)

Also referred to as Brundtland Commission.
Established: 1983, within the framework of UN. **Headquarters:** Geneva, Switzerland. **IGO.** **Members:** Commissioners in 23 countries. **Aims:** Re-examine the critical issues of environment and development and formulate innovative, concrete and realistic action proposals to deal with them; strengthen international cooperation on environment and development and assess and propose new forms of cooperation of existing patterns and influence policies and events in the direction of needed change; raise the level of understanding and commitment to action on the part of individuals, voluntary organizations, businesses, institutes and governments. **Activities:** Common perspectives on population; relationship between environmental management and economic development; mutually supportive relationship between environment and development; education, science and technological development; multidisciplinary approach to achieve the interdisciplinary judgements and evaluations that are needed for decision-making and actions. Transcending themes; interdependence; education and communication; sustainability; equity; security and environmental risks; international cooperation. **Publications:** *Our Common Future (1987)*.

World Meteorological Organization (WMO)
Established: 11 Oct. 1947. Since 1951 within the UN system. **Headquarters:** Geneva,
Switzerland. **IGO. Members:** Governments of 154 states and 5 territories. **Aims:** Facilitate
world-wide cooperation in the establishment of networks of stations for the making of
meteorological observations as well as hydrological and other geophysical observations
related to meteorology, and promote the establishment and maintenance of centres with
the provision of meteorological and related services.

Appendix B: Select bibliography

Allen, K.R., 1980, *Conservation and Management of Whales*, Butterworth & Co., London

Andresen, Steinar, 1989, 'Science and Politics in the International Management of Whales', *Marine Policy*, no 2, pp. 99–117

Andresen, Steinar, 1989, 'The Environmental North Sea Regime: A Successful Regional Approach?', The Fridtjof Nansen Institute, forthcoming in *Ocean Yearbook* **8**, 1989

Andresen Steinar and Fløistad, Brit, 1984, 'Overvåking av forurensnings-situasjonen i norske havområder: vektlegging, organisasjon, samordning', The Fridtjof Nansen Institute

Auburn, F.M, 1982, *Antarctic Law and Politics*, C. Hurst & Co. Publishers, London

Bankes, N.D., 1988, 'The Ozone Convention and Protocol: Further Steps Towards an International Law of the Atmosphere', *Resources*, **22** (Spring), 1-3

Beck, Peter J., 1986, *The International Politics of Antarctica*, Croom Helm, London & Sydney

Beek, J.G. Van, 1987, 'Historical Review of the Management Measures Taken by the International Whaling Commission', *Lutra 30*, 166-92

Bergesen, Helge Ole, Moe, Arild and Østreng, Willy, 1987, *Soviet Oil and Security Interests in the Barents Sea*, Frances Pinter, London

Birnie, Patricia, 1980, 'IWC -Survival and Growth', *Marine Policy*, vol. 4, no 1, January 1980

Birnie, Patricia, 1983, 'Countdown to Zero', *Marine Policy*, vol 7, no 1, January 1983

Birnie, Patricia, 1985, *International Regulation of Whaling*, Oceana Publications New York, vol.1-2

Bishop, Charles, 1959, 'Oceanography in Naval Warfare', US *Naval Institute Proceedings*, vol. 85, no. 5

Boehmer-Christiansen, Sonja, 1984, 'Marine Pollution Control in Europe — Regional Approaches, 1972-80', *Marine Policy*, vol. 8, no. 1

Boehmer-Christiansen, Sonja, 1986, 'An End to Radioactive Waste Disposal at Sea?', *Marine Policy*, vol. 10, no.2, pp. 119-31

Boehmer-Christiansen, Sonja, 1988a, 'The Politics of Environment and Energy in FR Germany: Forests versus Fossil Fuels', SPRU occasional paper no.28, University of Sussex

Boehmer-Christiansen, Sonja, 1988b, 'Black Mist and Acid Rain: Science as Fig Leaf of Policy', *The Political Quarterly*, vol.59, no.2, April- June 1988, pp 145-60.

Boehmer-Christiansen, Sonja A. and Skea Jim F., 1989, Acid Politics: an Anglo-German Comparison. To be published in 1989.

Bohlin, Ingemar, 1988, *Modern Polarforskning*, Første årsrapport in FRN-prosjektet, 'Ett vetenskapsteoretisktperspektiv på polarforskning', Institutionen før vetenskapsteori, Gothenburg University

Brown, Seyom, Cornell, Nina W., Fabian, Larry L. and Brown Weiss, Edith, 1977, *Regimes for the Ocean, Outer Space and Weather*, Brookings Institution, Washington DC

Buchanan, J. and Tullock, G., 1962, *The Calculus of Consent*, Ann Arbor, Michigan

Bupp, Irvin C., 1981, 'The Actual Growth and Probable Future of the Worldwide Nuclear Industry', *International Organization*, vol. 35, no. 1 (Winter), pp. 59-76

Butler, William E., 1971, *The Soviet Union and the Law of the Sea*, Johns Hopkins Press, Baltimore

Calabresi, Guido and Melamed, A. Douglas, 1972, 'Property Rules, Liability Rules and Inalienability: One View of the Cathedral', *Harvard Law Review*, **85**, 1089-128

Caldwell, Lynton Keith, 1972, *Defense of Earth: International Protection of the Biosphere*, Indiana University Press, Bloomington

Caldwell, Lynton Keith, 1984, *International Environmental Policy: Emergence and Dimensions*, Duke University Press, Durham

Carroll, John E. (ed.), 1988, *International Environmental Diplomacy*, Cambridge

University Press, Cambridge

Clark, R.B., 1984, 'North Sea Review', *Marine Pollution Bulletin*, vol.15, no.7, pp. 237-8

Clark W. and Munn, R., 1985, *Sustainable Development of the Biosphere*, Cambridge

Codding, George A. and Rutkowsky, Anthony M., 1982, *The International Telecommunication Union: An Experiment in International Cooperation*, Artech House, Dedham, MA

Colino, Richard R., 1984, 'The INTELSAT System: An Overview' in Joel Alper and Joseph N. Pelton (eds.), *The INTELSAT Global System*, (American Institute of Aeronautics and Astronautics, Inc., New York), vol. 93, 'Progress In Astronautics and Aeronautics', pp. 55-94

Collingridge, David, 1984, *Critical Decision Making*, Frances Pinter, London

Cook, James, 1985, 'Nuclear Follies', *FORBES*, 11 February, 1985, pp. 82-100

Crary, Albert, 1982, 'International Geophysical Year: Its Evolution and US Participation', *Antarctic Journal*, vol. XVII, no. 4, pp. 1-4

Cushing, D.H., 1983, 'The Outlook for Fisheries Research in the Next Ten Years' in B.J. Rothschild (ed.), *Global Fisheries: Perspectives for the 1980s*, Springer Verlag, New York, pp. 263-77

Demac, Donna A. (ed.), 1986, *Tracing New Orbits: Cooperation and Competition in Global Satellite Development*, Columbia University Press, New York

Devanney, J.W., 1975, *The OCS Petroleum Pie*, MIT Sea Grant Report No. MITSG 75-10, Cambridge

Dewry, David J., 1988, 'The Challenge of Antarctic Science' in *Oceanus,* vol. 31, no. 2

Douglas, Mary, 1986, *Risk Acceptability According to the Social Sciences*, Routledge and Kegan Paul, London

Downs, Anthony, 1972, 'Up and Down with Ecology: The "Issue-Attention Cycle"', *Public Interest*, **28**, 38-50

Dragesund, O., 1980, 'A Review of Management Practices and Research Activities on Norwegian Spring Spawning Herring', in B.R. Melteff and V.G. Wespestad (eds.), *Proceedings of the Alaska Herring Symposium*, Anchorage, Alaska, 19-21 February 1980, Alaska Sea Grant Report 80-4, pp. 207-38

Eckert, Ross D., 1979, *The Enclosure of Ocean Resources: Economics and the Law of the Sea*, Hoover Institution Press, Stanford

Elster, Jon, 1983, *Explaining Technical Change. Studies in Rationality and*

Social Change, Cambridge University Press. Cambridge, pp. 206-7

ENDS-Report 118, 1984, 'UK's Defensive Efforts Pay Off at North Sea Conference', November 1984

ENDS-Report 141, 1986, 'Opening Skirmishes on Health of the North Sea', October 1986

Energy 2000, 1987, 'A report to the World Commission on Environment and Development', Zed Books, London

FAO 1980, 'ACMRR Working Party on the Scientific Basis of Determining Management Measures', FAO Fish. Report 236

FAO 1987, 'Review of the State of World Fishery Resources', FAO Fish. Circ. **710**, Rev. 5

Galtung, Johan, 1965, 'Foreign Policy Opinion as a Function of Social Position', *Journal of Peace Research*, **2**, pp. 206-30

Gjelsvik, Tore, 1983, 'Scientific Research and Cooperation in Antarctica' in Rudiger Wolfrum (ed.), *Antarctic Challenge: Conflicting Interests, Cooperation, Environmental Protection, Economic Development*, Duncker & Humbolt, Berlin

Goldemberg, J. and Johansen, T. *et al.*, 1987, 'Energy for a Sustainable World', World Resources Institute

Goldie, L.F., 1958, 'International Relations in Antarctica', *Australian Quarterly*, vol. 30

Goldschmidt, Bertrand, 1977, 'A Historical Survey of Non proliferation Policies', *International Security*, vol. 2, no. 1 (Summer), pp 69-87

Gough, Michael, 1987, 'Environmental Epidemology: Separating Politics and Science', *Issues in Science and Technology*, Summer 1987, pp 21-31.

Gould, Laurence M., 1957, 'Antarctic Prospects', *The Geographical Review*, vol. XLVII, no. 1

Gulland, J.H., 1974, *The Management of Marine Fisheries*, University of Washington Press, Seattle

Gulland, J.A. (ed.), 1977, *Fish Population Dynamics*, John Wiley, New York

Gulland, J., 1988, 'The End of Whaling?', *New Scientist*, 29 October 1988, pp. 42-7

Haas, Ernst, 1980, 'Why Collaborate? Issue-Linkage and International Regimes', *World Politics*, vol. 32, no. 3, pp. 357-405

Hamilton, E.I., 1986, 'Science — A Time for Change?', *Marine Pollution Bulletin*, vol. 17, no 7, July 1986, pp. 295-98

Hardin, Russell, 1982, *Collective Action*, Johns Hopkins University Press, Baltimore

Haveman, Robert H. and Knopf, Kenyon A., 1978, *The Market System*, 3rd ed., Wiley, Santa Barbara

Hayward, Peter, 1984, 'Environmental Protection — Regional Approaches', *Marine Policy*, vol. 8, no. 2

Heap, John A, 1983, 'Cooperation in Antarctica: A Quarter of a Century's Experience' in Orrego Vicuna, Vicuna (ed.), *Antarctic Resources Policy: Scientific, Legal and Political Issues*, Cambridge University Press, Cambridge

Heap, John A., 1987, 'The Role of Scientific Advice for the Decision-Making Process in the Antactic Treaty System' in Rudiger Wolfrum (ed), *Antarctic Challenges III: Conflicting Interests, Cooperation, Environmental Protection, Economic Development*, Duncker & Humbolt, Berlin, pp. 21-8

Henrickson, Alan K., 1986, 'The Global Foundations for a Diplomacy of Consensus' in Alan K. Henrickson (ed.), *World Order: The Artisanship and Architecture of Global Diplomacy*, Scholarly Resources, Wilmington, pp. 217-44

Hermann, Charles F., 1969, 'International Crisis as a Situational Variable' in James N. Rosenau (ed.), *International Politics and Foreign Policy*, The Free Press, New York, pp. 409-21

Herscovici, Alan, 1985, *Second Nature: The Animal-Rights Controversy*, CBC Enterprises, Montreal

Hirschman, Albert O., 1970, *Exit, Voice, and Loyalty*, Harvard University Press, Cambridge MA

Hoel, A.H., 1985, *The International Whaling Commission 1972-1984: New Members, New Concerns*, The Fridtjof Nansen Institute, R:003-1985

Hollick, Ann L., 1981, *U.S. Foreign Policy and the Law of the Sea*, Princeton University Press, Princeton

Holt, Sidney, 1985, 'Whale Mining, Whale Saving', *Marine Policy*, vol.9 no.3, July 1985

Hygen, Johan B., 196A, 'Fridtjof Nansen's views of Civilization and Ethics, in Per Vogt, *Fridtjof Nansen, Explorer-Scientist-Humanitarian*, Dreyer, Oslo, 1969 International Agriculture Update, 1988, 'Creating and Sustaining a Green Revolution in Africa', University of Illinois, June 1988

Jacobson, Harold, 1973, 'The International Telecommunication Union' in Robert Cox and Harold Jacobson (eds.), *Decision-Making in International Organizations: The Anatomy of Influence*, Yale University Press, New Haven

Jacobson, Harold and Kay, David A., (eds.), 1983, *Environmental Protection: The*

International Dimension, American Society of International Law, New Jersey

Jager, Jill, 1988, 'Anticipating Climatic Change: Priorities for Action', *Environment*, September 1988, pp. 12-15 and pp. 30-3

Johnson, Rodney W., and Smith, Philip M., 1969, 'Antarctic Research and Lunar Exploration', *Advances in Space Science and Technology*, vol. 10, Academic Press Inc., New York

Jones, T.O., 1973, 'Coordinating Federal Arctic Research', *Arctic Bulletin*, vol. 1, no. 1

Jong, Folkert de, 1988, 'The Second Ministerial Conference on the Protection of the North Sea: An Historical Event?', *North Sea Monitor*, January 1988

Jordijk, L., 1988, 'Linking Policy and Science: A Model Approach to Acid Rain', *Environment*, vol. 30, no. 2

Kneese, Allen V. and Shultze, Charles L., 1975, *Pollution, Prices and Public Policy*, Brookings Institution, Washington DC

Koers, A.W., 1973, *International Regulation of Marine Fisheries*, Fishing News (Books) Ltd., West Byfleet, London

Kosloff, Laura H. and Trexler, Mark C., 1987, 'The Convention on International Trade in Endangered Species: No Carrot, But Where's the Stick?', *Environmental Law Reporter*

Krasner, Stephen D. (ed.), 1983, *International Regimes*, Cornell University Press, Ithaca

Larsen, Thor, 1978, *The World of the Polar Bear*, Hamlyn, London

Laws, R.M., 1987, 'Cooperation or Confrontation?' in D.W.H. Walton (ed.), *Antarctic Science*, Cambridge University Press, Cambridge

Levy, Stephen A., 1975, 'INTELSAT: Technology, Politics, and the Transformation of a Regime', *International Organization*, vol. 29, no. 3 (Summer), pp. 655-80

Long, Clarence D., 1977, 'Nuclear Proliferation: Can Congress Act in Time', *International Security*, vol. 1, no. 4 (Spring), pp. 52-76

Luhmann, Niklas, 1986, *Oekologische Kommunikation: Kann die moderne Gesellschaft sich auf okologische Gefaehrdungeinstellen?*, Westdeutscher Verlag, Opladen

Majone, G., 1985, 'International Institutions and the Environment' in Clark and Munn, 1985, *Sustainable Development of the Biosphere*, Cambridge

McHugh, J.L., 1974, 'The Role and History of the International Whaling Commission' in W.E. Schevill (ed.), *The Whale Problem: A Status Report*,

Harvard University Press, Cambridge MA, pp. 305-335

Miles, Edward, 1983a, 'On the Roles of International Organizations in the New Ocean Regime', in Choon-ho Park (ed.), *The Law of the Sea in the 1980s*, Law of the Sea Institute, Honolulu, pp. 383-445

Miles, Edward, 1983b, 'IOC Data and Information Exchange: Implications of the Law of the Sea Convention', *Marine Policy*, vol. 7, no. 2 (April), pp.75-86

Miles, Edward, 1987, *Science, Politics and International Ocean Management: The Uses of Scientific Knowledge in International Negotiations*, Institute of International Studies, University of California, Berkeley, Policy Papers in International Affairs, no. 33

Moltke, Konrad von, 1984, 'Needs and Action: Obstacles to International Policies', *World Resources Institute Journal*, **84**, Washington

Mueller, Dennis, C. 1979, *Public Choice*, Cambridge University Press, Cambridge

New Scientist, 1987, 'Pollution and Politics in the North Sea', 19 November 1987

Nye, Joseph S., 1981, 'Maintaining a Non-Proliferation Regime', *International Organization*, vol. 35, no. 1 (Winter), pp.15-38

Olsen, Johan P., 1983, *Organized Democracy*, Norwegian University Press, Oslo

Olson, Mancur, 1965, *The Logic of Collective Action*, Harvard University Press, Cambridge MA

Østreng, Willy, 1973, *De skandinaviske land i Arktis: Forutsetninger og muligheter for samarbeid*, Study AA:H007 in the publication series of the Fridtjof Nansen Institute

Østreng, Willy, 1978a, *Polhavet i internasjonal politikk*, publication AA:H012 in the publication series of the Fridtjof Nansen Institute

Østreng, Willy, 1978b, *Politics in High Latitudes: The Svalbard Archipelago*, C. Hurst, London

Østreng, Willy, 1983, 'Det varme Arktis' in Håkon Børde (ed.), *Svalbard og havområdene*, Gyldendal Norsk Forlag, Oslo

Østreng, Willy, 1984, 'Soviet Norwegian Relations in the Arctic', *International Journal*, vol. XXXIX, no 4 (Autumn).

Østreng, Willy, 1986, 'Delimitation Arrangements in Arctic Seas: Cases of Precedence or Securing or Strategic/Economic Interests?', *Marine Policy*, vol. 10, no. 2 (April), pp. 132-55

Østreng, Willy, 1987, *The Soviet Union in Arctic Waters: Security Implications for the Northern Flank of NATO*, occasional paper no. 36. The Law of the Sea Institute, University of Hawaii, Honolulu

Østreng, Willy, 1988/89, 'The Barents Sea in Soviet Rear-Deployment Strategy', forthcoming article in *Naval Forces. International Forum for Maritime Power*

Park, Chris C., 1987, *Acid Rain Rhetoric and Reality*, Methuen, London and New York

Parry, John T., 1986, 'Background, Perspective and Issues for Remote Sensing in the Tropics' in M. J. Eden and J. T. Parry (eds.), *Remote Sensing and Tropical Land Management*, John Wiley and Sons, New York

Pelton, Joseph N., 1977, 'Key Problems in Satellite Communications: Proliferation, Competition and Planning in an Uncertain Environment' in Joseph N. Pelton and Marcellus S. Snow (eds.), *Economic and Policy Problems in Satellite Communications*, Praeger Publishers, New York, pp. 93-123

Pepper, David, 1984, *The Roots of Modern Environmentalism*, Croom Helm, London

Phillip, David J.H., 1986, 'Are Environmental Conservation Organizations Necessary?', *Marine Pollution Bulletin*, vol.17, no 9, pp.387-8

Pollack, L. and Weiss, H., 1984, 'Communications Satellites: Countdown for INTELSAT VI', *Science*, vol. 223 (10 February), pp. 553-9

Polar Research Board, 1986, *Antarctic Treaty System: An Assessment*, National Academy Press, Washington DC

Pontecorvo, Giulio (ed.), 1986, *The New Order of the Oceans: The Advent of a Managed Environment*, Columbia University Press, New York.

Quigg, Philip W., 1983, *A Pole Apart: The Emerging Issue of Antarctica*, McGraw-Hill, New York

Rich, Robert F. (ed), 1981, *The Knowledge Cycle*, Sage Publications, Beverly Hills and London

Ries, Thomas, 1987, *The Soviet Military Operational Command Structure and its Application to Fenno-Scandia*, Report NUPI, Oslo, 20 August, pp. 61-2

Roberts, Marc J. *et al.*, 1984, 'Mapping Scientific Disputes That Affect Public Policymaking', *Science, Technology and Human Values*, pp 112-21

Roll-Hansen, Nils, 1986, *Sur nedbør — et storprosjekt i norsk miljø forskning*, NAVF, Oslo

Roll-Hansen, Nils, 1987, 'Ønsketenkning eller vitenskap. Subjektivismen i vitenskapsteori og forskningspolitikk', *Nytt norsk tidsskrift*, nr.2

Rothschild, B.J. (ed.), 1983, *Global Fisheries: Perspectives for the 1980s*, Springer-Verlag Inc., New York

Rowley, G.W., 1966, 'International Scientific Relations in the Arctic' in R.St. MacDonald (ed.), *The Arctic Frontier*, University of Toronto Press, Toronto

Ruggie, John Gerard, 1972, 'Collective Goods and Future International Collaboration', *American Political Science Review*, vol. 66, pp. 874-93

Ruggie, John Gerard, 1975, 'International Responses to Technology: Concepts and Trends', *International Organization*, vol.29, no. 3 (Summer)

Russell, Clifford S. (ed.), 1982, *Collective Decision Making: Applications from Public Choice Theory*, Johns Hopkins University Press, Baltimore

Sætevik, Sunneva, 1988, *Environmental Cooperation between the North Sea States*, Belhaven Press (Pinter Publishers), London

Sagers, Matthew J., 1988, 'New Notes', *Soviet Geography*, April, pp. 423-57

Sagoff, Mark, 1988, *The Economy of the Earth: Cambridge Studies in Philosophy and Public Policy*, Cambridge University Press, Cambridge

Sandler, Todd and Cauley, Jon, 1977, 'The Design of Supranational Structures: An Economic Perspective', *International Studies Quarterly*, **21**, 251-76

Scarff, J.E., 1977, 'The International Management of Whales, Dolphins and Porpoises: An Interdisciplinary Assessment', *Ecology Law Quarterly*, vol. 6

Scheinman, Lawrence, 1987, *The International Atomic Energy Agency and World Nuclear Order*, Resources for the Future, Washington DC

Schmandt, Jurgen, 1984, 'Regulation and Science', *Science, Technology and Human Values*, vol.9, issue 1 (Winter 1984)

Scott, Anthony, 1973, *Natural Resources: The Economics of Conservation*, McClelland and Stewart, Toronto, Chapter 8

Scott, Anthony, 1976, 'Transfrontier Pollution: Are New Institutions Necessary?' in *Economics of Transfrontier Pollution*, OECD, Paris, pp.178-218

Sebek, Viktor, 1983, 'Bridging the Gap Between Environmental Science and Policy-making: Why Public Policy Often Fails to Reflect Current Scientific Knowledge', *Ambio*, vol. 12, no. 2

Sebenius, James, 1983, 'Negotiation Arithmetic: Adding and Subtracting Parties and Issues', *International Organization*, **37**, 281-316

Smith, Phillip M., 1969, 'Prospects for International Cooperation on the Moon: The Antarctic Analogy', *Bulletin of the Atomic Scientists*, vol. XXV, bn.7

Sperling, K.R., 1986, 'Protection of the North Sea: Balance and Prospects', *Marine Pollution Bulletin*, vol. 17, no.6

Titus, James G. (ed.), 1986, *Effects of Changes in Stratospheric Ozone and Global Climate*, vol. 1, United States Environmental Protection Agency and United

Nations Environment Programme, Washington DC

Tønnesen, I. and Johnsen, A., 1959-70, *Den moderne hvalfangsts historie. Opprinnelse og utvikling*, Sandefjord, vol.1-5

Underdal, Arild, 1979, 'Issues Determine Politics Determine Policies: The Case for a "Rationalistic" Approach to the Study of Foreign Policy Decision-Making', *Cooperation and Conflict*, **14**, pp.1-9

Underdal, Arild, 1980a, *The Politics of International Fisheries Management*, Oslo

Underdal, Arild, 1980b, 'Integrated Marine Policy; What, Why and How?', *Marine Policy*, no. 3, July 1980, pp. 159-69

Underdal, Arild, 1984, 'Causes of Negotiation Failure', *Internasjonal Politikk*, Temahefte I, Oslo, pp. 81-97

Underdal, Arild, 1987, 'International Cooperation: Transforming "Needs" into "Deeds"', *Journal of Peace Research*, vol. 24, no.2, June 1987

Vicuna, Orrego Vicuna (ed.), 1983, *Antarctic Resources Policy: Scientific, Legal and Political Issues*, Cambridge University Press, Cambridge

Vogel, David, 1986, *National Styles of Regulation: Environmental Policy in Great Britain and the United States*, Cornell University Press, London

Warner, William W., 1983, *Distant Water: The Fate of the North Atlantic Fisherman*, Little, Brown, Boston

Washburn, A.L. and Weller, Gunther, 1986, 'Arctic Research in the National Interest', *Science*, vol. 233, 8 August

Went, A.E.J., 1979, *Seventy Years of Growing. A History of the International Council for the Exploration of the Sea 1902-1972*, Andr. Fred & Fils Copenhagen

Wihlborg, Clas G. and Wijkman, Per Magnus, 1981, 'Outer Space Resources in Efficient and Equitable Use: New Frontiers for Old Principles', *Journal of Law and Economics*, vol.24, no. 1 (April), pp.23-43

Wildavsky, A., 1962, 'The Analysis of Issue Contexts in theStudy of Decision-Making', *Journal of Politics*, **24**

Wildawsky, A. and Tenenbaum, E., 1981, *The Politics of Mistrust: Estimating American Oil and Gas Resources*, Sage Publications, Beverly Hills and London

Withers, David and Weiss, Hans J., 1984, 'INTELSAT and the ITU', in Joel Alper and Joseph N. Pelton (eds.), *The INTELSAT Global Satellite System*, American Institute of Aeronautics and Astronautics, inc. New York, pp.270-310

Wohlstetter, Albert, 1968, 'Strength, Interest and New Technologies', *ADELPHI PAPERS*, September 1968

Wooster, Warren, 1986, 'Immiscible Investigators: Oceanographers, Meteorologists, and Fishery Scientists' in Edward Miles, Robert Pealy and Robert Stokes (eds.), *Natural Resource Economics and Policy Applications*, University of Washington Press, Seattle and London, pp. 374-87

Wooster, Warren (ed.), 1988, *Fishery Science and Management: Objectives and Limitations*, Springer-Verlag, New York

World Commission on Environment and Development, 1987, *Our Common Future*, Oxford University Press, Oxford

Young, Oran R., 1979, *Compliance and Public Authority: A Theory with International Applications*, Johns Hopkins University Press, Baltimore

Young, Oran R., 1979, and Fisher, Roger, 1981, *Improving Compliance with International Law*, University Press of Virginia, Charlottesville

Young, Oran, 1982, *Resource Regimes: Natural Resources and Social Institutions*, University of California Press, Berkeley

Young, Oran R., 1988, *International Cooperation: Building Regimes for Natural Resources and the Environment*, Cornell University Press, Ithaca

Zacher, Mark W. 1987. "Trade Gaps, Analytic Gaps: Regime Analysis and International Commodity Trade Regulation", *International Organization* 41, 173-202

Index